Old Zion Evangelical Lutheran Church (Harrold's)

HISTORY OF OLD ZION EVANGELICAL LUTHERAN CHURCH

HISTORY OF OLD ZION EVANGELICAL LUTHERAN CHURCH

in Hempfield Township, Westmoreland County, Pennsylvania.
Near Harrold's

By

William Arter Zundel M.A., B.D.

Pastor of St. John's Evangelical Lutheran Church
Maywood, Illinois

Field Missionary for Montana

KALPAZ

ISBN: 978-93-5128-852-7(PB)

First Published in 1922
Indian Reprint in 2017

Published by

Kalpaz Publications
C-30, Satyawati Nagar,
Delhi – 110052
E-mail: kalpaz@hotmail.com
Website: kalpazpublications.com
Ph.: +91-9212142040

Cataloging in Publication Data—DK
Courtesy: D.K. Agencies (P) Ltd. <docinfo@dkagencies.com>

Zundel, William Arter, 1878-1949, **author.**
History of old Zion Evangelical Lutheran Church in Hempfield Township, Westmoreland County, Pennsylvania, near Harrold's / by William Arter Zundel (M.A., B.D.).
pages cm
"First published in 1922"—Title page verso.
ISBN 9789351288527

1. Zion Evangelical Lutheran Church (Hempfield Township, Westmoreland Co., Pa).—History. 2. Hempfield (Westmoreland County, Pa. : Township)—Church history. I. Title.

BX8076.H4Z8 2017 DDC 284.174881

PREFACE

For many years, the authentic records of Old Zion Evangelical Lutheran Church have been locked in the German language in the old Church Register.

This old register had been carelessly handled for many years and was thought by many to have been lost or destroyed. But it found friends that knew its value and preserved it.

The volume came into our hands some years ago and we at once set about to translate its contents.

We have made diligent search for authentic information concerning this church. The early history has been enlarged and made as full as possible. To a casual observer it will seem that incidents of other places should have no place in this narrative, but they contribute valuable information concerning the times, and show the problems and difficulties peculiar to all pioneer life.

Much of this history was written before the World War and is not in any way affected by the animosities of recent years. The record of Old Zion for patriotism stands clear from the bloody Revolution to the World War and the muster rolls of her country bear the names of her sons who served their country well.

In recording the synodical affiliation of Old Zion, there has been an effort to make clear, for the first time, the real synodical connections of the church throughout the years. Fidelity to truth and historical fact necessitated references to unpleasant events of the past and our readers will realize that few participants had a full knowledge of the situation and the facts during the period of strife. We have taken pains to present both sides of the controversy and also to state the plain and full facts of history. The division of the church is a cold historical fact and requires an account of its cause and effects.

We have made no effort to include the history of the St. John's Reformed Church. We hope one of her sons will some day write the history of her long life and glowing achievements. For about one hundred years Old Zion and St. John's Churches have lived together in peace and harmony in the same house of worship and burying their dead in the same God's Acre.

Since the strife in the eighties and the division, a new generation has grown up; they have been educated in the same schools and associated together on all occasions. They have inter-married and, except for the two organizations, have forgotten the strife of the past. Both congregations now belong to the same Synod and the United Lutheran Church in America.

It may be the pleasure of some future historian to relate how the two congregations united their forces for a greater "Zion oder Herold's Kirche" of the future.

Suitable recognition has been given to the sources of information that we have used. However, especial mention should be made of the painstaking efforts of the late Charles Strohbach of Freedom, Pa., who assisted materially in the translation of the old Church Register. Special care has been taken to preserve the old forms of names and to give literal translations. The names given in the several Appendices will be valuable in tracing family genealogies; they are also valuable as legal evidence.

Valuable aid has been rendered by the historian of the Pittsburgh Synod, Rev. Duncan M. Kemerer, and the council and committee of Old Zion's Lutheran Church and others.

Acknowledgements are made of the services of H. M. Zundel, who furnished many cuts and contributed many recent facts of Chapter XVI and aided in the general work of publication.

The work connected herewith has been a labor of love, a token of gratitude to the Mother Church that baptized us into the Kingdom of God and nourished us in the faith, whose portals have been the doorway to Heaven for hundreds of saints during her history of one hundred and fifty years.

LIST OF AUTHORITIES CONSULTED

Original Parish Register.

Southern Conference History, Rev. W. F. Ulery, Church Register Co., Greensburg, Pa.,—1903.

History Pittsburgh Synod of the General Synod of the Evangelical Lutheran Church, Rev. Ellis B. Burgess, Philadelphia,—1904.

The German Element in the United States, by Albert Bernhardt Faust, Two Volumes, Houghton Mifflin Company, Boston and New York,—1909.

Col. Henry Bouquet and His Campaigns by Rev. Cyrus Cort, Steinman and Hensel, Printers,—1883, Lancaster, Pa.

History of Westmoreland County, Pennsylvania, by John N. Boucher, The Lewis Publishing Company, New York and Chicago,—1906, Three Volumes.

The Frontier Forts of Western Pennsylvania by George Dallas Albert, Report of the Commission to locate the site of the Frontier Forts of Pennsylvania.

A History of the Reformed Church within the Bounds of Westmoreland Classis, edited by a Committee of Classis, Reformed Church Publication Board, Philadelphia,—1877.

A History of the Evangelical Lutheran Church in the United States by Rev. Henry Eyster Jacobs, D.D., L.L.D., Charles Scribner's Sons, New York,—1902.

The Lutheran Cyclopedia, edited by Rev. Henry Eyster Jacobs, D.D., L.L.D., and Rev. John A. W. Haas, B.D., Charles Scribner's Sons, New York,—1911.

The Broken Platform by Rev. John N. Hoffman, Lindsey and Blakeston, Philadelphia,—1856.

The Formulation of the General Synod's Confessional Basis by Rev. J. S. Neve, D.D., German Literary Board, Burlington, Iowa,—1911.

Documentary History, Lutheran Ministerium of Pennsylvania, Philadelphia,—1898.

Documentary History of the General Council of the Evangelical Lutheran Church in North America, S. E. Ochsenford, D.D., Philadelphia,—1912.

Geschichte der Allgemeinen, Evang. Lutherischen Synode von Ohio und Anderen Staaten, Peter und Schmidt, Columbus, Ohio,—1900.

Border Warfare in Pennsylvania during the Revolution, L. S. Shimmell, Ph.D., Harrisburg, Pa.,—1901.

Who Are the Pennsylvania-Germans? By Theodore E. Schmank, Lancaster, Pa.,—1910, New Era Printing Co.

The Domestic Life and Characteristics of the Pennsylvania—German Pioneer, by Rev. F. J. F. Schantz, D.D., Lancaster, Pa.,—1900 by Pennsylvania—German Society.

Albertus Magnus, bewahrte und Approbirte Sympatetische und Natuerliche Egyptische Geheimnisse fuer Menschen und Vieh.

Fuer Staedter und Landleute Fuenfte vermehrte und verbesserte Auflage, — — Brabrand.

History of the Pittsburg Synod of the Reformed Church in the United States. Rev. David B. Lady, D.D. Chas. M. Henry Printing Co., Greensburg, Pa.,—1920.

Lutheran Symbols or American Lutheranism Vindicated, by S. S. Schmucker, D.D., T. Newton Kurtz, Baltimore,—1856.

Life and Times of Henry Melchior Muehlenberg, by William J. Mann, D.D. G. W. Frederick, Philadelphia,—1888.

The Life of Rev. H. Harbaugh, D.D., by Linn Harbaugh, Esq. Reformed Church Publishing Board, Philadelphia, Pa.,—1900.

History of the Joint Synod of Ohio, by C. V. Sheatsley. Lutheran Book Concern, Columbus, Ohio,—1919.

Hallesche Nachrichten.

Regina, the German Captive, Rev. B. Weiser. General Council Publishing Board, Philadelphia, Pa.,—1919.

CONTENTS

		Page
Chapter I.	The Location	1
Chapter II.	Early German Colonists	5
Chapter III.	Explorations and Early Settlements in Westmoreland County	13
Chapter IV.	Zion Church Settlement	30
Chapter V.	Frontier Conditions	44
Chapter VI.	The Red Revolutionary War	58
Chapter VII.	Forts and Blockhouses	80
Chapter VIII.	Social Life of the Pioneers	90
Chapter IX.	The Patriarchs	95
Chapter X.	Property Affairs and Relations with the Reformed Church	110
Chapter XI.	Synodical Relations	114
Chapter XII.	Contending for the Faith	125
Chapter XIII.	Rebuilding	137
Chapter XIV.	Our Sister Church	147
Chapter XV.	The Fruitage	150
Chapter XVI.	The Sunday School, Cemeteries and Reformed Pastors, etc.	155
Chapter XVII.	Education among the German Elements in Western Pennsylvania	164
Appendix A.	Early Baptisms	187
Appendix B.	Communicants	231
Appendix C.	Confirmants	247
Appendix D.	Taufschein	256
Appendix E.	Annual Settlements	258

CHAPTER I

The Location

Great is the Lord, and greatly to be praised, in the city of our God, in the mountain of his holiness. Beautiful for situation, the joy of the whole earth, is Mount Zion. Walk about Zion, and go round about her; tell the towers thereof. Mark ye well her bulwarks; consider her palaces; that ye may tell it to the generation following. For this God is our God for ever and ever; he will be our guide even unto death. Psalm 48.

Glorious things are spoken of thee, O city of God. Selah. And of Zion it shall be said, this and that man was born in her: and the highest himself shall establish her. The Lord shall count, when he writeth up the people, that this man was born there. Selah. Psalm 87.

Moved by religious motives and fascinated by the magnificent scenic beauty of the location, the founders, like David of old, called their new home "Zion Church Settlement;" in the midst of which they set apart land, styling it "Good Purpose," for the establishment of their Church and school. Zion Church meant to them all that Mount Zion meant to David.

This new Mount Zion was to them beautiful for situation. Nestled on a sheltered southeastern slope of a long range of hills that separate the headquarters of the Sewickley and the Brush Creek streams, Zion Church has a magnificent landscape before her. At the foot of the hill lies a fertile valley, which at that time, was covered with a magnificent forest of

Birds-eye View of Portion of "Good Purpose" (Harrold's)

oaks, hickory, poplar, beech, walnut, maple and other hardwood trees. A brook of clear cool water flowed in a winding course away into the distance until it joined other tributaries of the Sewickley Creek. Beyond the valley rose the foothills of the Alleghenies and beyond on the horizon the Blue Mountains rose in grandeur. In springtime the opening buds and unfolding leaves gave an ever changing variety, while in the fall when the frost touched vegetation there appeared a gorgeous display of the most beautiful colors nature has ever devised for the delight of the eye of man.

The Rocky Mountains may speak of power and magnitude; the plains may excell in distances and unlimited range of vision; the sea may in its various moods awe or please the heart of man but the Pennsylvania hills in autumn, backed by the Blue Mountains, and clothed in natures holiday attire, speak peace, love, beauty and contentment.

Here the seasons are at their best. Four seasons of distinct climate. Rain in plentiful quantities; yet no rainy season. Spring and summers warm enough for an abundant growth of vegetation; yet not long enough to be enervating. Boosters may write of the wonderful climate of other countries and state, but here nature boosts for herself. What country can boast of a finer stand of forests of various hard woods? Or a larger variety of desirable wild animals and birds? Here was the hunters paradise; a fit explanation of the efforts of the Whites to conquer and the Reds to maintain this happy hunting ground through fifty years of the most deadly conflict between the Red men and the White men for the control of a continent.

The soil that grows oaks and the various hard woods, is fertile; a land of oak and limestone has been the delight of the German settler from that day to this. Deer, bear, wolves, beaver, wild turkey were plentiful. Small game and fur bearing animals still abound.

Few countries are blessed so richly and abundantly by nature. Amid the trees of wonderful hard wood there roamed abundant game. The soil was fertile and abounded in limestone with which to renew the fertility. Beneath the soil nature stored up wondrous veins of coal and iron, which has made the Ohio Valley the heart of the iron and steel industry. Yet deeper in the earth, abundance of oil and gas has been found.

With a climate unexcelled, and such wondrous natural resources we may well commend the shrewdness and sagacity of our forefathers who originally settled here.

CHAPTER II

Early German Colonists

Columbus, an Italian, re-discovered America; Martin Waldseemueller, a German, named the new found land, "America." Spaniards, English, French, Dutch and Swedes made settlements. The Germans made no settlement as a nation. They came as a people to make their homes under other flags than their own. Though the most numerous of all peoples that came to America they never colonized under a German flag.[1]

There were German settlers at Port Royal, in South Carolina, in 1562. There were a number of Germans at Jamestown in 1607. Germans were also among the Dutch of New Netherland; one was the first governor, Peter Minuit, and another Jacob Leisler became governor.

Minuit was born at Wesel on the Rhine, and was a protestant. He bought the Island of Manhattan from the Indians for about $24.00. Later he was a friend of Gustavus Adolphus, the Swedish King who was planning a colony for America.[2] The associations of Minuit at this time would lead us to infer that he was of the same faith as the Swedes, i. e. A Lutheran. In 1638 he planted the Swedish Colony on the Delaware. Since many German cities of the Baltic co-operated in the Swedish settlement we may infer that some Germans were among them. John Printz the first

---

[1]From 30 to 40 per cent of American blood is Teutonic. See Lutheran Influence in American Affairs by the author.

[2]The German Element in the United States. (1) Note:—Faust. (1).

governor, according to trustworthy authority, was a German nobleman.—Johahn Printz von Buchau.

John Lederer was sent out by Governor Sir William Berkley of Virginia, to explore the land south and west of the James river in 1669-70. Peter Fabian, a Swiss-German was a member of an exploring expedition sent out by the English Carolina Company in 1663. The report is probably written by Fabian because the distances are recorded by the standard of the German mile. A German by the name of Hiens was with LaSalle in Texas in 1687.

Germans settled in large numbers in Pennsylvania, New York, Virginia, Maryland, North Carolina, South Carolina, Georgia and New Jersey. By the aid of Hofrat Heinrich Ehrenfried Luther, of Frankfort-on-the-Main, German settlers were secured to settle on the Kennebec River in Massachusetts, (now Maine) some also settled around Boston.[3] The wanderlust of the early Angles and Saxons who conquered Britain, Gaul and Rome was not lacking in the Teutons that came to America. We find them on the frontier from Maine to Georgia.

As there was no census in those early days it is difficult to estimate the number of Germans in the Colonies before the Revolution. The Continental Congress in 1776 estimated the population at 2,243,000 whites and 500,000 slaves. This estimate is considered too high. Bancroft estimates the population in 1775 to be 2,100,000. Charles A. Hanna, in his book "The Scotch-Irish," estimates the Scotch-Irish population of the colonies at 385,000, which is evidently too high. Faust (German Element in the United States) estimates the German element in 1775 as follows:

---

[3]Israel Bissel, probably a descendant of these settlers, is the man sent by Eldridge Gerry, who warned Hancock of the coming of the British. Bissel delivered his message at 9 o'clock at night, just one hour before Paul Revere started.

New England	1,500
New York	25,000
Pennsylvania	110,000
New Jersey	15,000
Maryland and Delaware	20,000
Virginia and West Virginia	25,000
North Carolina	8,000
South Carolina	15,000
Georgia	5,000
Total	225,000

"Future researches in the colonial history of the Germans will undoubtedly reveal larger numbers than have been given above, but the attempt has been made here to confine the estimate within limits that are clearly incontestable." Fausts figures are too low. There were many settlements on the frontiers not included in his estimates.

Some historians have invented the fiction that the Germans were not on the frontier in pre-revolutionary times, but a careful survey shows that they were on the extreme frontier, from Maine to Georgia. Though the English and Scotch-Irish held most of the appointive positions and therefore wrote the official reports, from which historians heretofore have mainly drawn their data, a closer study reveals a differing history.

In New York the Germans on the Mohawk, Schoharie and German Flats stood the brunt of the Indian wars. In Pennsylvania the Germans were as far west as any settlers. The Wetzel's, Zanes and Henry's at Wheeling and settlers in Westmoreland were pioneers (which see later). In Virginia, the Carolinas and Georgia the original explorers and settlers were Germans. The Royal American Regiment not only fought in all the frontier contests but garrisoned the frontier forts for many years.

"As we study on the map the location of the Germans before the Revolution, two facts impress themselves. In the first place, the Germans were in the possession of most of the best land for farming purposes. They had cultivated the great limestone areas reaching from northeast to southwest, the most fertile lands in the colonies. The middle sections of Pennsylvania were in their possession, those which became the granary of the colonies in the coming Revolutionary War, and subsequently the foundation of the financial prosperity of the new nation. The Shenandoah and Mohawk valleys were the rivals of the farm-lands of Pennsylvania, while the German countries of North and South Carolina pushed them hard for agricultural honors. The Germans in these sections supplanted all other nationalities through their superior industry, skill, and material resources acquired through habits of economy."

"Even before the Revolution the value of the midland Pennsylvania counties as provision-houses for armies was recognized by the following incident. In 1758 an army was raised for the taking of Fort Duquesne, near which Braddock had met disaster three years before. The question arose whether the army starting from Pennsylvania should go straight through the woods, hewing a new road, or should march thirty-four miles southwestwardly to Fort Cumberland in Maryland, and thence follow the road made by Braddock. It was in accordance with the interests of Pennsylvania that the new road be made; while Virginia was unwilling to see a highway cut for her rival that would lead into the rich lands of the Ohio, claimed by Virginia. Washington, who was then at Fort Cumberland with a part of his regiment, earnestly advocated taking the old road, while the Quartermaster-General, Sir William SinClair, advised in favor of the Pennsylvania route. The generals in command, Forbes and Bouquet, decided for a particular reason to take the straight course. It was shorter and when once made **would furnish readier and more abundant supplies of food and forage:** but to make it would consume a vast amount of time and labor. As later events proved, it was not British success in battle, but mainly the advantage of position, the possibility of getting supplies and holding out longer, advantages beyond the reach of the French, that forced the latter to evacuate Fort Duquesne."[4]

Dr. Benjamin Rush, the noted Philadelphia physician, one of the signers of the Declaration of Independence; surgeon in the Revolutionary Army, etc., says the Pennsylvania farms produced millions of dollars, which after 1780 made possible the foundation of the Bank of North America. The first bank in America, chartered 1781. Washington's "honest friend," Christoph Ludwig, baker-general of the army, who provided all the bread for the patriot army, drew his supplies of grain directly from the Pennsylvania German farms.[5] "The second striking fact which impresses itself in a study of the map is the occupancy by the German settlers of almost the entire frontier area from Maine to Georgia." "The credit for defending the American frontier has very commonly been accorded to the Scotch and Irish settlers. From the map, based upon a careful study of the location of the German settlers, it appears that the Scotch and Irish could not have had a larger share in the defense of the frontier than the Germans, when the whole extent of the frontier line is considered. There were certain reasons why so large a percentage of the German immigration settled on the frontier. Similar causes operating for the bulk of the Scotch, Irish and Huguenot immigrants. They were poor, and were obliged to go where land was cheap or where squatters could maintain their independence."

Dr. Benjamin Rush, like the historian Tacitus wrote a modern "Germania" of the Pennsylvania Germans. It was

---

[4]Faust, Vol. 1, Page 266. [5]Faust—Page 267, Vol. 1.

entitled "An account of the manners of the German inhabitants of Pennsylvania, written in 1789." The author treats his subject under sixteen heads. He discusses "a few particulars in which the German farmers differ from most of the other farmers of Pennsylvania."

1. (Housing horses and cattle). In settling a tract of land the Germans always provide large and suitable accommodations for their horses and cattle, before they lay out much money in building a house for themselves. The next generation builds a large and convenient stone house.

2. (Good land). "They always prefer good land, or that land on which there is a large quantity of meadow ground. By attention to the cultivation of grass, they often grow rich on farms, on which their predecessors have nearly starved. They prefer purchasing farms with some improvements, to settling on a new tract of land." (This latter statement did not hold true for the frontier regions, only the older regions in Eastern Pennsylvania).

3. (Methods of clearing land). "In clearing new land they do not girdle or belt the trees simply, and leave them to perish in the ground, as is the custom of their English or Irish neighbors; but they generally cut them down and burn them." Underwood and brush they would pull out by the roots.

4. (Good feeding). They feed their horses and cows well. "A German horse is known in every part of the state." Indeed, he seems to feel with his lord the pleasure and pride of his extraordinary size and fat.

5. Fences). "The fences of a German farm are generally high and well built so that his fields seldom suffer from the inroads of his own or his neighbors horses and cattle."

6. (Use of wood). "The German farmers are great economists of wood." They do not waste it in large fireplaces

but burn it in stoves, using about one fourth to one fifth as much.

7. (Comfort of cattle). "They keep their horses and cattle as warm as possible in winter, by which they save feed."

8. (Economy). "The Germans live frugally in their homes with respect to diet, furniture and dress."

9. (Gardens). Kitchen gardening the Germans introduced altogether. Their gardens contained useful vegetables at every season of the year. "Pennsylvania is indebted to the Germans for the principal part of her knowledge in horticulture."

10. (Few hired men). The Germans seldom hire men to work upon their farms. The wives and daughters of the German farmers frequently forsake for a while their dairy and spinning wheel and join their husbands and brothers in the labor of the fields.[6]

11. (Wagons). "A large and strong wagon covered with cloth is an essential part of the furniture of a German farm. These Conestoga wagons became the "prairie schooner" of a later date.

12. (Children). "The favorable influence of agriculture, as conducted by the Germans, in extending the most happiness, is manifested by the joy expressed at the birth of a child. No dread of poverty or distrust of Providence from an increasing family, depress the spirits of this industrious and frugal people."

13. (Love of labor). "Germans produced in their children not only the habits of labor but a love for it. When a young man asks the consent of his father to marry the girl of his choice, he does not inquire so much whether she be rich or poor, or whether she possess any personal or mental accomplishments, but whether she be industrious and acquainted with the duties of a good housewife."

---

[6]Cf. Whittier's poem "Maud Muller."

14. (Patrimony). "The Germans set a great value upon patrimonial property." The idea prevails that a house and home should be possessed by a succession of generations.

15. (Superstition). "The German farmers are very much influenced in planting and pruning trees, also in sowing and reaping, by the age and appearance of the moon." They used the divining rod to find water. Thus: Taking a last years growth of a forked peach branch the two branches are grasped firmly with thumbs outward then the whole forked branch is twisted backward toward the body and upward, bringing the thumbs toward each other, then revolving them downward, backward and upward. This gives the peachfork a decided twist with the heavy base branch standing upward and slightly forward. Now the practitioner walks over the ground and when the vein of water is reached the peach base branch will twist downward toward the water. Magic arts of healing were also practiced. One book of magic is entitled "Albertus Magnus tried and approved sympathetic and natural Egyptian secrets, for man and beast." But it must not be understood that the German settler was more superstitious than other frontier men of the day. The entire country was oppressed with witchcraft and magic. The American Indian had his medicine man, who was nothing else than a witch and magician. The colonists elsewhere were burning witches about this time. Even today, people consult the horoscope and avoid Friday and the thirteenth as unlucky.

16. (Barns). "A German farm may be distinguished from the farms of the other citizens of the state by the superior size of their barns, the plain but compact form of their houses, the height of their enclosures, the extent of their orchard, the fertility of their fields, the luxuriance of their meadows, all of which have a general appearance of plenty and neatness in everything that belongs to them."[7]

---

[7]Faust.

CHAPTER III

Explorations and Early Settlements in Westmoreland County, Pennsylvania

While the English, Dutch and Swedes were settling the Atlantic Seaboard, the French were busy exploring the great interior of America. Moving from Canada as a base, their expeditions under Joliet, Marquette, LaSalle and Hennepin, explored and fortified the great Mississippi Valley from the Great Lakes to the Gulf of Mexico, and the Ohio Valley from its tributaries to its entrance into the Mississippi. Hence, while England claimed the Atlantic seaboard and the hinterland, France also claimed the Ohio and Mississippi Valleys by virtue of explorations.

In 1689 war broke out in Europe between France and England. One of the objects was the possession of India and America. This war (1689-1763), called The Hundred Years War, was taken up by their respective Colonies in America. The fourth section of this conflict (1754-1763) was known as the French and Indian War, and had for its purpose the control of the interior of the North American continent.

The French had built a line of Forts from Quebec to the Lakes and from thence to the Gulf of Mexico. To protect the Ohio Valley they erected Forts at Presque Isle on Lake Erie, Fort Le Boeuf, Fort Venango, a Fort on French Creek, and contemplated building a fort at the junction of the Allegheny and Monongahela Rivers.

Conrad Weiser, a German from the Palatine, and trusted Indian Agent, after pacifying the six nations in 1745 and regaining their friendship, was sent by the Governor of Pennsylvania in 1748, to treat with the Indians of the Ohio Valley. Weiser traveled through the mountains to the Ohio, and from thence to Logg's Town near Legionville on the Ohio river. His mission was to keep the Indians from an alliance with the French. He gathered full data of the French forts and settlements, and secured information concerning the intentions of the enemy. This information was invaluable when representatives of seven English colonies met in council with the chiefs of the Six Nations in order to secure an Alliance with the Six Nations against the French and Indians of the Ohio Valley. Weiser was able to repeat in the language of the Mohawks his experience with the French and Indians of the Ohio Valley, and he roused the animosity of the Six Nations against them, taking advantage of the Indians greed for land.[1]

Johanan Conrad Weiser, Jr., was born November 2, 1696 at Afstaedt, Germany. He migrated to America with his father in 1710. In November 1713 his father was visited by Quagnant, a chief of the Maquas, or Six Nations, who, taking a great fancy to Conrad, requested that he might accompany him back. He did so, remaining with the tribe some eight months, during which time he suffered much but learned their language and customs thoroughly, and was adopted by them. This experience was invaluable to his country later. From 1732 until his death he was the recognized head of the Indian bureau of the English Government in the province. Respected alike by red man and white, because of his unquestioned ability and uprightness, he maintained peace until war was unavoidable, and was even then instrumental in bringing its horrors to a close at the earliest possible date. He held many offices of trust and honor. At the outbreak of the French and Indian war, he was commissioned Lieut.-Colonel October

[1]Faust-German Element in the U. S., Vol. 1, page 273.

31, 1755, and given command of the First Batalion, Pennsylvania Regiment and assigned to protect the frontier along the Blue Mountains. He was a sincere and earnest Christian, and a Lutheran. His daughter, Anna Maria, married Henry Melchior Muhlenberg, the great organizer of the Lutheran Church in those times. He died suddenly in 1760.[2]

Another German who nobly served the colonies during the Indian trouble was Christian Frederick Post, a member of the Moravian Brotherhood. He made a journey to Kushkushkee on Beaver Creek northwest of Fort Duquesne, to visit the Indians and to persuade them to remain neutral in the coming war between the French and Indians. In spite of the intrigues of the French, he accomplished his purpose, the Delawares remained peaceful. This made possible the great Council at Easton. This council sent a message of peace to the tribes of the Ohio. Frederick Post with several white and Indian companions was chosen to bear it. The French had stirred up the Indians and were present with peace offers from the French Commander when Post arrived. "There was a grand council at which the French officer was present, and Post delivered the peace message from the council at Easton with another, with which Forbes had charged him. The message pleased all the hearers except the French captain. The overtures of peace were accepted, and the Delawares, Shawanoes and Mingoes were no longer enemies of the English."[3]

This peace was especially important because it occurred immediately after the defeat and capture of Major Grant at Fort Duquesne. The desertion of the Indian allies led to the evacuation of Fort Duquesne and its capture by Gen. Forbes.

---

[2]Lutheran Cyclopedia.
[3]Parkman's Montcalm and Wolf quoted by Faust, etc.

In 1761 Post and Heckewelder attempted to found a mission in Stark County, Ohio, but failed on account of Pontiac's war. In the autumn of 1767 Post returned to his Western Indian congregation and remained there, the first pioneer. In the following year David Zeisberger founded an Indian congregation at Goshocking on the Allegheny River. About 1771 Gnadenhuetten and Salem, Ohio, were founded. The Indians were taught the arts of peace, to read and write, also to speak English and German. In 1775 the congregations numbered 414 persons.

In 1782 the Wyandots under the Scotch-Irish renegade, Simon Girty, ravaged the settlements of the upper Ohio. Evil tongues spread the report that the Christian Indians, who had come back to the Muskingum, had taken part in these savage raids. A conspiracy was former to destroy the Moravian villages. Early in March 1782 a company of volunteers gathered together under the command of Colonel David Williamson of Washington Co. This company decended upon the Christian Indian village of Gnadenhuetten by stealth. Finding a few peaceful Indians on the outskirts of the town they slew them and took the town by surprise. The Indians were told that they would be taken to Fort Pitt, and that they should summon the settlers from the other towns of Salem and Schoenbrunn. Those of Salem came, the others fled. All were now seized and herded like sheep in two large barns, the men in one and the women and children in another. A mock trial was held by Williamson, in which the question was put, whether the captives should be taken to Fort Pitt or murdered. Williamson asked those who wished to spare the Indians to step out of the ranks, but only eighteen men showed any inclination toward mercy and humanity. The cowards next decided upon the plan of massacre. Some favored burning them in the barns, but the majority, **greedy for scalps,** preferred to act as executioners. After giving the prisoners a brief time to prepare for death the assasins entered the prison barns and with club and knife butchered every man, woman and child. The only survivors were two boys, one had concealed himself under the floor and the other revived after being partially scalped. There was but one German in this company of over 80 men, a man named Bilderbach.[3a]

"Colonel Williamson was afterwards elected to office in Washington County and it is said died in jail as a debtor. County Lieutenant John Cannon was among them. It is said that the fiend who killed the fourteen with a mallet, was at the time a County Commissioner and justice of Washington County, and that he was subsequently elected Sheriff of the County. John Cannon founded Cannonsburg and from him the Academy so noted in the past took its name. Now this outrage, the blackest in Pennsylvania annals, was committed by a people who prided themselves on their advancement, wealth and culture, and who looked with scorn on the Dutch, i. e. Germans who in their dealings with the Indians, followed as far as possible the policy of William Penn."[4]

The Ohio Company organized in 1748, received a grant of 500,000 acres south of the Ohio and west of the Monongahela rivers. This scheme was a speculation in futures as clearly as the gambling in futures of grain. The land had never been purchased from the Indians, was not explored nor surveyed. The historic importance of this company is overstated. Likewise the journey of Washington assumes large importance only by retrospection. True he performed his duty well, but he furnished little information that others had not already attained. The conquest of the Ohio did not proceed from Virginia, but from Pennsylvania. The military success of Washington in the Ohio country is not as brilliant as that of Col. Bouquet. It is the subsequent successes of

[3a]Faust German Element in U. S. Vol. 1, page 402.
[4]Boucher, History of Westmoreland County.

Washington that lends additional interest to his Ohio country work.

The Ohio company wished to colonize their grant with a hundred families of Pennsylvania Germans but the offer was rejected because they objected to supporting an English (Episcopal) clergymen. They proposed to furnish the families if they were allowed their own pastors.

In 1755 occurred Braddock's defeat. Among the provincials troops were a number of Germans. The Kimmels are said to have been with Braddock's Army and to have settled in Westmoreland shortly afterward.

In 1758 General Forbes marched against Fort Duquesne. The new route was chosen because it was shorter and connected with a large source of supplies (see Chapter II). Major Grant, sent out by order of Bouquet to learn the strength of the enemy was captured and a large part of his force destroyed. Flushed with success the French, now under Command of De Vitri, attacked the Camp at Loyalhanna, now Ligonier. It is noteworthy that while De Vitri had 1200 soldiers, only 200 Indians accompanied him, and through the efforts of Christian Frederick Post the Indian allies left Fort Pitt, making the evacuation of the Fort necessary. The attack at Camp Loyalhanna was unsuccessful.

Forbes arrived at Loyalhanna on November 6th. The outlook was gloomy and Washington says an abandonment of the expedition was contemplated. But through captives it was learned of the weakness of the French Fort and the desertion of the Indian allies, therefore, Forbes pressed on and when the scouts reached the Fort they found it abandoned and set on fire.

Capt. Beaujeu with about 200 French and Canadians and 600 Indians defeated Braddock's Army of 1200 picked soldiers. General Forbes could not have had more than about 4000 effective soldiers and the French had at least 1200 men.

If the thousands of Indians had remained loyal to the French, they could have withstood a siege until re-enforcements could have arrived; for the French and Indians commanded the waterways. Posts work in winning the Indians to a peace with the English had a decisive influence on the campaign.

"Bouquet writes to Chief Justice Allen, November 25, 1758, quoted from Parkham; Montcalm and Wolfe, Vol. II, page 161: "After God, the success of this expedition is entirely due to the general (Gen. Forbes) who by bringing about the treaty with the Indians at Easton struck the French a stunning blow, wisely delayed our advance to wait the effects of that treaty, secured all our posts, and left nothing to chance, and resisted the urgent solicitation to take Braddock's road, which would have been our destruction. In all his measures he has shown the greatest prudence, firmness and ability."[5]

Immediately following Forbes army came the first real settlers of the territory now called Westmoreland County. The Pennsylvania and Virginia soldiers of this army were largely disbanded in the early part of 1759. Many of them with their families immediately started west in pursuit of new homes. Many pushed on west to the Ohio valley. Those who stopped here settled mainly along the Forbes road and south of it. Some never returned with Forbes at all. Some of them settled without any right, on choice land, which they expected to own by right of occupancy. To others was granted land by what was called military permits. The following is a military permit. "By Arthur St. Clair, Late Lieutenant in his Majesty's Sixtieth Regiment of foot, having care of His Majesty's Fort at Ligonier. I have given permission to Frederick Rohrer to cultivate a certain piece of land in the neighborhood of Fort Ligonier, over a certain creek, which empties into the Loyalhanna known by the name of Coal Pit

[5]Faust, Vol. 1, page 278.

Creek; beginning at a White Oak standing on a spring and marked with three letters F. X. R., and running from thence to another tree marked with the same letters and standing on another spring called Falling Spring, and from these two marked trees to the said Coal Pit Creek supposed to contain two hundred acres: He the said Frederick Rohrer being willing to submit to all orders of the Commander in Chief, the Commanding officer of the District and of the Garrison. Given under my hand at Ligonier this 11th day of April 1767. Ar. St. Clair.[6]

The entire country was overrun by the Indians and it is natural that the first settlers should build cabins around the forts, such as Ligonier and Fort Pitt. But soon the hardy soldiers and others dared to seek out the rich lands south of the Forbes road. Andrew Byerly, whose land warrant was No. 36 for 236 acres, settled in the Brush Creek valley along the Forbes road in 1759. Christopher Rudebaugh and several others followed closely and took up lands. John Herold sold lands near Greensburg to Detars in 1760. Andrew Harmon settled in the Ligonier Valley in 1769. Michael Rodenbaugh came about 1760. Christopher and Daniel Herold settled near Youngwood about the same time. Christopher Walthour came in 1764 and purchased a mill site from John Rodenbaugh, at the junction of Bushy Run and Brush Creek. John Peter Miller came in 1764. John Wagle came in 1765. The Kimmels came with Braddock's army in 1755, withdrew and became hunters and farmers and many other German settlers whose names appear on the early church register came at this early date.

The Indian war called "Pontiac's Conspiracy" drove these early settlers back to the forts. Pontiac was Chief of the Ottawa tribe. He fought with the French at Braddock's defeat. In military matters he was a Napoleon and in diplomacy

[6]Boucher History of Westmoreland County.

a Bismarck. Parkman rates him as the ablest leader the Indians ever produced. His home centered about Detroit. Eighteen nations or tribes entered in the Conspiracy. From part of the Six Nations of New York down to the Gulf of Mexico the Conspiracy ran strong. It was planned that a blow should be struck suddenly at all the Forts in the Ohio and Lake region. This storm burst upon the settlers in the Spring of 1763. Nine forts and posts were captured by stratagem or assaults. Detroit, Niagara and Fort Pitt were attacked about the same time.

Pittsburgh was then but a village. In July 21, 1760 the population of Pittsburgh consisted of:

Houses	146
Unfinished Houses	19
Huts	36
Total	201
Number of men	88
Number of women	29
Number of male children	14
Number of female children	18
Total	141

Exclusive of those in the Fort.

Fort Pitt was commanded by Captain Simeon Ecuyer, a Swiss officer and a small garrison of 330 soldiers, traders and backwoodsmen.

On the date May 29, 1763 Captain Ecuyer writes to Colonel Bouquet about the uprising of the Indians and adds "Just as I had finished my letter three men came in from Clapham's with the Melancholy News, that yesterday, at three o'clock in the afternoon, the Indians murdered Clapham, and every body in his house: These three men were out at work, and escaped through the woods. I immediately armed them, and sent them to assist our people at Bushy Run. The Indians have told Byerly to leave his place in four days, or he and his family would all be murdered: I am uneasy for the little posts —as for this I will answer for it." S. Ecuyer.[7]

"As Ecuyer states, Byerly had received warning but his family was in no condition to be moved. Mrs. Byerly had just been confined and the departure was delayed as long as possible, indeed until certain death was imminent if the flight should be any longer postponed. Byerly had gone with a small party (perhaps Clapham's men referred to above) to bury some persons who had been killed at some distance from his station. A friendly Indian who had often received a bowl of milk and bread from Mrs. Byerly came to the house after dark and informed the family that they would all be killed if they did not make their escape before daylight. Mrs. Byerly got up from her sick couch and wrote the tidings on the door of the house for the information of her husband when he should return. A horse was saddled on which the mother with her tender babe three days old in her arms, was placed, and a child not two years old was fastened behind her.

"Michael Byerly was a good sized lad, but Jacob was only three years old and had a painful stone bruise on one of his feet. With the aid of his older brother who held him by the hand and sometimes carried him on his back, the little fellow, however, managed to make good time through the wilderness to Fort Ligonier, about thirty miles distant. But although he reached his ninety-ninth year he never forgot that race for life in his childhood, nor did he feel like giving quarter to hostile Indians, one of whom he killed on an island in the Allegheny in a fight under Lieutenant Hardin in 1779, although the savage begged for quarters.

[7]Frontier Forts.

"Milk cows were highly prized by frontier families in those days, and the Byerly family made a desperate effort to coax and drive their small herd along to Fort Ligonier. But the howling savages got so close that they were obliged to leave the cattle in the woods to be destroyed by the Indians. Byerly in some way eluded the Indians and joined his family in the retreat. They barely escaped with their lives. The first night they spent in the stockade, and in the morning the bullets of the pursuers struck the gates as the family pressed into the fort."[8]

Lieutenant Archibald Blane with a detachment of Royal Americans commanded the Fort. Colonel Bouquet of the first battalion of Royal Americans had his headquarters at Philadelphia at this time. The Royal Americans, broken into detachment, had held the line of forts and posts on the western frontier for over six years. As soon as the outbreak became known Bouquet started westward. Part of the 42nd Regiment of Royal Highlanders and the 77th Montgomerys Highlanders were added to his command.

About Carlisle all was consternation. Reports came in of the Indian ravages. The country between the mountains and the Susquehanna was abandoned. Two thousand families left their homes and fled. At Shippensburg on July 25, 1763 there were 1384 fugitives. At Bedford conditions were similar.

Wendel (Uhrig) Ourry of Bedford sent a detachment to relieve Fort Ligonier. Bouquet also threw forward thirty men for the same purpose. On August 2 Bouquet reached Ligonier with his army. Leaving there his heavier baggage he started, August 4th, to relieve Fort Pitt. A band of frontiersmen and scouts led the way. These were supported by a band of pioneers. The wagons and cattle were in the center

---

[8]Col. Henry Bouquet and his campaign, Cort.

guarded by the Highlanders, a rear guard of backwoodsmen brought up the rear.

The Highlanders were brave men but knew little of Indian fighting. Bouquet wrote "I cannot send a Highlander out of my sight without running the risk of losing the man, which exposes me to surprises from the skulking villains I have to deal with."

Andrew Byerly accompanied the army. By one o'clock the army was approaching Bushy Run. Byerly with eighteen men of the Royal Americans was in the advance, when suddenly this advance guard was fired upon from ambush. Twelve out of the eighteen men fell before the other columns could come up. Bouquet formed his men for the defense. The Highlanders were brave but they furnished an open target for the Indians. They charged repeatedly with bayonets but the savage gave way only to return again when the Scotchmen returned to their line. About sixty men fell that afternoon, and many of the officers were killed and wounded. Lieutenant Dow of the Royal Americans was seriously wounded after killing three Indians.

That night the army suffered much from thirst. Byerly, at great risk, brought several hatsfull of water from a neighboring spring which allayed the thirst of the wounded. The next day the battle was renewed at dawn. By stratagem Bouquet drew the savages from their protection and attacked them on front and flank. The Indians fought bravely but could not withstand the bayonet charge in front and the flank fire. Seeing that they had been entrapped, the Indians broke and fled, leaving sixty dead on the field. Bouquet's army lost fifty killed, sixty wounded and five missing. The casualties among the Highlanders were greater than among the Royal Americans and Rangers: the latter fought in Indian fashion while the former used open tactics.

In a few days the army pressed on and relieved Fort Pitt. "The battle of Bushy Run, says Parkman, was one of the best contested actions ever fought between white men and Indians." Colonel Bouquet and Gen. Herkimer rank among the very foremost Indian fighters. Of Herkimer, Washington says, "It was Herkimer who first reversed the gloomy scene." (Burgoynes campaign).

A word should be said of the Royal American Regiment. "This regiment was authorized by act of Parliament. It was to consist of four battalions of one thousand each, and intended to be raised chiefly of the Germans and Swiss, who, for many years past, had come to America, where waste land had been assigned them on the frontiers. They were generally strong, hardy men, accustomed to the climate. It was necessary to appoint some officers, especially subalterns who understood military discipline and could speak the German language: and as a sufficient number could not be found among the English officers, it was further necessary to bring over and grant commissions to several German and Swiss officers and engineers."[9]

Later the Royal American regiment became the Sixtieth Rifles. "The rifle, in 1775, was used only along the frontiers of Pennsylvania and the Southern Colonies. It had been introduced into Pennsylvania about 1700 by **Swiss and Palatine immigrants.** The frontiersmen improved it and made out of it a superior type of firearms. Over every cabin door hung a well made and correctly-sighted rifle. As soon as a boy was big enough to level it, he was given powder and ball to shoot squirrels. These were the "expert riflemen" organized by Act of Congress June 14, 1775, into a corps of nine companies. In one short month, the first company, Nagel's Berks County "Dutchmen" was at Cambridge, and in

[9]Smollett's History of England, page 111-475. (Frontier Forts, page 253).

less than sixty days nine companies of backwoodsmen from Pennsylvania, Maryland and Virginia were at Boston. At a review, a company of these riflemen, while on a quick advance, fired their balls into object of seven inch diameter at a distance of 250 yards. They were the nucleus of the American army, absolutely loyal to the American cause and knowing no fatherland but the wilderness."[10]

"The Royal American Regiment was a new corps raised in the colonies, largely among the Germans of Pennsylvania. Its officers were from Europe; and of the most conspicuous among them was Lieut. Col. Bouquet, a brave and accomplished swiss, who commanded one of the four battallions of which the regiment was composed." A list of the campaigns of this regiment is given:

"1757 First Battalion in Indian wars.
Five companies under Stanwix in Pennsylvania.
Third Battallion at Fort Hunter and Fort William Henry.
Second and Fourth at Louisbourg.
First Battalion under Bouquet in South Carolina.
First and Fourth at Crown Point and Ticonderoga.
1758 Second and Third Battallions at Louisbourg.
First and Fourth under Bouquet and Forbes at Fort Duquesne.
1759 Fourth Battallion under Prideaux at Fort Niagara.
Second and Third under Wolfe at Quebec.
Fourth under Haldiman at Oswego.
First under Amherst at Lake Champlain.
Fourth under Sir William Johnson, Bouquet, Stanwix and Wolfe at Quebec.
1760 First, Second and Third at Quebec.
1761 First in Virginia.

[10]Border Warfare in Pennsylvania Shimmel.

1762 Third at Martinique and Havana.
1763 First under Bouquet at Bushy Run and Pittsburgh."[11]

Many from this regiment took up lands in Westmoreland County. "At one time Michael Schlatter, pioneer of the Reformed Church, resigned his congregation because of difficulties with the Holland Synod, and became Chaplain under Colonel Louden, in the Royal American Regiment, fourth battalion in the campaign against Nova Scotia and Louisburg. He held a similar position during the Revolutionary War."[12]

"From this time (1764) until the regular opening of the land office (1769) trouble was apprehended by reason of settlers occupying territory in various parts of the country, particularly territory on the Monongahela and Youghougheny, in violation of the treaty rights of the Indians. Complaint being made, the Governor of Virginia, as well as Gen. Gage, the commander in chief of the British forces in America, used every reasonable exertion to have the settlers peaceably removed. Various conferences and treaties were held during this period between the agents of these officials and the Indians, at and about Fort Pitt. It was provided that the penalties that were attached to the violation of these laws, or treaty obligations, did not extend to those who had settled on the main communication leading to Fort Pitt, under the permission of the Commander-in-Chief, nor to settlements made by George Croghan, Esq., Deputy superintendent under Sir William Johnson, upon the Ohio above said fort."[13]

"On February 13, 1768 an act was passed which provided that any one having settled here without permission, and who should neglect to remove after a legal notice was served on him to do so, should, after being convicted of such neglect, be punished with death without the benefit of the clergy."[14]

---

[11]Frontier Forts.
[12]Faust.
[13]Frontier Forts.
[14]Boucher History of Westmoreland County.

Because of the impending troubles a council was called at Fort Stanwix in New York in the fall of 1768. Sir William Johnson met the Indian Chiefs and made a treaty with them November 5, 1768 which restored peace and harmony once more. By this treaty all territory from a point where the Susquehanna crosses the New York line, down to the southwest corner of Pennsylvania, including the Allegheny, Conemaugh, Monongahela and Youghougheny River valleys, was conveyed to the Proprietaries. This is called "The New Purchase." To us it is the most important of all purchases and was the last made by the Penns from the Indians. The sum paid to the Indians is said to have been $10,000 in presents and money and unlimited rum."[15]

This "New Purchase" was opened for settlement April 3, 1769 and several thousand warrants were applied for the first day.

"Fully two hundred families of Pennsylvania Germans, chiefly from the counties of Northampton, Berks, Lehigh, Franklin, Lancaster, Adams and York, crossed the mountains from 1769 to 1772, and took up lands, some of these Germans being from Maryland and Virginia and a few came direct from the Fatherland. The great majority of these earliest settlers located in Westmoreland, Fayette and Allegheny counties. The first settlements were Fort Pitt in Allegheny County. Harold's Brush Creek and Ligonier Valley in Westmoreland County; and German township in Fayette County. Other settlements effected soon after were Ridge, Schwab's, Kuendigs, Hoffman's Seanor's, Greensburg (then Newtown) Manor, and Beamer's in Westmoreland County; Bethlehem and Stecher's in Allegheny County; West Salem in Allegheny County; Buechle's in Butler County; Rupp's and Crooked Creek in Armstrong County, and Brush Valley, Germany and In-

[15]Boucher History of Westmoreland County.

diana in Indiana County. The German settlements of Clarion, Mercer, Crawford and Erie Counties were made at a still later period."[16]

---

[16]History of the Pittsburgh Synod of the General Synod of the Evangelical Lutheran Church—Burgess.

CHAPTER IV

Zion Church Settlement

The settlement around the present Herold's Church was made as early as 1750–60 and although these early settlers were driven eastward by the Indian attacks, they returned with Bouquet and reoccupied their farms. Much land was preempted by "tomahawk" right and military permit before this section was opened for settlement on April 3, 1769. After this formal opening, many more settlers arrived.

The interest of these early German settlers in religion is shown in that in the year 1765 or before, they preempted 158 acres of the choicest land for Church purposes; this they styled "Good Purpose." A warrant for this tract was granted August 22, 1785, and patented May 23, 1789. This land was preempted and patented for the Lutheran Church alone. In fact, it seems as if there were but few German Reformed in the settlement at this time, as there are no authentic records of the German Reformed Church until the coming of Rev. John William Weber, who arrived early in June, 1783.

It has been supposed that the records kept by Balthasar Meyer, the Lutheran Schoolmaster, included the German Reformed, as well as the Lutheran baptisms; but this is not the case; for we read in the History of the Reformed Church, Page 40, Edition of 1877: "These teachers were even constrained, as we have seen in the case above given, if there were no minister, to administer infant baptism when it was thought necessary. This was probably more the case with

Lutherans than with the Reformed, **who seldom or never permitted lay baptism."**

Fac-simile of Taufschein of Johann George Eisenman, of Zion Church Settlement

Indeed, the records of Balthaser Meyer show that it was the established rule and custom to have children baptised at an early age. (See appendices A and D). There are also documents extant which show that the Lutheran doctrine of Baptismal Regeneration was well known and practiced in these early times as we read from the Taufschein of "John George Eisenmann, born 28 of May in the year of our Lord 1788 and on the 13th of July was through the washing of Holy Baptism baptized into the congregation of Christ as a living member and as a young branch received." The Baptism witnesses were, in this sacred ordinance, the honorable John Peter Eisenmann and Anna Barbara, his wife; uncle and aunt of the child. This uncle presents the Taufschein to the child and upon it we read further this advice which he gives, "Take care of your soul and think that you, through the sacrament of Baptism, by Jesus, are received. It is only water which is externally used, but the blood of Jesus Christ internally, so that your soul, virtuous and clean, may enter the Kingdom of Heaven. Through grace you are born anew. You are chosen to be an heir of heaven through Jesus Christ, the son of God, etc." Further we read, "The Baptism gives you new life, to live in that new life forever. Here in time and there in eternity."

Another fact of great weight in determining that these early records are Lutheran is that Balthasar Meyer was a Lutheran, which is shown when he ordains Anton Ulrich Luetge to the Lutheran ministry. Then again when Rev. Weber came to the settlement in 1783, he started a separate record of Baptisms which is paralel to, but not recorded in this book.

We must remember that although the Lutheran and German Reformed congregations later worshipped in the same building and owned the property jointly, they were not a Union Church. They were two congregations, distinct in doctrine and organization, with each its own Pastor; and the record begun by Balthasar Meyer and continued by the Lutheran Pastors does not contain any records of the Reformed Church, except the records of the yearly settlement;

and these relate to the financial conditions of the two congregations and the joint property. These are signed by the officers of both congregations. (See appendix E.)

Doubtless both parties to the settlement retained copies, and the Lutheran copy was inserted in this book.

We have no reason to doubt that some of the earlier German Reformed also brought their children to the Lutheran schoolmaster for baptism, just as later, the Lutheran and Reformed pastors baptized all children brought to them for that purpose.

The first entry in this old Lutheran record is as follows:

"Register of all children in Zion Church settlement, baptized by Balthasar Meyer, schoolmaster, from the second of August, 1772, until — — — — — . (See appendix A). The last entry in the handwriting of Balthasar Meyer is in the year 1792, the fourth of June. The record indicates in the year 1784 the advent of a regular Lutheran Minister, Rev. Anton Ulrich Luetge, but it seems that schoolmaster Meyer still continued to baptize children and entered the baptisms that he performed up until the fourth of June, 1792.

In 1784 a new baptismal list is begun, the heading is as follows:

"Record of such children, who were baptized in Zion's Church in Hempfield Township, Westmoreland County in the state of Pennsylvania, by the Reverend preachers." Inasmuch as Rev. John William Weber was keeping a separate record of baptisms of the Reformed Church, we are led to believe that this is Rev. Luetge's list of Baptisms. It is kept in the same handwriting until the 10th of September, 1791. We have identified the handwriting of this list as that of Karl Scheibeler, schoolmaster. It was customary in those days to have the schoolmaster keep the Church Records.

Fac-simile of Record of First Baptisms at Zion Church Settlement

"It was resolved that each congregation have its own Church Record, and that it be kept by the teacher of the congregation."[1]

[1]Minutes of the Evangelical Lutheran Ministerium of Pennsylvania and adjacent states, 1793.

Rev. Luetge's name appears in this list as God father, as follows:

	Parents	God-Parents
Hanna Friderica		Anton Ulrich Luetge
Born Feb. 18, 1785,	John Samuel Mau	Sophia Luisa, his wife.
Bapt. Mar. 6, 1785.	Eva Catharina, his wife	John Spielman
		Catharina, his wife.

The record of the Baptisms is continuous from 1772 until the present.

The first communion record is headed as follows:

"Record of communicants in Herold's or Zion's Church in Hempfield Township, Westmoreland County, in the year of our Lord and Savior, Jesus Christ, 1791, 11th October." (See appendix B).

This record continues to the present.

The record of confirmants is begun as follows:

"Record of the Confirmants, who on the 26th of May, 1792, in Hempfield Township, Westmoreland County, in the Herold's or Zion's Church, by Pastor Steck, Evangelical Lutheran preacher, were confirmed and blessed, and on the following day, the 27th of May, for the first time partook of the Lord's Supper." (See appendix C).

The record of confirmants is continuous until the present.

The Church in the House

During the period of 1750 to 1772, we may speak of the congregation as the **"Church in the house,"** when services were held in the house, for people who would preempt 158 acres of the choicest land for "Good Purpose" would not neglect the worship of God.

The Church in the School

From 1772 to 1782, we have the period of the **"Church in the school."** The interests of the settlement centered in the school. A schoolhouse was erected in 1772 and a schoolmaster secured. Balthasar Meyer became the first schoolmaster and the religious leader of the settlement. The first formal records of the Church were made by him when he recorded the Baptisms which he performed.

The old schoolhouse was located about three hundred feet south of and slightly eastward of the present public school building.

The following description of the schoolhouse the author received from Mrs. Salome Miller, nee Leasure, of Armbrust, Pa., in the year 1912. Mrs. Miller was then in her ninety-third year of age, but was well preserved in health and had a remarkably clear memory. She was a pupil of "Grandpap" Zundel.

Mrs. Miller remembered the old schoolhouse at Herold's. It was first built as a one room log building. There was one door facing the east and one window opposite the door. The floor was of puncheon, the seats of hewn logs made into benches. At first the window lights were of greased paper, later we read in the Annual settlement of the Church, of an item of expenditure "for glass in schoolhouse, 8 shillings." This was in 1792. As glass was then a novelty, this item shows how highly these settlers rated their school and how progressive they were to improve its equipment. It is probable that this was the only schoolhouse west of the Alleghenies that had a glass window.

About the time John Michael Zundel became schoolmaster, probably in order to furnish him a home, a second story was added to the schoolhouse. This second story extended beyond the main building in order to afford protection to the doorway to the school room and also to give room for an entrance to the second story. This entrance to the second story was not very elaborate. It consisted of a trap door in the floor of the extended second story and a ladder which would be drawn up at night. There was no provision for a stove or fireplace in the second story; the only heat obtainable was from the fireplace in the schoolroom below. The cooking for the family was done outside the house in an open fireplace. Thus, in winter and summer it was necessary for the schoolmaster and his good helpmeet, upon arising in the morning, to open the trap door, let down the ladder, then descend to the ground outside the schoolhouse, clear away the snow, if it be winter, then build a fire from the glowing embers secured in the schoolhouse fireplace or start the fire anew with flint and steel and punk, and finally prepare the morning meal.

In this second story of the schoolhouse, schoolmaster Zundel lived many years. Here his children were born and reared until the eldest was probably fourteen years of age. Notwithstanding such hardships, John Michael Zundel lived to see his eighty-seventh year, and became the progenitor of a long line of school teachers, some of whom have succeeded him in the Herold's School.

After moving from the schoolhouse in 1827, he lived for a time on the "Yar" Adam Schneider farm and later lived with his daughter near Mt. Pleasant, Pa., and was buried in the private cemetery on the Schneider farm.

Balthasar Meyer was never ordained nor even licensed to preach the gospel. That he instructed the young, baptized infants, and read sermons are well established facts; but there is no evidence that he administered the Lord's Supper.

The longing for the Lord's Supper must have been the ruling motive of the settlers when they had schoolmaster Meyer set apart the exhorter Anton Ulrich Luetge to the Ministry.

Anton Ulrich Luetge was born in Germany and educated at the Halle University for the Foreign Mission field, but later decided to come to America. He settled in Franklin County and in 1782 settled in the Zion Settlement in Westmoreland County. It is said that Mr. Luetge also practiced medicine in connection with his pastoral work. In 1789, he removed to

Schippensburg, Pa., then in 1794 to Chamberstown, Pa., where he died in 1795. His widow appealed to the Ministerium for aid and was granted sums at stated intervals.

There is no record of the ordination or of the action of the congregation regarding the election of Mr. Luetge. That the procedure was not regular is shown by the records of the Evangelical Lutheran Ministerium, 1785. "Mr. Luetge, who has been ordained by a preacher named Meyer, asked in writing for admission into the Ministerium. But it was resolved that the United Ministerium did not want to have anything further to do with him."

In 1788 the minutes make the following reference: "Mr. Luetge, who for some years was stationed in Westmoreland County as preacher, reported himself to the Synod, and asked to be received. He had been ordained by a certain Meyer, who himself was not ordained. The Ministerium declared his ordination invalid, and requested from him a written outline on Mark 1:15: 'Repent ye, and believe the Gospel.'" On the following day, after the outline was read and considered, "The case of Mr. Luetge was again taken up and on motion, resolved to give him a license to preach and to baptize, on the following conditions:

1. That he shall improve his knowledge of Greek.
2. Keep a diary of his official acts.
3. Present to the Ministerium testimonials from the elders and deacons of the congregations in which he preaches."

Mr. Luetge complied with these conditions and was continued on the rolls of the Ministerium as a Licentiate.

The action of the Ministerium seems severe, yet it was necessary in those days because of the many bad men and false prophets that aspired to the ministry. In spite of such severe methods and all diligent watchfulness, wicked men did occasionally secure entrance to congregations as pastors, to the great scandal and harm of the Church. Then again our fathers were zealous to maintain an educated ministry. The difference between a licentiate and an ordained minister was chiefly that of education and experience.

"No. 30—That licensed candidate who is convinced that, by private application, he has advanced sufficiently to be able to undergo the examination referred to above in No. 27, may, in a spirit of meekness, make known his desire to be ordained in open session, but never without the afore-mentioned conviction as to a knowledge of the ancient languages and theology. No one will in future be ordained without both these requirements, unless in a very extraordinary instance, or the most urgent necessity."—Constitution of the Ministerium, 1781.

At the same meeting of the Ministerium that Mr. Luetge was licenced, it was "Resolved that the ordinandi and licentiates must sign a revers, which shall be entered on the Protocol." (Page 223.)

"The contents of the revers are:

1. To preach the Word of God in its purity, according to Law and Gospel, as it is explained in its chief points in the Augsburg Confession and the other Symbolical Books.

(Thus, we see that the first preacher west of the Alleghenies was solemnly pledged to the unaltered Augsburg Confession and the Symbolical books.)

2. Diligently to instruct children, visit the sick, care for souls and administer Holy Baptism according to the command of Christ.

3. Diligently to exercise himself in Knowledge.

4. To adorn the office with a Christian life.

5. Not to leave or go beyond the congregations which were entrusted to him in the license.

6. To record the most noteworthy occurrences of his ministry in a journal and annually present this to the Synodical Meeting, also to appear personally as often as asked.

7. To renew the license annually." (Page 188.)

The Synod also resolved (1788) "That the licentiates are obliged to attend each Synodical Meeting, and that they have a right to present matters and make comments, but not to vote."

In 1789 "Pastor Schulz moved that the licentiates should hand in to the Ministerium their journals and four complete sermons each year, as otherwise the Ministerium had no opportunity to judge correctly of their presentation of divine truth. This motion was generally approved and accepted." (Page 227.)

This whole matter of licensing candidates had a useful purpose in the early unsettled days of our fathers when ministers were scarce and the people demanded the services of their schoolmasters and others, but it has no place in a settled, well ordered state of the Church.

Mr. Luetge was called to Schippensburg, Cumberland County, in 1789. In the year 1791, we read "A letter from the congregation in Schippensburg was read in which the Ministerium was requested again to renew the license of Mr. Luetge, who also asked for it in person, whereupon it was unanimously —Resolved, That Mr. Luetge's license be renewed for one year."

In 1794, Anton Luetge is accredited to Chamberstown.

In 1796 we read, "Various Congregations now vacant: eg. — — — Gruensburg, Herold's Broshkrick, and Ridge, which the late Mr. Luetge served."

Thus, we see that the Ministerium never recognized the lay-ordination of Mr. Anton U. Luetge, and Mr. Luetge died as a licentiate.

The Church in the Sanctuary

We can readily see how the Indian attacks and the unsettled conditions of affairs would affect the work of the Church.

School houses were built at Zion settlement, Newton, now Greensburg, and at Brusch Creek, and schools were held at other points in Forts, Blockhouses, and private houses, or cabins for a few months during the year. The children were baptized by the schoolmasters and the older children were taught and catechized in the schools. Doubtless, these schools were also centers of worship and lay-preaching,—but the people longed for a church home.

A log church was begun at an early date but its completion was hindered by Indian troubles and other embarrassments, until the arrival of Rev. Luetge. It is said that when work was resumed after the Indian troubles, a goodsized oak sapling was found growing within the walls, indicating that the work had been retarded many years. During his pastorate, the building was completed.

"One of the old pastors of Harrold's congregation has made the following record concerning this church. 'The church building erected was rather spacious, but had only one door. The floor was made of puncheon, the seats were hewn logs. There was a gallery on the right side, open in front; it had rough seats to which a rude stairway led. At first there was only a plain table as an altar, but the present pastor remembers an altar there during the time of his ministerial service. The original pulpit was of the wine glass pattern, surmounted with a sounding board, painted a blue, with a canopy, showing the sun, moon, and stars in white.[2] The windows of the church were often broken and left unrepaired, so that squirrels and birds had free access to the inside of the church. They were often seen sporting about in the church, diverting themselves and the young people during the services."[3] This log church was used until the new stone church was built in 1830.

During Rev. Luetge's pastorate, there were probably four or five schoolmasters in the parish. Balthasar Meyer continued

[2]This old Pulpit has been traced and found by the aid of H. M. Zundel and Nicholaus Long. It is now restored and kept in the church. [3]Ulery Hist. Southern Conference.

to teach and baptize children. Karl Scheibeler taught in Greensburg and at Harrold's; because the list of baptisms beginning 1784 are entered by his hand in the Church register. John Michael Zundel and George Bushyager taught at Brush Creek and John Michael Zundel taught at Herold's from about 1810 to 1828.

Rev. Luetge was called to Schippensburg, Cumberland County, in 1789 and was reported from that field in 1791.

Quaint Old Pulpit from Old Log Church

Note on Old Pulpit.

This is the original pulpit of the old log church, built about 1782: It was elevated on a log three feet in diameter and three feet long, set upright, crude steps, four in number, led up to it. There was a small seat on the side opposite the entrance. The pulpit proper, shown in the cut, is the original, but the base and steps have been supplied in its rebuilding. This pulpit was used in the old log church until 1830.

When the new stone church was built the old pulpit was given to the Muelheisen Church. The elder Tobias Long and Philip Muelheisen were largely influential in the founding of the "Milliron" Church. Tobias Long the son of the elder Tobias Long named above who is now (May 1922) still living at the age of 88 years, says. "As a boy, but a few years after the old pulpit was brought to the "Milliron" Church, I often heard father and others speak of its early history, how it had for years been used in the old log church and then, after building the old stone church was brought here."

Comrade Nicholas Long, a veteran of the Civil War, also recalls the tradition of the old Pulpit. He says that many times he has heard the venerable Rev. H. E. F. Voight preach from the pulpit.

Mrs. Reuben Miller, nee Sarah Gangaware, daughter of Joseph Gangaware, who attended the Herold Church, deserves great credit for preserving the old pulpit for the present generation. When repairs were made to the "Milliron" Church, many years ago, the old pulpit was discarded. She could not bear to see it desecrated, so she had it hauled to her home on a sled. First it was placed at the end of an old fashioned cider press. Then it was next stored in her cellar. When the home was remodeled it was then stored under the porch, where it was found by Nicholaus Long, H. M. Zundel and Jacob E. Wincman, as the author had suggested. The pulpit is now preserved as a precious treasure of its early history in Old Zion's Church. It is probably the oldest pulpit west of the Allegheny mountains.

CHAPTER V

Frontier Conditions

The march of civilization westward is shown by the erection of counties. In 1682 Penn found Philadelphia, Bucks, and Chester Counties. Then followed, westward, Lancaster County in 1729, York County in 1749, Cumberland County in 1750, Bedford in 1772, and Westmoreland, beyond the mountains in 1773. This county embraced nearly all of Pennsylvania west of the mountains.

The first officers were appointed by Governor Richard Penn.

The scramble of politicians for office and salaried positions was as keen then as now. The Scotch-Irish take to politics as keenly as the German takes to a farm. Indeed, it was fortunate that there were Scotch-Irish and English to take the offices, else, so far as the Germans were concerned, Westmoreland would have been as unfortunate as Germantown was in 1703. Pastorius wrote to William Penn complaining of the difficulty in getting his people to serve as public officers, and expressing the hope that the arrival of new immigrants might relieve the situation.

"Fines and importations becoming necessary to secure officeholders, seems an embarrassment almost inconceivable to later generations of men, yet this historical fact emphasizes a trait often exhibited by the Germans in the United States." "December 1, 1694, Paul Wulff was elected clerk, but declining without good cause, he was fined three pounds by the General Court."[1]

Under the distracted conditions of a "border" settlement, it would be ridiculous to assert that the appointive and elective officers were always representative of the best men on the border. Politics was then more potent than now, since the Proprietaries lived at a distance and were necessarily out of immediate touch with actual conditions. Some of the barbarous penalties surely did not reflect credit upon the early courts. The election of the notorious murderer Williamson and some of his pals to office in Washington County outraged the decency even of "border" life. The conduct of some of the commanding officers in the west during these times was of such a nature as to bring the rebuke of state officials and frequent removals by the commander-in-chief. While the savage was scalping the helpless settlers, some of these commanders were playing politics for position.

The trustees to locate and erect the public buildings, appointed by the State, were Robert Hanna, Joseph Erwin, John Cavett, George Wilson, and Samuel Sloan. Now Hanna, Erwin, and Sloan stood together and decided that Hanna's house should be the county seat and Erwin should keep the tavern at Hannastown. What Sloan got out of the deal we are not told.

For many years, the settlement at Germantown did not have a jail, nor did they need one. From this place also went out the first protest, on American soil, against negro slavery; but the rigor and majesty of English law, "the accumlated wisdom of the ages," as administered by such judges as Hanna, Lochry, Sloan, and Cavett, required all the instrumentalities of torture used at the time.

"John Smith, charged with stealing and pleaded guilty, was sentenced to receive thirty-nine lashes on the bare back,

[1]Faust, Vol. 1059.

well laid on, and his ears were then to be cut off and nailed to the pillory, and he was to stand one hour in the pillory." "In January, 1774, William Howard suffered one hour in the pillory, after having received thirty lashes on the bare back, well laid on."

"In October, 1775, Elizabeth Smith was ordered to receive fifteen lashes on the bare back, well laid on."[2]

Three kinds of bond servants were brought to Westmoreland County—negro slaves, indentured servants, and redemptioners. The indentured servant could be bound for life or a period of years. It ranged in severity all the way from a voluntary act to involuntary slavery. The redemptioners were those who "indentured" themselves for a period of years, in return for the expense of ship passage to America. They redeemed themselves by a term of service to their creditor.

This "bondage" servant system sometimes brought undesirable people to the frontier, but in the main, it brought good workers whose only failing was the misfortune to be poor.

The "undesirables" of the frontier were largely the rowdies and criminals of the more settled sections of the east, who sought refuge on the frontier; thus it has been even to this day on the frontier in America.

In 1774 began what is known as Dunmore's War. Lord Dunmore was governor of Virginia. As the southern border of Pennsylvania was not then extended west of the mountains, Virginia and Pennsylvania both laid claim to the territory of the Ohio, Monongahela, and Youghiogheny valleys. At this time, Dunmore sent John Connolly to Pittsburgh. In January, 1774, he took the city, raised an army and called the place Fort Dunmore. He called the militia together ostensibly to fight the Indians, but really to fight for Virginia. St.

---

[2]Boucher History of Westmoreland County.

Clair, who had charge of Pennsylvania's interest, had Connolly arrested. He gave bail and went to Virginia, where Dunmore appointed him a justice. Returning to the west, he arrived at Hanna's town and refused to permit the Pennsylvania court to meet. He arrested the judges and sent them to Virginia. This naturally aroused the people, not only because they would thus lose title to their lands, but because of a threatened Indian attack. It appears, however, that the Indian attack threatened only the Virginians, but our people did not know this, and it would be easy for a scalping party to mistake a Pennsylvanian for a Virginian.

Connolly had called out the militia but had mobilized it at Kitanning, hence the settlers were left defenseless. Indignation meetings were held at many places and petitions sent to the Governor. An indignation meeting was held at Fort Allen and a petition was sent to Governor Penn, signed by the following persons. Doubtless other well known men were in the militia at Kitanning.

"Wendel Oury, Christopher Trubee, Frantz Raupp, Nicholas Scheuer, John Lafferty, John Bendeary, Conrad Houck, James Waterms, John Redeck, Adam George, Nicholas Allimang, Adam Uhrig, Stofel Urich, John Golden, Peter Urich, Martin Hunts, Michael Konel, Heinrich Kleyn, Conrad Hister, Hans Gunckee, Peter Kassner, Peter Uber, John Krausher, Heinrich Schmit Jacob Schmit, Jacob Kuemel, John Moffey, Adam Bricker, Peter Wannemacher, Philip Klingelschmit, Peter Klingelschmit, Peter Altman, Anthony Altman, Joseph Paukkek, Brent Reis, Baltzer Mayer, Jacob Hauser, Peter Altmann, Christian Baum, George Crier, Peter Rosch, Joseph Kutz, Adam Meire, Daniel Wilers, Thomas Williams, Michael Hatz, George Mondarf, William Hanson, William Altman, Marx Breinig, Johannes Breinig, Samuel Lewisch, Anthony Walter, Jacob Welcker, George Bender, Nicholas Junt, Michael Hann, David Marshall, Heinrich Sil, Richard Archbold, Conrad Linck, Friedrich Marschal, Hannes Breinig, Kasper Mickendorf, Jacob Schraber, Daniel Matiss, Heinrich Schram, Peter Schelhammer, Jacob Meylin, Dewalt Macklin, Hannes Kostwitz, Jacob Schram, Ludwig Aterman, Hans Sil, Jacob Stroh, Christopher Herolt, Gerhart Tames."[3]

On June 12, 1774, St. Clair writes to Governor Penn: "An idle report of Indians having been seen within the Partys, has drove them every one into some little fort or other—and many hundreds out of the country altogether. This has obliged me to call in the Partys from where they were posted, and have stationed them, twenty men at Turtle Creek, twenty at Proctor's, and twenty at Ligonier, as these places are now the Frontier toward the Allegheny, all that great Country, between that road and the river, being totally abandoned, except by a few who are associated with the people who murdered the Indian. (Wipey a friendly Indian). And are shut up in a small Fort on Conymack, equally afraid of the Indians and the officers of justice."[4]

Dunmore's war lasted until 1775, when it was ended by the Continental Congress, and the boundary line was fixed in 1780 as it is today.[5]

It was during or prior to Dunmore's War that Fort Allen was built.

The Revolution

Notwithstanding the distractions of Indian wars and Dunmore's war, the people west of the Alleghenies were alive to the issues of the Colonies and the Mother country. The news of the battle of Lexington traveled fast, but we doubt if the news had reached Westmoreland, before the call went out for a general meeting at Hannastown for May 16, 1775. Here, a year before the Declaration of Independence, the following resolutions were adopted:

---

[3]Burgess History of the Pittsburgh Synod, General Synod.
[4]Frontier Forts.
[5]Frontier Forts, page 189.

"Meeting of the inhabitants of Westmoreland County, Pennsylvania. At a general meeting of the inhabitants of the County of Westmoreland, held at Hanna's town the 16th day of May, 1775, for taking into consideration the very alarming situation of the country, occasioned by the dispute with Great Britain:"[6]

"Resolved unanimously, That the Parliament of Great Britain, by several late acts, have declared the inhabitants of Massachusetts Bay to be in rebellion; and the Ministry, by endeavoring to enforce these acts, have attempted to reduce the said inhabitants to a more wretched state of slavery than ever before existed in any state or country. Not content with violating their Constitutional and Chartered privileges, they would strip them of the rights of humanity, exposing lives to the wanton and unpunishable sport of licentious soldiery, and depriving them of the very means of sustenance.

"Resolved unanimously that there is no reason to doubt but the same system of tyranny and oppression will, should it meet with success in Massachusetts Bay, be extended to every other part of America: it is, therefore, become the indispensable duty of every American, of every man who has any public virtue or love of his country, or for posterity, by every means which God has put in his power, to resist and oppose the execution of it; that for us, we will be ready to oppose it with our lives, and fortunes, and the better to enable us to accomplish it, we will immediately form ourselves into a military body, to consist of companies to be made up out of the several townships under the following association, which is declared to be the Association of Westmoreland County.

"We declare to the world, that we do not mean by this Association to deviate from that loyalty which we hold it our bounded duty to observe; but, animated with the love of

[6]Frontier Forts.

liberty, it is no less our duty to maintain and defend our just rights, which with sorrow we have seen of late wantonly violated in many instances by a wicked Ministry and a corrupt Parliament, and transmit them entire to our posterity, for which purpose we do agree and associate together.

"Possessed with the most unshaken loyalty and fidelity to His Majesty, King George the Third, whom we acknowledge to be our lawful and rightful King, and who we wish may long be the beloved sovereign of a free and happy people throughout the whole British Empire; we declare to the world that we do not mean by this association to deviate from that loyalty which we hold it to be our bounden duty to observe; but, animated with the love of liberty, it is no less our duty to maintain and defend our just rights (which with sorrow, we have seen of late wantonly violated in many instances by a wicked Ministry and a corrupt Parliament) and transmit them entire to our posterity, for which purposes we do agree and associate together.

"1. To arm and form ourselves into a regiment or regiments, and choose officers to command us.

2. We will with alacrity, endeavor to make ourselves masters of the manuel exercise, and such evolutions as shall be necessary to enable us to act in a body with concert; and to that end we will meet at such times and places as shall be appointed, either for the companies or regiment, by the officers commanding each when chosen.

3. That should our country be invaded by a foreign enemy, or should troops be sent from Great Britain to enforce the late arbitrary acts of Parliament, we will cheerfully submit to a military discipline, and to the utmost of our power, resist and oppose them, or either of them, and will coincide with any plan that may be formed for the defense of America in general or Pennsylvania in particular.

4. That we do not desire any innovation, but only that things may be restored to, and go on in the same way as before the era of the Stamp Act, when Boston grew great and America was happy. As a proof of this disposition, we will quietly submit to the laws by which we have been accustomed to be governed before that period, and will, in our several or associate capacities, be ready when called on to assist the civil magistrates in carrying the same into execution.

5. That when the British Parliament shall have repealed their late obnoxious statutes, and shall recede from their claim to tax us, and make laws for us in every instance, or when some general plan of union or reconciliation has been formed and accepted by America, this, our association, shall be dissolved; but till then, it shall remain in full force; and to the observation of it we bind ourselves by everything dear and sacred amongst men. No licensed murder; no famine introduced by law.

Resolved, That on Wednesday, the 24th instant, the township meet to accede to the said association and choose their officers."[7]

Some investigators have denied the authenticity of these resolutions, but there is nothing in them that need disturb the equanimity of the historian. It is clear, from the document itself, that the "meeting" had no news of the battle of Lexington. The phrases "No licensed murder" refers to the Boston massacre, and "No famine introduced by law" refers to the closing of the Port of Boston. This meeting and resolutions are the result of the work of the "Committees of Correspondence" with headquarters, doubtless, at Boston. It seems that the "Committee of Correspondence" had sent about the same request and information to many other places throughout the land. A similar meeting was called at Pittsburg on the same day, May 16, 1775.[8] "At Hanover, Pa., the

[7]Boucher, page 124. [8]Border Warfare in Pennsylvania, page 43.

Scotch-Irish and German borderers resolved among other things 'that in the event of Great Britain attempting to force unjust laws upon us by the strength of arms, our cause we leave to Heaven and our Rifles'."

On June 16, 1774, a meeting took place at Woodstock, Va., Rev. Peter Muehlenberg, Lutheran pastor, presided and afterwards was Chairman of the Committee on Resolutions. "Rev. Muehlenberg was an intimate friend of Patrick Henry and Colonel George Washington. With the former he laid deep plans of sedition; with the latter he shot bucks in the Blue Ridge Mountains."

The following extracts show the spirit pervading the resolutions.

"That we will pay due submission to such acts of government as His Majesty has a right by law to exercise over his subjects, and to such only.

That it is the inherent right of British subjects to be governed and taxed by representatives chosen by themselves only, and that every act of the British Parliament respecting the internal policy of American is a dangerous and unconstitutional invasion of our rights and privileges.

That the enforcing the execution of said acts of Parliament by a military power will have a necessary tendency to cause a civil war, thereby dissolving that union, which has so long happily subsisted between the mother country and her colonies; and that we will most heartily and unanimously concur with our suffering brethren in Boston and every other part of North America, who are the immediate victims of tyranny, in promoting all proper measures to avert such dreadful calamities, to procure redress of our grievances, and to secure our common liberties."[9]

The Committee of safety and correspondence appointed for the county consisted of Peter Muehlenberg, Chairman,

---

[9]Faust, page 292.

Francis Slaughter, Abraham Bird, T. Beale, J. Tipton, and Abraham Bowman.

Similar resolutions were adopted in Virginia as follows: Fredericksburg, June 1. Prince William County, June 8, 1775.

"The Mecklenburg, North Carolina, Declaration of Independence, so called, was written May 20 and adopted May 31, 1775. This declaration is said not to imply. complete independence of Great Britain."[10]

The militia raised by means of these Associations was called "Associators." Doubtless the Minute Men of Lexington and Concord belonged to the same general organization as the Associators. Hence, we see that the Hanna'stown meeting.was but a part of the work of the Committee of Correspondence and part of a widespread movement. Nor does the Hanna'stown document go as far and express the fundamental issues as clearly, as the Woodstock document.

Who wrote the Hanna'stown Resolutions is not known. Some have claimed that St. Clair wrote them, but his correspondence denies that fact and shows him rather cynical and unsympathetic.

In a letter to Joseph Shippen, Jr., from Ligonier, May 18, 1775, he says, "Yesterday, we had a county meeting and have come to resolutions to arm and discipline, and have formed an Association, which I suppose you will soon see in the papers. God grant an end may be speedily put to any necessity to such proceedings. I doubt their utility, and am almost as much afraid of success in this contest as of being vanquished."[11]

To Governor Penn, May 25th, 1775, he writes, "We have nothing but musters and committees all over the country, and everything seems to be running into the wildest confusion. If

[10]Standard Encyclopedia.
[11]Frontier Forts.

some conciliating plan is not adopted by the Congress, America has seen her golden days; they may return, but will be preceded by scenes of horror. An Association is formed in this country for defense of American Liberty. I got a clause added, by which they bind themselves to assist the civil magistrates in the execution of the laws they have been accustomed to be governed by."[12]

St. Clair was the representative of the Proprietors in this county and he evidently feared a reaction against the Penns as well as against the mother country. At least, he safeguarded his employer's interests.

When the war was actually begun, Westmoreland men enlisted in the first and second Battalions of Pennsylvania troops, in the Third Pennsylvania Regiment, in the Pennsylvania Rifle Regiment, in the Second Pennsylvania Regiment, and the Eighth Pennsylvania Regiment.[13] This last Regiment was mustered at Pittsburg, 1776, for the defense of the border against the Indians, but was later marched to New Jersey to aid Washington. There were ten companies which numbered 681 soldiers in all. Captain David Kilgore's company had 58 men; Captain Samuel Miller's had 85; Captain Van Swearingen's had 74; Captain Joseph Piggott's had 59; Captain Wendel Ourry's had 59; Captain Andrew Mann's 62; Captain James Montgomery's 59; Captain Michael Huffnagle's 74; Captain John Finley's 79; and Captain Basil Prather's 73.[14]

After more than a year's service in the east, the Eighth Regiment was sent back to Pittsburgh to defend the border.[15] Westmoreland men served in nearly all the campaigns from Quebec to Georgia. Wherever, during the Revolution, we read of "Riflemen," there we may expect to find the German and Swiss, for the rifle was a weapon introduced into

[12]Frontier Forts.
[13]Boucher, Vol. I, page 139.
[14]Boucher, Vol. I, page 138.
[15]Boucher, Vol. I, page 138.

America by them and none ever surpassed these hardy pioneers in the accuracy of its use.

There are several interesting features of the Revolutionary War that we should know. The first is that Washington's bodyguard was made up of Germans. There had been suspects in the first bodyguard and plots to seize the person of the Commander-in-chief. On the advice of Washington's private secretary and adjutant, Reed, who was of German descent, a troop was formed consisting entirely of Germans, called the Independent Troop of Horse, and placed under the command of Major Barth. Van Heer, a Prussian, who had served as cavalry Lieutenant under Frederick the Great in the Seven Year's War. Van Heer recruited most of his men in the Pennsylvania German counties, Berks and Lancaster. They began to serve in the spring of 1778, and were honorably discharged at the end of the war, twelve of them serving longer than any other American soldiers, having the honor of escorting the Commander-in-Chief to his home at Mount Vernon. These twelve men each received presents of arms, accoutrements, and a horse, as we learn from a written record in the possession of the family of one of the twelve, Ludwig Boyer (or Beyer). In the pension lists of 1828, a number of names of soldiers belonging to Van Heer's troop (fourteen officers and fifty-three men) are given. Boyer was granted a pension, one hundred pounds annually; Jacob Fox (Fuchs), who had lost his discharge, brought as witness two former comrades, Burckhardt and Trischer, who swore that they had belonged to Van Heer's corps and that that troop was the bodyguard of Washington.

Colonel John Johnson, by birth an Irishman, president of the Historical and Philosophical Society of Ohio and personal friend of Washington, said that not a single officer or soldier of this troop understood a word of English and that it was commanded by Major Van Heer, a Prussian.[16] The descendents of Ludwig Boyer lived in Piqua, Ohio, and he doubtless came west after the war. The Boyers and Fuchs were familiar names in our settlement.

Another incident not generally known is the presence of German troops at Yorktown, both with the Americans and with the French. Under Rochambeau served the Royal German Regiment of Zweibruecken, a battalion of grenadiers of Kur-Trier of the Regiment Saar. Several divisions of Alsatians and Lotharingians, and the "Independent Horse" legion.

Nelson's company of Westmoreland riflemen fought at Germantown, Brandywine, Monmouth, Stony Point, and Yorktown, with General Wayne. This Second Pennsylvania Regiment fought with St. Clair in Canada. The Third Pennsylvania Regiment was with Wayne at Yorktown. At the siege of Yorktown, Baron Steuben was the only American officer who had ever been present at a siege. He had served under Frederick the Great and gave up a lucrative position in order to volunteer his services to Congress. He became the organizer, drill-master, and Inspector-General of Washington's army, and his tactics and discipline saved Washington's army at Monmouth, where the familiar voice of Steuben rallied General Lee's retreating division. His discipline saved Lafayette's army in Virgina. He literally created an army for General Greene in the South. Steuben was in command in the trenches when the British raised the white flag at Yorktown. Steuben's brigade consisted of Wayne's Pennsylvania Regiment, Muehlenberg's Virginians, and Gist's Marylanders, the brigade being at least one-half German.[17]

The last principal British redoubt was stormed by Prince Wilhelm von Zweibruecken and his grenadiers and yagers. This redoubt was defended by the Hessians, and it is reliably reported that "commands were given in the German language

[16]Faust, Vol. I, page 299. [17]Faust, Vol. I, page 348.

on either side when the redoubt was captured."[18] "After Steuben had received the first overture of peace from Cornwallis, Lafayette requested that he be permitted to supersede Steuben, but the latter, knowing that by the etiquette of military custom he was entitled to the place until the surrender, referred the matter to Washington. Washington decided in favor of Steuben. The latter was not impelled by personal vanity, nor did the Prussian feel antagonistic to the Frenchman, but he possessed a large measure of pride in his Americans. He wanted the American Soldiery, his pupils in military tactics and discipline, to be honored as the recipients of the enemy's suit of surrender." In our cemeteries lie the mortal remains of brave men who saw the British raise the white flag at Yorktown and who rejoiced in the honor that fell to Steuben's American brigade.

---

[18]Faust, Vol. I, page 347, 348.

CHAPTER VI

The Red Revolutionary War

While the Americans and British were fighting in a more or less civilized fashion along the seaboard, the red allies of the British, and the British themselves, were fighting a savage war on the frontiers.

"During the summer of 1777 occurred the violent and atrocious outbreak of the savages, instigated by the British in order to harass the frontiers and to divert the attention of these people from the contest of the east to the defense of their own hearths, and from now on to the close of the war this frontier knew no peace."[1]

"Gov. Hamilton, at Detroit, to whom the entire management of frontier affairs had been entrusted, was ordered by Guy Carleton, October 6th, 1776, to enlist the Indians and have them ready for spring. The purpose of this attack on the frontier was to weaken the main army of the 'Rebels' and facilitate the operations of Howe and Burgoyne. Hamilton was fully aware of the importance of his part and played it well. He soon asquired the hatred of the 'buckskins,' who held him in abhorence, and nicknamed him the 'hair-buyer' general. That he deserved this name is disputed; but scalps were bought and paid for at Detroit. There is an account of an Indian, who, by dividing a large scalp into two, got $50.00 for each half at Detroit."[2] "Franklin in his list of twenty-six British atrocities, gives the 10th and 14th as—

[1]Frontier Forts.
[2]Border Warfare, page 68.

'The King of England, giving audience to his Secretary of War, who presents him a schedule entitled **Account of Scalps;** which he receives very graciously.'

'The commanding officer at Niagara, sitting in state, a table before him, his soldiers and savages bring him scalps of the Wyoming families and presenting them. Money on the table with which he pays for them.'[3]

The following is an inventory of scalps taken by the Seneca Indians, which accidentally fell into American hands. Lot 1—forty-three scalps of soldiers of Congress killed in battle, also sixty-two scalps of farmers who had been killed in their houses.

Lot 2—Ninety-eight scalps of farmers killed in their houses, surprised by day, not by night as the first lot. The red color applied to the hoops of wood, which were used to stretch the scalp, indicated the difference.

Lot 3—Contained ninety-seven scalps of farmers killed in their fields, different colors denoting whether killed by tomahawk or rifle ball.

Lot 4—Contained one hundred and two scalps of farmers, most of them young men.

Lot 5—Contained eighty-eight scalps of women, those with blue hoops cut from the heads of mothers.

Lot 6—Contained one hundred and ninety-three scalps of boys of different ages killed with clubs or hatchets, some with knives or bullets.

Lot 7—Contained two hundred and eleven scalps of girls, large and small, and

Lot 8—One hundred and twenty-two scalps of various kinds, among them twenty-nine babes's scalps, carefully stretched on small white hoops.

---

[3]Border Warfare, page 69.

The entire bundle including the total of 1,062 scalps, fell into the hands of a New England expedition against the Indians, and a prayer was found, addressed to the British governor (Haldimond)—"Father, we wish that you send these scalps to the Great King that he may look at them and be refreshed at their sight, recognize our fidelity, and be convinced that his presents have not been bestowed upon a thankless people."[4]

The Senecas were one of the tribes of the Six Nations. It is thought that Kiashuta, a head chief of the Senecas, led the Indian attack at Hanna'stown. He was also in Pontiac's conspiracy.

The Senecas occupied Western New York and the upper Allegheny region.

The British Government took the initiative in offering premiums for scalps, for it was not until 1780 that Pennsylvania offered $1,000.00 for every Indian scalp. This was to encourage scouts, rangers, and militia to invade the Indian territory and thus relieve the frontier. This was a dangerous plan, as is seen in the case of Williamson and his gang when they murdered the Christian Indians in Ohio to obtain the bounty for their scalps in 1782.

The bounty frequently led to the slaughter of friendly Indians, thus the "roughnecks" of the border frequently brought shame and counter-attacks upon the honest settlers of the frontier. "On this question, Colonel Broadhead, in a letter to President Reed, (of Pennsylvania) says that about forty friendly Delaware Indians had come to assist the white settlers in the frontier war, and that a party of about forty white men from the region of Hanna's town attempted to destroy them, and were only prevented from doing so by his soldiers. He says in the same letter that he could have gotten one hundred Indians to join him, had it not been for

[4]Faust, Vol. I, page 316.

such open enmity as was evinced by these men from Hanna's town. Among the Hanna's town party were Captains Irwin and Jack, Lieutenant Brownlee, and Ensign Guthrie." This enmity was the cause of Brownlee's death, when captured at Fort Miller. When inadvertently, his name was mentioned by a fellow captive, the Indians immediately tomahawked him. "Judge Wilkinson, in the American Pioneer, says the scalp bounty law was brought into disrepute by killing friendly Indians to sell their scalps."[5] Another factor that increased the sufferings of the settlers in Westmoreland County in those revolutionary days was the constant bickering, contention, and playing politics among the military commanders at Fort Pitt and the counties surrounding. "President Reed in a letter to Lochry, says, 'It is with much concern that we hear that when troops are raised for your protection, they are permitted to loiter away their time in taverns or straggling about the country.'[6] There were charges of misappropriation of supplies, and rather frequent changes in commanders. President Reed disapproved of retaining the troops at Hannastown and asked that they be sent where they could be of more service. Lieutenant Lochry built a magazine and blockhouse on his own farm in Unity Township to keep the army stores and ammunition. He either did not fully trust the garrisons with its right use, or was providing for his own safety. President Reed disapproved of his plan and directed that the stores and munitions should be kept in the garrisons.

In November, 1777, Archibald Lochry, county Lieutenant of Westmoreland, writes to President Wharton as follows: "The distressed situation of our country is such, that we have no prospect but desolation and destruction. The whole country on the north side of the road (Forbes road) from the Alle-

[5]Boucher, Vol. I, page 147.
[6]Boucher, Vol. I, page 149. History of Westmoreland County.

gheny Mts. to the river is all kept close in forts; and can get no subsistance from their plantations; they have made application to us requesting to be put under pay and receive rations, and as we could see no other way to keep the people from flying and letting the country be evacuated, we were obliged to adopt these measures (requesting your Excellency to give the necessary orders to enable us to put them in execution)—if these very measures are not adopted, I see no other method that can secure the people from giving up the country. These people, while they support these frontiers, are certainly serving the public, and certainly cannot continue long so to do unless supported by the public."[7]

In 1778 an attack was made upon Hannastown at which time Eve Ourry (Uhrig) saved the fort. "Eve Oury was granted a special pension of forty dollars per year by Act of April 1, 1846. The act itself recites that it was granted for heroic bravery and risking her life in defense of the garrison of Hannastown Fort in 1778, when it was attacked by a large number of Indians, and that by her fortitude, she performed efficient service in driving away the Indians, and thus saved the inmates from a horrid butchery by the merciless and savage foe."[8] She was a daughter of Francis Oury (Uhrig) and died at Shieldsburg, in 1848, and is buried at Congruity.

"Colonel Lochry writes to President Reed, May 1, 1779, that not less than forty people had been killed, wounded, and captured that spring, and that the enemy had killed people within three hundred yards of Hanna's town."

"It was on March 28, 1778, that Alexander McKee, Matthew Elliott, and Simon Girty fled from the vicinity of Fort Pitt to the enemy and incited the Indians against the settlers. These three renegades afterwards proved themselves

---

[7]Frontier Forts.
[8]Boucher, Vol. I, page 170.
[9]Border Warfare, page 104.

active servants of the British Government, bringing untold misery to the frontiers, not only while the Revolution continued, but throughout the Indian War which followed that struggle."[10]

Under date of June 25th, 1779, Col. Broadhead reports that "Captain Brady with twenty white men and one young Delaware Chief (all well painted) set out toward the Seneca country and some of the Indian warriors came in to the inhabitants. They killed a soldier between Forts Crawford and Hand, and proceeded towards the Sewickley settlement where they killed a woman and four children and took two children prisoners."[11]

This is doubtless the official account of the Henry Massacre.

The Henry Massacre

The attack on the Henry (Heinrich) home has often been rehearsed in our hearing. The scene of the tragedy was within sight of the author's boyhood home. The little cemetery on the hillside on the John G. Miller farm contains the earthly remains of the Henry family. We can still trace the sight of the burned cabin upon the freshly ploughed land. The story is as follows:

Frederick Henry (Heinrich), of Northampton, Burlington County, New Jersey, settled, shortly after 1770, in the Herold settlement, about two miles north of the schoolhouse (now the John G. Miller farm; the A. M. Zundel farm and Solomon Bender farm were parts of the original tract). In time, the new settlers cleared some land and erected a house and stables. Four children cheered this lonely settlement. During the Spring of 1779, when the husband, Frederick Henry, was compelled to leave home to take some grist to a distant mill, a

[10]Frontier Forts.
[11]Frontier Forts, page 338 and Border Warfare, page 108.

band of Indians, perhaps Senecas, descended upon the helpless home.

As was their custom, the Indians sneaked up to the house to ascertain if the men were home and on guard. Now, the Henry's had a large cock that frequently came to the door of the home to be fed. Mrs. Henry, seeing some feathers moving near the door, sent one of the children to shoo away the big rooster, whereupon the Indians, decked out in the feathers of their war head-gear, burst in upon the helpless family. Mrs. Henry bravely attempted to defend her little ones, whereupon she was "tomahawked" and scalped in the presence of her small children.

One child, seeing the Indians coming at the door, fled into the corn field and hid among the corn, and thus escaped, the Indians being in a hurry, fearing the wrath of the settlers.

The Indians now took the three children captive, and after firing the buildings, started on their journey toward the Indian country. It soon developed that the youngest child, a mere infant, would be too much bother to the Indians, so when it began to cry, a big Indian took it by its feet and dashed its brains out against a maple tree on the Solomon Bender farm, now owned by William Henry.

This tree was held sacred by the pioneers and it stood until recent times (about 1900).

The other two children were carried away.

Immediately upon the return of Henry, a posse of settlers started out in pursuit of the Indians. One account relates that the Indians were in their camp above Pittsburgh on the Allegheny, and after a lively skirmish, the children were recaptured, and the murderer of the wife and child identified; tied to a tree, and despatched by the daughter, Anna Margaret, then about nine years old.[12]

---

[12]The eldest child recorded in Baptismal record of Frederick Hinrich and Catherine his wife was Sarah, born October 24, 1777.

Anna Margaret Henry married Adam Steiner in 1793 and her daughter, Sarah, became the wife of George Eisenmann.

Another account agrees with the report of Col. Broadhead, that Captain Brady, with twenty white men and a Delaware Chief, effected the capture. We may surmise that when the neighbors of the Henry and Haines families assembled, (for the Haines homestead had been attacked the same time and two children slain. The neighborhood pathway leading from the Haines home to the Henry home, guiding the savages to unprotected Henry home) they followed the savages trail to the Allegheny river and there was joined by Brady and the Delaware Chief. Since the invasion of the Indian country was hazardous, the whole party disguised as Indians, followed the trail, and slew the Indians and captured the children.

The Indians were sometimes more merciful than their savage white allies. The commander of Detroit offered bounty for scalps, but none for "fresh meat," i. e. live captives; hence, the Indians would march their captives, carrying the plunder, to the vicinity of Detroit and then kill the captives and take their scalps to the commander for bounty. The English paid $50.00 per scalp.

Ofttimes the prisoners were taken to the Indian villages where they became the slaves of the village, unless adopted by some Indian. When adopted, the captives were treated well.

When Bouquet made his campaign to the Muskingum in 1764 he secured the release of many captives.

"McCullough, one of the captives, in his narrative, says that Rhoda Boyd and Elizabeth Studibaker escaped from the whites and went back to the Indians. Mary Jemison, who had married among them, fled with her half-breed children and hid until the troops left the country. One of the Virginia volun-

Margaretta Elizabeth was born August 13, 1778. Catherine, daughter of Frederick Hinrich and Margaretta his wife was born February 6, 1789.

teers had lost his wife and a child two years old, in an Indian foray in to the settlement six months before. What transports filled their hearts when he met her with a babe three months old at her breast! Quickly, he took her to his tent, and furnished suitable clothing for her and her babe. But, what had become of the two-year-old darling captured with its mother? She could not tell, except that it had been separated from her and taken elsewhere after their captivity. A few days later, a child was brought in which was supposed to be the one in question. The mother was sent for, and at first was not certain that it was her child, but after carefully scrutinizing it, she recognized its features, and was so overcome with joy that she dropped her young babe and, catching up the newly found child, she clasped it to her heart, and with a flood of tears, carried it off. The father, picking up the child that she had let fall, followed his overjoyed wife and thus again the family circle was unbroken. The rough soldiers, and even the stolid savages were moved to feelings of sympathetic tenderness by such touches of human nature, which make the whole world of mankind akin."[13]

The captives that were unidentified and claimed at Pittsburgh, were taken by the volunteer soldiery to Carlisle.

To Carlisle came Frau Hartmann, who had lost a child, a little daughter nine years before; after scrutinizing the captives carefully, she recognized a girl as her long lost child. But the child had long since, in her servile captivity, forgotten even the face of her mother. Although the mother begged and entreated with all the eloquence of a mother's heart, she could not arouse any recognition within the maiden. The sorrowful plight of the mother soon came to the ears of Bouquet whose sympathy was aroused, and seeking her, he spoke to her kindly and offered his help. The mother opened her heart and lamented

---

[13]Cort.

that the child she had so often sung to sleep would not recognize her and had forgoten her.

Bouquet asked the mother if she could recall some melody that she had sung to the girl in her childhood. Frau Hartmann sang the old church hymn "Allein und doch nicht ganz alleine Bin ich in meiner Einsamkeit." The child listening intently, and when the words were uttered,—"G'nug, dasz bei mir, wann ich allein, Gott und viel tausend Engel sein," the girl remembered them and with a cry of recognition, she rushed into the arms of her devoted mother.

The hymn, with a translation by Rev. Samuel R. Fisher, D.D., is as follows:[14]

Allein und doch nicht ganz alleine
Bin ich in meiner Einsamkeit,
Denn wann ich ganz verlassen scheine,
Vertreibt mir Jesu selbst die Zeit.
Ich bin bei Ihm, und Er bei mir,
So kommt mir gar nicht einsam fuer.

Alone and yet not all alone
Am I, in solitude though drear,
For when no one seems me to own
My Jesus will himself be near.
I am with Him and He with me,
I, therefore, cannot lonely be.

Komm ich zur Welt; man redt von Sachen,
So nur Eitelkeit gericht;
Da muss sich lassen das verlachen,
Der etwas von den Himmel spricht.
Drum wuensch ich lieber ganz allein,
Als bei der Welt ohn Gott zu sein.

---

[14]Cort, page 71.

Seek I the world? Of things they speak,
Which are on vanity intent;
Here he is scorned and spurned as weak,
Whose mind on heavenly things is bent,
I rather would my lone way plod,
Than share the world without my God.

Verkehrte koennen leicht verkehren,
Wer greifet Pech ohn kleben an?
Wie solt ich dann dahin begehren,
Wo man Gott bald vergessen kann?
Gesellschaft, die verdaechtig scheint,
Wird oefters nach dein fall beweint.

With ease do perverts perverts make;
Who handles pitch his hands will soil;
Why then, should I with those partake,
Who of His honor God despoil?
Society which we suspect,
We often afterwards reject.

Wer wollte denn nun recht erkennen,
Dass ich stets in Gesellschaft bin?
Und will die Welt mich einsam nennen,
So thu' sie es nur immerhin.
G'nug, dass bei mir, wann ich allein,
Gott und viel tausend Engel sein.

Who will not then with candor own,
I have companions all I crave?
And will the world still deem me lone?
Then let it thus forever rave.
Enough! I've God and angel's host,
Whose number can its thousands boast.

The women of the border were no less heroic than the men.

Maria Ludwig was the daughter of John George Ludwig and, as a maiden, served as a maid in Dr. William Irvine's family in Carlisle, Pennsylvania, and was generally called "Molly." About the outbreak of the Revolution, she married William Hays. Her husband became a gunner in an artillery company and Molly returned, after a time, to serve in Gen. Irvine's family. She received news that her husband had been severely wounded, wherefore she started out to find him. She nursed him and after that, for seven years, she accompanied him from battlefield to battlefield. She was utterly fearless brought water and food to the soldiers, and helped to carry away the wounded and care for them. "Here comes Molly with her pitcher" was a refreshing sound in the heat of battle, that made her known throughout the army as Moll Pitcher. At the battle of Monmouth, when her husband was wounded and there was no assistance available for serving the cannon, she herself set about putting the piece in position and loading it, while those about her were in doubt whether to stand or to retreat. Rallied by her example, they continued the battle until reinforcements arrived."[15]

Another incident shows the heroic character of the frontier woman.

Ebenezer Zane (Zahn) had established the first permanent foothold on the Ohio River in 1769, building a blockhouse on the present site of Wheeling. The fort was attacked in 1782 by a band of forty British soldiers and one hundred and eighty-six Indians. The particular hero of the siege was Elizabeth Zane, sister of Ebenezer. The latter at the time lived about forty yards distant, in a house which was used as a magazine for the fort, which was left in command of Silas Zane. The

---

[15]Faust, Vol. I, page 341.

ammunition of the fort being exhausted, it was proposed that one of the swiftest runners get a new supply from the magazine. Elizabeth Zane insisted on being allowed to go instead. "You have not one man to spare," she said, "a woman will not be missed in the defense of the fort."

She rushed out when an opportunity presented itself, and reached the house. There Colonel Ebenezer Zane fastened a tablecloth about her waist, into which he emptied a keg of powder; then, with her precious burden, she succeeded in safely returning to the fort amid a shower of bullets, several of which passed through her clothes."[16]

"Among the numerous stories of heroism on the frontier there is none more memorable than that told of Johann Christian Schell. He lived with his wife and six sons about three miles to the northeast of Fort Dayton (German Flats, N.Y.) in what was called Schell's Bush. It was in August, 1781, when most settlers had retreated for safety to the forts, or to more easterly settlements. He decided to breast the storm relying upon his sure eye and strong arm. Schell's blockhouse was strong, well built, and well adapted for defense against ordinary attacks. His house was stored with weapons and ammunition. He was at work in the field with his sons one day when the enemy appeared. The two youngest sons, twins eight years of age, could not follow their father and elder brothers fast enough, and were taken captive and dragged off to Canada. It was two o'clock in the afternoon when about forty-eight Indians and sixteen Tories attacked the house. Their leader was Donald MacDonald. While Schell and his four sons shot off their rifles, his wife reloaded them. Almost every shot hit its mark, but the enemy were so numerous as not to feel their losses. Finally MacDonald himself succeeded in reaching the door, which he tried to pry open with a lever. During the at-

[16]Faust, Vol. I, page 419.

tempt, he was shot in the leg. Quick as a flash, Schell unbolted the door and pulled the wounded Captain into his house. This success rescued the besieged from the danger of fire, for MacDonald would in such an event, have been burned also. MacDonald's ammunition also fell into the hands of Schell, which was fortunate, for he had only a few shots left. The last effort of the enemy having failed, the brave family were giyen a respite from their bloody labors. While father and sons were getting their rifles ready for another attack, the mother began to sing the battle hymn of the Reformation "Ein feste Burg ist unser Gott." "A mighty fortress is our God." The men fell in and Luther's martial hymn echoed through the woods with tremendous power.

Ein feste Burg ist unser Gott,
Ein gute Wehr und Waffen;
Er hilft uns frei aus aller Not,
Die uns jetzt hat betroffen.
Der alt boese Feind
Mit Ernst er's jetzt meint;
Grosz Macht und viel List
Sein grausam Ruestung ist;
Auf Erd ist nicht sein's gleichen.

A mighty fortress is our God,
A trusty shield and weapon;
He helps us free from every need
That hath us now o'ertaken.
The old bitter foe
Means us deadly woe;
Deep guile and great might
Are his dread arms in fight
On earth is not his equal.

Mit uns'rer Macht ist nichts getan;
Wir sind gar bald verloren.

Es streit't fuer uns der rechte Mann,
Den Gott hat selbst erkoren.
Fragst du, wer der ist?
Er heiszt Jesus Christ.
Der Herr Zebaoth
Und ist kein ander Gott;
Das Feld musz er behalten!

With might of ours can naught be done,
Soon were our loss effected;
But for us fights the Valiant One
Whom God Himself elected.
Ask ye, Who is this?
Jesus Christ it is,
Of Sabaoth Lord,
And there's none other God;
He holds the field forever.

Und wenn die Welt voll Teufel waer,
Und wollt' uns gar verschlingen,
So fuerchten wir uns nicht so sehr,
Es soll uns doch gelingen.
Der Fuerst dieser Welt,
Wie sau'r er sich stellt,
Thut er uns doch nicht;
Das macht, er ist gericht';
Ein Woertlein kann ihn faellen!

Though devils all the world should fill
All watching to devour us,
We tremble not, we fear no ill,
They cannot overpower us.
This world's prince may still
Scowl fierce as he will,

He can harm us none,
He's judged, the deed is done
One little word o'erthrows him.

Das Wort sie sollen lassen stahn
Und kein'n Dank dazu haben;
Er ist bei uns wohl auf dem Plan
Mit seinem Geist und Gaben.
Nehmen sie den Leib,
Gut, Ehr', Kind und Weib,
Lasz fahren dahin!
Sie haben's kein'n Gewinn;
Das Reich musz uns doch bleiben!
(Dr. Martin Luther.)

The Word they still shall let remain
And not a thank have for it,
He's by our side upon the plain,
With His good gifts and Spirit.
Take they then our life,
Goods, fame, child and wife;
When their worst is done,
They yet have nothing won,
The Kingdom ours remaineth.
(Authorized English translation, Church Book.)

This hymn inspired them to renewed effort. "The Tories and Indians now pushed some of their guns through the shot-holes of the house, at a moment when the men had withdrawn to load. The courageous mother, seeing the danger, seized an axe and struck it upon the guns, bending the barrels, and giving her men time to reload. Darkness soon set in, and the besieged family sang with lusty voices as if they were confident relief were coming from Fort Dayton. The attacking party, not being able to see through the woods, and discouraged by the loss of their leader, withdrew into the forest, taking with them the two youngest sons of Schell. During the night, the latter with his family wisely withdrew to Fort Dayton. The next morning, MacDonald was brought into the fort and remained a hostage for the two sons. This courageous defense, with its inspiring singing, stands out as one of the bright spots in the long tale of suffering which the Mohawk settlers were called to endure. Not always was bravery so well rewarded. Even Schell himself, a year later, died from the effects of a wound received from another marauding party of Indians."[17]

Such were the dangers our forefathers had to meet.

In the summer of 1781 occurred the illfated Clark expedition into the Ohio country against the Indians. In this expedition, Col. Lochry and many of his company of Westmoreland men lost their lives.

The disasterous Crawford Expedition against Sandusky occurred in 1782.

On the 13th of July, 1782, a party of about one hundred and fifty Indians and white renegades among whom was the Renegade Connolly (Shimmel places the total enemy strength at 300 Indians and 60 Tories[18] attacked Hanna's town and Millers station. At Hanna's town, the alarm was given in time so that the people fled to the Fort. The few huts in the village were burned, but the Fort under the leadership of Michael Huffnagle held out. A part of the enemy force went to Millers station and surprised a wedding party and took the station and many prisoners.

From a historian's viewpoint, we cannot refrain from an explanation regarding all the historical accounts of the burning of Hanna'stown that we have ever seen.

Why are certain men written into the story in capital letters and others in six-point type, as it were? Why hesitate to give Michael Huffnagle the credit for his leadership at that time?

---

[17]Faust, Vol. I, page 318.
[18]Border Warfare, page 139,

In reading the histories of the times, one is amazed to find certain nationalities written up and others downward. Doubtless, the Scotch-Irish deserve great credit for their work on the frontier and elsewhere to our nation; we would not pluck a laurel from their wreath of achievement, but at the same time, why are there so many slurring remarks thrown against the German element and their achievements in the early history of our country? From the time of John Smith at Jamestown, Virginia, to the present, there has been an ungallant and unworthy attitude among many writers toward the achievements of the German, Swiss, and Scandinavian settlers in this country.

This discrimination also holds as regards religions. Our school histories tell us of the religion of the Cavaliers and Puritans. They make special mention that Roger Williams was a Baptist, that Maryland was settled by the Catholics, New York by Dutch Calvinists, but what the religion of the Saltzburger and of the Swedes of the Delaware was, nothing is said.

Here is a sample of the treatment of the situation in the Province of Pennsylvania in 1776. Shimmel's Border Warfare in Pennsylvania, page 42—"There were three political parties more or less defined, in the Province in 1775: (1) the friends of the existing Government, composed chiefly of the adherents of the Proprietaries, Royalists from conscientious opinion and from religious scruples, and the greater portion of the Society of Friends; (2) the Revolutionary or active movement party; (3) a class of men, earnestly devoted to the cause of the Colonies, but more or less anxious for reconciliation. The first and third were greatly in the majority. The first comprised the Quakers, who, with the Proprietary party, at that time controlled the Assembly. The Germans, from a sense of gratitude to Penn for their homes and liberties, acted with the Quakers. The third party comprised nearly all of those who were recognized as the political leaders of the day—Franklin, Dickinson, Reed, Morris, Mifflin, McKean, Clymer, and others. The second class were the Scotch-Irish, but they were far removed from the seat of the Government, and before the declaration of independence, had very little political influence."

"The Quakers and the German sects were opposed to war on account of religious scruples. This fact had caused a bitter feeling against them on the part of the Scotch-Irish."

Taking the three divisions as in the main correct, we dissent to the place assigned the German element. It is true that the Germans were grateful for their lands and liberties. They, then as now, were loyal to the "powers that be," but they never belonged to class one as did the Quakers and English. The older German settlements were whole souled with Franklin and his party. They were **never** "Tories." In the opinion of John Adams, in which Thomas McKean, Chief Justice of Pennsylvania, etc., coincided, the people of New York and Pennsylvania were very equally divided between the Tory and Democratic parties, and nearly one-third of the whole population of the colonies, at the time of the Revolution were Tories. There were very few Tories among the Germans in Pennsylvania. There were pacific sectarians, such as Mennonites, Quakers, Dunkards, Seventh-Day Baptists, and others, who were opposed to war from religious principles, but few indeed were Tories.

Now Schimmel says that "before the declaration of independence, the Scotch-Irish party (second class) had very little political influence." Who, then, influenced Pennsylvania to become the keystone state in Independence? Was it the Tory party? No. The Quakers and pacific sects? No. Then the Germans, after all, must have been on the patriots' side. Muehlenberg and Schlatter were leaders for the Revolutionary cause. The Lutheran and Reformed churches followed their leadership.

In 1776 the population of Pennsylvania was 341,000. (Congressional census.) It is estimated (above) that one-half were Tories, leaving 170,500 for the patriotic cause. Hanna, "Scotch-Irish in North Ireland and North America," estimates the Scotch-Irish population at 100,000. Faust, German Element in the United States,[19] accounts for at least 110,000 Germans in population of Pennsylvania. The testimony of Benjamin Franklin, Dr. Rush, the historian Proud as well as Muehlenberg's report to Halle, all agree that the German population of Pennsylvania in 1775 was at least one-third of the whole. Now, if we accept the statements of the historians that one-half the population of Pennsylvania was Tory, that the Scotch-Irish had little influence before 1775, then it remains that it was the German element that swung the old Keystone State into the arch of Liberty.

We think John Adams's estimate that one-half the population were Tories is entirely too high. In the heat of conflict, doubtless the Quakers and German pacific sects were rated as tories, on the principle that "he that is not with me is against me" in arms. As stated above, there were some Germans who, for religious reasons, were opposed to war, but who performed pacific duties such as raising grain, etc., but there were very few German Tories. Here on the frontier we read of no German renegade Tories among the Indians, while the roll of renegades and Tories,—Girty, Elliot, McKee, Butler, Mac Donald, Connoley, Croghan, Guy Johnson, John Gibson, and others, attest to the fact that not all English and Scotch-Irish settlers were Patriots.

Dr. Shimmel's classification would lead us to infer that the Scotch-Irish were the Revolutionary party and that the Germans belonged to the party desiring reconciliation. Upon this basis, the Scotch-Irish had little influence in the famous Han-

[19]Vol. II, page 285.

nastown Resolutions and the other Resolutions at Hanover and Woodstock, for these resolutions explicitly state the principle of reconciliation; and queer enough, at each meeting the Germans were an important factor. The statements, frequently made, that the Scotch-Irish were the frontiersmen of America, exclusive of the Germans, is but the fiction of over-zealous partisan writers. The same influences that brought the one group brought the other also, namely, cheap lands and independence.

On June 22, 1782, about a month before the burning of Hannastown, a meeting was held at Fort Walthour and a petition sent to General Irvine, then commander at Fort Pitt. The petition states "That since the commencement of the present war, the unabated fury of the savages hath been so particularly directed against us, that we are at last, reduced to such a degree of despondency and distress, that we are now ready to sink under the insupportable pressure of this very great calamity. . . .. That the season of our harvest is now fast approaching, in which we must endeavor to gather in our scanty crops, or otherwise subject ourselves to another calamity equally terrible to that of the scalping-knife . . . and from fatal experience, our fears suggest to us every misery that has usually accompanied that season. . . .

Wherefore, we humbly pray for such an augmentation of our guard through the course of the harvest-season as will enable them to render us some essential service. . . .

And, as we have hitherto been accustomed to the protection of the continental troops during the harvest-season we further pray, that we may be favored with a guard of your soldiers, if it is not inconsistent with other duties enjoined on you."[20]

---

[20]Frontier Forts.

A small force of continentals was stationed at Turtle Creek. These were intended to protect all that settlement round about. The petition was signed by the following:

"George, Chrisopher, Joseph, and Michael Waldhauer, Abraham and Joseph Studebedker, Michael and Jacob Byerly, John and Jacob Ruthdorf, Frederick Williard, — — — — — Wiesskoph, Abram Schneider, Peter and Jacob Loutzenheiser, Hanover Davis, Conrad Zulten, Garret Pendegrast, and John Kammerer."[21]

---

[21]Washington Irving Correspondence—Butterfield, pages 300-301, quoted from Cort. Col. Henry Bouquet and His Campaigns.

CHAPTER VII

Forts and Blockhouses

This chapter is taken largely from Frontier Forts by Albert.

Walthour's Fort

Walthour's Fort was located eight miles west of Greensburg on the turnpike to Pittsburgh, twenty-three miles east of Pittsburgh and four miles south of Harrison City. It was built on the farm of Christopher Waldhour. Christopher and his brother George Waldhour, the Studebakers, Kunkles, Byerlys, Williards, Irwins, Hibergers, Wentlings, Bauchmans, Gongawares, Fritchmans, Buzzards, Kifers, etc., belonged to that settlement.

"It would appear that the region about this fort suffered most during the seasons 1781-1782, and especially just before the destruction of Hannastown. Many petitions, sent to Gen. Irvine from citizens of Washington and Westmoreland counties, show in a clear light, the dangers and exposures of the border throughout this period. Of these petitions there was one from Brush Creek, dated June 22, 1782 (see Chapter 6) of which Mr. Butterfield, the erudite historian of the Western Department says: 'This petition, so unexceptionally elegant in diction, as well as powerfully strong and clear in the points stated, is signed by nineteen borderers, mostly Germans. The document itself is in a bold and beautiful hand. It would be hard to find in all the Revolutionary records of the west a more forcible statement of border troubles, in a few words, than this."[1]

To this Fort belongs the **story of the Lame Indian**[2] as given by H. H. Brackenridge.

"In Pittsburgh, Pennsylvania, about the year 1782, one evening just at twilight, there was found sitting in a porch, an Indian with a light pole in his hand. He spoke in broken English to the person of the house who first came out, and asked for milk. The person (a girl) ran in and returning with others of the family, they came to see what it was that had something like the appearance of a human skeleton. He was to the last degree emaciated, with scarcely the semblence of flesh upon his bones. One of his limbs had been wounded; and it had been on one foot and by the help of the pole that he had made his way to this place. Being questioned, he appeared too weak to give an account of himself, but asked for milk, which was given him, and word sent to the commanding officer of the garrison at that place (Gen. William Irvine), who sent a guard and had him taken to the garrison; after having had food and now being able to give some account of himself, he was questioned by the interpreter (Joseph Nicholson). He related that he had been on Beaver river trapping, and had a difference with a Mingoe Indian who had shot him in the leg, because he had said he wished to come to the white people. Being told that he must tell the truth, and that in doing so he would fare the better, he gave the following account, to-wit:

That he was one of a party who had struck the settlement in the last moon, and attacked a fort and killed some and took some prisoners.

This appeared to be a fort known by the name of Walthour's fort by the account which he gave, which is at the

[1]Washington Irving Cor., page 301.
[2]Frontier Forts, page 363.

distance of twenty-three miles from the town on the Pennsylvania road towards Philadelphia, and within eight miles of what is now called Greensburg. He stated that it was there that he received his wound.

The fact was that the old man Walthour, his daughter, and two sons were at work in the field, having their guns at some distance and which they seized, on the appearance of the Indians, and made towards the fort. This was one of these stockades or blockhouses to which a few families of the neighborhood collected in times of danger, and going to their fields in the day, returned at night to this place of security.

These persons in the field were pursued by the Indians and the young woman taken. The old man with his sons kept up a fire as they retreated and had got to the distance of about a hundred yards from the fort when the old man fell. An Indian had got upon him and was about to take his scalp, when one in the fort directing his rifle, fired upon the Indian who made a horried yell and made off, limping on one foot. This was in fact the very Indian, as it now appeared that had come to the town. He confessed the fact, and said, that on the party with which he was, being pursued, he had hid himself in the bushes a few yards from the path, along which the people from the fort in pursuit of them came. After the mischief was done, a party of our people had pursued the Indians to the Allegheny river, tracing their course, and had found the body of the young woman whom they had taken prisoner, but had tomahawked and left. The Indian, as we have said, continuing his story to the interpreter, gave us to understand that he lay three days without moving from the place where he first threw himself into the bushes, until the pursuit might be over, lest he should be tracked; that after this he had got along on his hands and feet, until he found this pole in the marsh, which he had used to assist him, and in the meantime had lived on berries and roots; that he had come to a post some distance from here, where a detachment of soldiers were stationed and thought of giving himself up, and lay all day on a hill above the place thinking whether he would or not, but seeing that they were all militia men and no regulars, he did not venture. The Indians knew well the distinction between regulars and militia, and from these last, they expected no quarter.

The post of which he spoke was about twelve miles from Pittsburgh on the Pennsylvania road at the crossing of what is called Turtle Creek. It was now thirty-eight days since the affair of Walthour's fort and during that time this miserable creature had subsisted on plants and roots and had made his way on one foot by the help of a pole. According to his account, he had first attempted a course to his own country by crossing the Allegheny river, a considerable distance above the town, but strength failing to accomplish this, he had wished to gain the garrison where the regular troops were; having been to this place before the war; and, in fact, he was now known to some of the garrison by the name of Davy. I saw the Indian in the garrison after his confession, some days, and was struck with the endeavors of the creature to conciliate good will by smiling and affecting placability and a friendly disposition.

The question was now what to do with him. From the mode of war carried on by the savages, they are not entitled to the law of nations. But are we not bound by the laws of nature, to spare those that are in our power; and does not our right to put to death cease, when an enemy ceases to have it in his power to injure us? This diable boiteux, or devil on two sticks, as they may be called—his leg and his pole—would not seem likely to come to war again.

"In the meantime the widow (Mrs. Mary Willard) of the man who had been killed at Walthour's fort and mother of the young woman who had been taken prisoner and found tomahawked, accompanied by a deputation of the people of the settlement, came to the garrison, and, addressing themselves to the commanding officer, demanded that the Indian should be delivered up that it might be done with him as the widow and mother and relations of the deceased should think proper. After much deliberation, and the country being greatly dissatisfied that he was spared, and a great clamour prevailing through the settlement, it was thought advisable to let them take him, and he was accordingly delivered up to the militia of the party, which came to demand him. He was put on a horse and carried off with a view to take him to the spot where the first mischief had been done (Walthour's fort). But, as they were carrying him along, his leg, the fracture of which by this time was almost healed, the surgeon of the garrison having attended it, was broken again by a fall from the horse which had happened some way in the carrying him.

The intention of the people was to summon a jury of the country and try him, at least for the sake of form, but as they alleged, in order to ascertain whether he was the identical Indian that had been of the party of Walthour's fort; though it was not very probable that he would have an impartial trial, there having been a considerable prepossession against him. The circumstance of being an Indian would have been sufficient evidence to condemn him.

The idea was, in case of a verdict against him, which seemed morally certain, to execute him, according to the Indian manner, by torture and burning. For the fate of Colonel William Crawford and others was at this time in the minds of the people, and they thought retaliation a principle of natural justice. But, while the jury were collecting, some time must elapse, that night at least; for he was brought to the fort, or blockhouse, in the evening.

According, a strong guard was appointed to take care of him, while in the meantime, one who had been deputed sheriff went to summon a jury, and others to collect wood and materials for the burning, and to fix the place, which was to be the identical spot where he had received his wound, while about to scalp the man he had shot in the field, just as he was raising his scalp halloo, twisting his hand in the hair of the head, and brandishing the scalping-knife.

It is to be presumed that the guard may be said to be off their guard somewhat on account of the lameness of the prisoner and the seeming impossibility that he could escape; but so it was, that while engaged in conversation on the burning, that was to take place, or by some other means inattentive, he had climbed up at the remote corner of the blockhouse, where he was, and got to the joists, and thence upon the wall-plate of the blockhouse, and thence, as was supposed, got down on the outside between the roof and the wall-plate, for the blockhouse is so constructed that the roof overjuts the wall of the blockhouse, resting on the ends of the joists that protrude a foot or two beyond the wall, for the purpose of those within firing down upon the Indians, who may approach the house to set fire to it, or attempt the door. But, so it was that, towards morning, the Indian was missed, and when the jury met, there was no Indian to be brought before them. Search had been made by the guard everywhere, and the jury joined in the search, and the militia went out in all directions, in order to track his course and regain the prisoner. But no discovery could be made and the guard were blamed for the want of vigilence; though some supposed that he had been let go on the principle of humanity that they might not be under the necessity of burning him.

The search had been abandoned; but three days afterward, when a lad, looking for his horses, saw an Indian with a pole or long stick, just getting on one of them by the help of a log or trunk of a fallen tree; he had made a bridle of bark as it appeared, which was on the horse's head and with which and his stick guiding the horse, he set off at a smart trot, in a direction towards the frontier of the settlement. The boy was afraid to discover himself, or reclaim the horse, but ran home and gave the alarm, on which a party in the course of the day was collected and set out in pursuit of the Indian.

They tracked the horse until it was dark, and were then obliged to lie by; and in the morning, taking it again, they tracked the horse as before but found the course varied, taking into branches of streams to prevent pursuit and which greatly delayed them, requiring considerable time tracing the stream to find where the horse had taken the bank and come out; sometimes taking along hard ridges, though not directly in his course, where the tracks of the horse could not be seen; in this manner he had got on to the Allegheny river where they found the horse with the bark bridle, where he appeared to have been left but a short time before. The sweat was scarcely dry upon his sides; for the weather was warm and he appeared to have been ridden hard; the distance he had come was about ninety miles. It was presumed the Indian had swam the river, into the uninhabited (and what was then called the Indian) country, where it was unsafe for the small party that were in pursuit to follow.

"After the war, I took some pains to inform myself whether he had made his way good to the Indian towns, the nearest of which was Sandusky, at a distance of about two hundred miles; but it appeared that after all his efforts, he had been unsuccessful and had not reached home. He had been drowned in the river or famished in the woods, or his broken limb had occassioned his death."

The following was the order issued by Gen. Irvine:

"You are hereby enjoined and required to take the Indian delivered into your charge, by my order, and carry him safe into the settlement of Brush Creek. You will afterwards warn two justices of the peace and request their attendance at such place as they shall think proper to appoint, with several other reputable inhabitants. Until this is done and their advice and direction had in the matter, you are, at your peril, not to hurt him nor suffer any person to do it. Given under my hand at Fort Pitt, July 21, 1782.

To Joseph Studibaker, Frances Birely, Henry Willard and Frederick Willard."

Rugh's Blockhouse

Michael Rugh came to Westmoreland in 1772 from Northampton County, Pennsylvania. He early built a large two-story log house a little south of the present barn and a little above the spring on the farm of John Rugh, about two miles south of Greensburg and near the County Home.

Michael Rugh was a man of some prominence, especially in the latter part of the Revolution. He was elected coroner in 1781, and was also later in the same year, one of the commissioners of Purchases and a Common Pleas judge. There is an unbroken tradition of the people's fleeing to Rugh's Blockhouse from all the surrounding country after the attack on Hannastown.

Fort Allen, Hempfield Township

Fort Allen was the name given to a structure erected in "Hempfield Township, Westmoreland County, between Wendel Oury's and Christopher Truby's" at the same time that Fort Shippen, at Capt. John Proctor's, Shield's Fort, and others of like character were erected, that is, in the summer of 1774. This structure was probably a stronghouse, or a blockhouse erected for the emergency and never required, so far as is known, for public use. It was named probably in honor of Andrew Allen, Esq., of the Supreme Executive Council. From the names of the signers (see Chapter 5), the locality was manifestly in the German settlement of Hempfield Township, to the west of New Town (Greensburg). No other mention of this place by that name is found (see Rupp, West Pa. Appx.). All knowledge of its exact location has passed away.[8]

The site of Fort Allen was probably about four hundred yards south of the school house, slightly westward at a spring, on the northern slope, on the Church farm. A building stood here at an early time. We ourselves have seen foundation stones and rotting logs at this location. Some school sessions were held here also.

The proximity to a spring and doubtless the cleared ground made this location superior to the school house site, which was surrounded by forrest and had no spring nearby.

Kepple's Blockhouse

Kepple's Blockhouse was located on the farm of Michael Kepple in Hempfield Township about a mile and a half from Greensburg on the road to Salem (Delmont P. O.).

Stokeley's Blockhouse

was located near Waltz's Mill.

McDowell's Blockhouse

was at Madison.

Marchand's Blockhouse

was situated on the Doctor David Marchand farm, on the north fork of the Little Sewickley in Millersdale, Hempfield Township, about four miles west of Greensburg. It was used during the Revolution and as a refuge against the Indians. Rev. Cyrus Cort writes: "It is one of the traditions of our family that my great grandfather, John Yost Cort, had charge, in perlious times, of the women and children in that fort."

---

[8]Frontier Forts.

Philip Klingensmith's House

Col. James Perry writes to President Reed from Westmoreland County.

"Savikley (Sewickley) July 2, 1781. This morning a small garrison at Philip Clingensmith's about eight miles from this, and four or five from Hannastown, consisting of between twenty and thirty men, women, and children was destroyed; only three made their escape. The particulars I cannot well inform you, as the party that we sent to bury the dead are not yet returned and I wait every moment to hear or perhaps see them strike at some other place. The party was supposed to be about seventeen, and I am apt to think there are still more of them in the settlements.

The location of the fort was probably on the farm of Daniel Mull, Penn Township. Some think the location was on the North Eastern part of Jeannette.

List of Forts and Blockhouses

connected with the German settlement.

Fort Ligonier.
Wallace's Fort, erected 1774, Derry Township.
Barr's Fort, 1769, about one mile from New Derry.
Palmer's Fort, 1774, Fairfield Township.
Shield's Fort, 1774, New Alexandria.
Walthour's Fort, eight miles west of Greensburg.
Rugh's Blockhouse, south of Greensburg.
Fort Allen, 1774, at Harrolds.
Kepple Blockhouse, 1½ miles north of Greensburg.
Stockeley's Blockhouse, near Waltz's Mills.
McDowell's Blockhouse, Madison.
Marchand's Blockhouse, Millersdale.
Fort Shippen, 1774, Unity Township.
Lochry's Blockhouse, 1781, Unity Township.
Klingensmith's House, 1770 (?) Jeannette.
Fort Reed, Hannastown.

CHAPTER VIII

Social Life of a Pioneer

Strenuous and dangerous as were the lives of the Pioneers, they had their social side with appropriate relaxation and amusement.

While it was customary for each family to live on its own farm, there were numerous occasions when neighboring families would unite. Partly by necessity to handle large logs, partly for social reasons the settlers would gather together for "log-rolling." The German settlers cut down the trees and burned them instead of girdling them and permitting the dead tree to stand, as the English and Scotch-Irish did. These log-rollings were contests of strength among the young men and the blazing logs furnished the light for the evening entertainment of the young folks.

The marriage of a young couple brought the country side together, the first day was the bride's day celebrated at the home of the bride, the second day was groom's day and the "Infair" was celebrated at the home of the groom. All the delicacies of the times were served. There was abundance of wild game and other meat, corn-bread, pone, white bread, vegetables and fruits of the season. Cider and whisky in abundance. We may be assured that these hard-working Pioneers ate and drank heartily. A wedding party was broken up at Millers station and many of the guests taken prisoner, when Hannastown was attacked in 1782.

Another get-to-gether time was for a house or barn raising, when the crowd would be divided into contending groups, each vying with the other to get their log hewn and fitted into place first and we may be sure the young men did their best for the maidens were interested and cast many an approving glance and smile as they prepared the meals in the woods nearby.

Young people always have some way of meeting each other. Besides the long journeys to church and the "Kinderlehre" which we may be sure were improved to their own satisfaction for those early pioneers did not complain of a walk of five or six miles through the woods, and the records show that many were confirmed at from eighteen to thirty years of age; and we know that many a youth and maiden learned other things than Luther's Five Parts at the "Kinderlehre" and shortly after confirmation the pastor would have the pleasure of uniting two lives in holy wedlock.

Then there were singing schools, Spelling Bees, Apple Butter parties, Corn roasting parties, Frolics to cut grain or do some unusual labor for some settler. Altogether the lives of the pioneers were not dull except when the Indians were on the warpath.

For the women, they had their pride in culinary skill, spinning and housekeeping, which included the kitchen garden; the German settlers introduced the kitchen garden into America. It was the duty and privilege of every bride to spin her own trousseau. While the interests of the pioneer woman largely belonged to "Kirche, Kind and Kueche," this does not imply that their lives were narrow and sad. We pity the woman who would rather work with a dead typewriter, sell dead drygoods, than minister to a living family in the home and teach the living soul of a child to love its Savior and its mother.

The men had many diversions that exhibited their endurance and skill. The boy learned how to shoot by "barking" squirrels, i. e. when a squirrel clung to the side of a

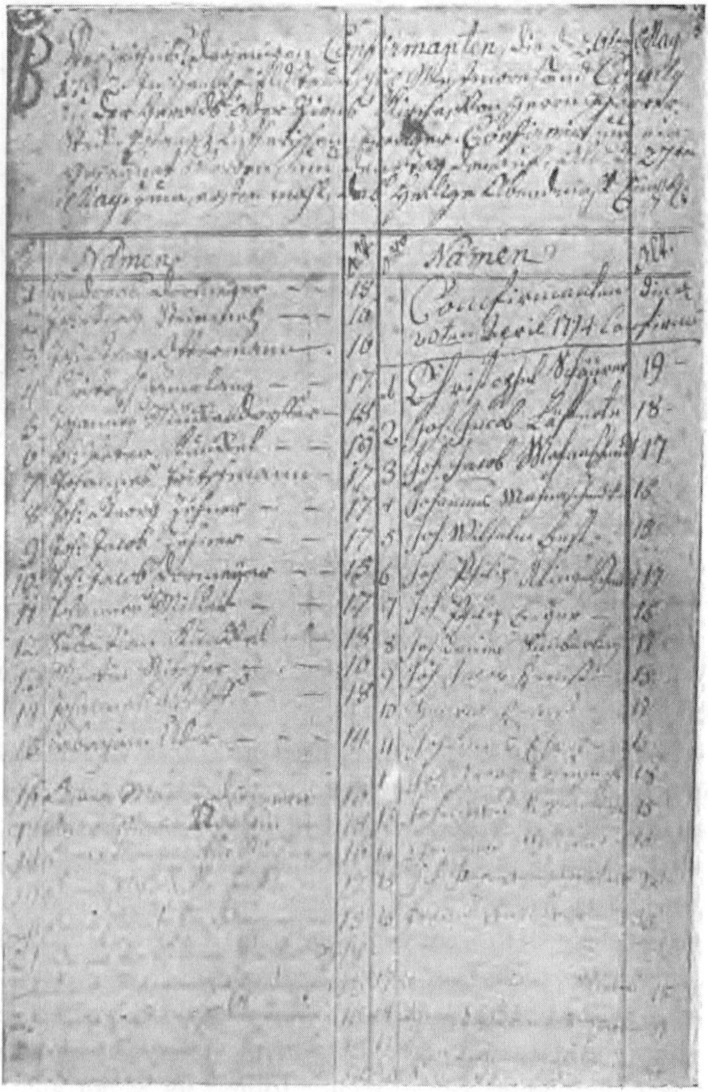

Fac-simile of Record of First Confirmants 'Zion or Herold's Church"

tree the hunter would shoot so that the rifle ball would strike the bark under the squirrel, thus stunning the squirrel. So skillful were these settlers with the rifle that no matter how tall the tree, they would either "bark" the squirrel or shoot off its head. Then deer and bear hunting and trapping fur bearing animals kept the men busy in winter and added to the income, for the furs had a ready sale and could be bartered for salt, sugar and other home necessities that they themselves could not produce.

During the Indian wars and the Revolution the men were busy defending their country. Many fought in the armies of the east and the others defended the frontier against the savage British, Tories and Indians. Goaded on by the scalping of helpless women and children they often fought superior numbers at great odds and as a consequence often times failed and lost their lives. Many names that appear on the early church rolls were removed in this way and no kin were left to perpetuate their names and achievements. If a brief mention of the fact were made in the official reports, historians have "edited" it out of the narrative.

Inured to hardship and danger many of the early settlers, like the Wetzel's and Brady's thoroughly enjoyed hunting the Indian. It was dangerous sport but the thrills of narrow escapes afforded great enjoyment. Competition in shooting was always a stirring sport which led to practical ends. Shooting matches for prizes were quite frequent.

The early German settlers were home lovers and found their chief joy in providing for its comfort and enjoying the company of wife and children around the open fireplace during the long winter evenings. Notwithstanding the German's inclination to build a good barn for the cattle, his house was superior to many of his contemporaries. It is interesting to note the efforts made to beautify the home. The German's library was superior to that of his contemporary and he kept abreast of the times through his German newspaper. Men and women of fine culture and great literary and scientific ability were found in the humble log cabins.

In general there was a deep fervent piety among the early settlers. They brought their Bibles, prayer books and religion with them into the wilderness. They built the first church and schoolhouse in Greensburg and the first church in Pittsburgh. Their schoolhouse at Harold's was one of the very first, probably the first, west of the mountains.

CHAPTER IX

The Patriarchs

Rev. John Michael Steck, 1791-1830.

Rev. John Michael Steck became pastor September 24, 1791, and served until July 14, 1830.

Rev. Steck was born on the 5th of October, 1756 in Germantown, Pennsylvania, where he was also brought up and received his proparatory education. He studied theology under Dr. Helmuth of Philadelphia.

"In 1784, Rev. Steck was licensed, and accepted a call from Chambersburg, Franklin County, where he labored successfully for four years. In 1788, he was sent as a missionary to Bedford County, which then included the territory now Somerset and Fulton counties, where he labored for four years with great diligence, and remarkable success. He preached wherever he found settlements of German people."[1]

In the summer of 1791, he received a call from the field in Westmoreland County and entered upon his work September 24, 1791.

He held his first communion Oct. 11, 1791, at which time there were 80 communicants (see appendix B).

He confirmed his first Catechetical Class on the 26th of May, 1792, there being 43 in the class (see appendix C).

In the Minutes of the Ministerium of Pennsylvania in 1796, we read, "Resolved, 9th, that Mr. Johann Michael Steck,

---

[1]Ullery, Southern Conference History.

Fac-simile of Record of First Communicants "Zion or Herold's Church"

as licensed candidate, serve Greensburg, Herold's Bruschkirk, Ridge, at Jacobskrik and at Allegany, in Westmoreland County."

In 1798, "Licensed candidate Joh. Michael Steck, from Gruensburg" attended the Ministerium with Jacob Stroh as delegate. At this time, Mr. Steck reports:

335 baptized members
333 communicant members.
67 confirmations
37 funerals

In the minutes of 1801 we read "A letter from four congregations in Westmoreland County, Pennsylvania, was read; they testify to their satisfaction with Mr. Steck, and beg that his absence be excused, because of sickliness."

In his report for 1801 Mr. Steg (Steck) from Greensburg reports:

Baptisms	174
Confirmations	77
Communicants	928
Funerals	17

Mr. Steg's license was renewed.

In 1806 Mr. Jacob Ruch accompanied Mr. Steck to the 59th Convention at Hagerstown, Md.

"Mr. Jacob Ruch handed in a letter from the congregations in and about Greensburg in Westmoreland County, Pennsylvania, a good testimonial for their preacher, Mr. Joh. Michael Steck. They asked to be permitted to keep him, and that he may remain a member of the Reverend Ministerium."

At this meeting Mr. Steck reported:

Baptisms	246
Confirmations	63
Communicants	500
Funerals	27
Schools	3

As with Rev. Luetge so with Rev. Steck, he became a member of the Ministerium of Pennsylvania and was pledged to the unaltered Augsburg Confession and the other Symbolical Books of the Lutheran Church. This petition of the congregations is a tacit acknowledgement that they were in harmony with the faith and practices of the Confessional Lutheran Church. Their appeal and the sending of delegates shows that they acknowledged and appreciated their membership in the Ministerium of Pennsylvania.

Zion Lutheran Church was founded upon and always sustained the full Confessional position of the unaltered Augsburg Confession and the Symbolical Books of the Evangelical Lutheran Church.

"On June 3rd, 1806, the Ministerium "Resolved that Mr. Joh. Michael Steck shall be ordained this evening."

"Joh. Mich. Steck handed in the license and one sermon." "In the evening Mr. Joh. Mich. Steck was solemnly consecrated to the ministry in the Church." This is witnessed by J. Heinr, Helmuth, President, and Jacob Goering, P. T. Secretary.

In 1812 Rev. Steck reports:[2]

Baptisms	296
Confirmations	100
Communicants	472
Funerals	30

In December 1812 the ministers of the "frontier" met in Special Conference in Washington County. Rev. Steck was Secretary of the Conference. These conferences continued until 1818 when they culminated in the formation of the Ohio Synod.[3]

---

[2]Minutes Lutheran Ministerium of Pennsylvania.

[3]The Fourth Special Conference met in Greensburg, Pennsylvania, October 22-25, 1814. The powers of the Conference were enlarged by the Ministerium of Pennsylvania.

In 1818 when the Ohio Synod was formed, Rev. Steck and his congregations withdrew from the Ministerium of Pennsylvania and joined in forming the new Synod. The Ohio Synod met in Greensburg, Pennsylvania, in 1822. J. P. Schmucker and Steck, Jr., were sent as delegates to the General Synod.

The congregation remained in connection with the Ohio Synod until the formation of the Pittsburgh Synod in 1845.

Rev. John Michael Steck was truly a "bishop." He labored in a field that now includes Westmoreland, Fayette, Allegheny, Beaver, Butler, Armstrong, Indiana, Clarion, and Mercer Counties. He was truly a man of God. He labored faithfully until the Lord called him home, a period of nearly thirty-nine years.

It was during his closing ministry that the new stone church was built. The building committeemen were Jacob Haines and Bernard Thomas. The corner-stone was laid May 28th, 1829, and the church was dedicated in 1830. Rev. J. G. C. Schweitzerbarth preached the Lutheran sermon and Rev. H. E. F. Voight, the Reformed sermon at the dedication. The church was a tall, almost square stone building with a gallery on three sides. It was heated by two stoves, the stove pipes extending up to the ceiling, where they entered chimneys and extended through the combs of the roof.

There were two entrances; on the east side and the west side. The main floor was divided into four sections by the aisles which led to the chancel. One of these sections on the northeast side was termed the "Old Men's Corner." The other opposite, on the northwest side was the "Old Women's Corner." The younger women, girls, and children sat under the gallery on the south side, while the middle-aged men and boys "hiked" to the gallery.

In the chancel place, to the north central part, was a large rectangular altar, painted white; behind this besides the chairs for the preachers, was the pulpit. The pulpit was

Old Stone Church

a high wine glass pattern with steps leading up to it. It rested against the wall in the north central side. It was the custom for the minister to conduct the opening service at the altar and

Wine Glass Pulpit from Old Stone Church

during the singing of the hymn before the sermon to mount the steps and enter the pulpit.

In the early days the services of the two denominations was so similar that the only difference some people could see was in the use of the Lord's Prayer. One denomination said "Unser Vater" and the other "Vater Unser."

In the early days before hymn books were common, the minister used to "line the hymns," i. e., read a line of the hymn, then the congregation led by some sweet-voiced matron, would sing that line; then another line would be read, and sung in like manner;—thus through the hymn. Humorous incidents are recorded of the mistakes that sometimes oc-

George Eisaman
(Fourth Teacher at Harrold's)

curred. It is related of one old minister that upon taking up his hymn book, he apologized, saying, "My eyes are weak, the light is dim, I can scarcely see to read this hymn." Whereupon, the congregation, thinking this was the first line of the hymn, began to sing the line.

Happy and accomplished was the man or woman who could "keep the 'air' " of the tune and lead the singing. We can still see father Isaac Wentzel leading the singing and beating time to the "buckwheat" notes. Before him, George Eisaman taught school and led the singing. He, doubtless, led the singing at the dedication. The new church cost about $3,000.00.

This church was repaired, painted, and papered in 1855.

Before the completion of the church, Rev. Steck's health began to fail and in the summer following the dedication, on July 14, 1830, he fell asleep. Before his death, at the request of the congregation, his son, Rev. Michael John Steck, was called as his assistant. Upon the death of the father, the son became the regular pastor and was soon as beloved as his father.[4]

A fitting obituary of Rev. John Michael Steck appears in the Minutes of the Ministerium of Ohio, 1830, as follows in part: "This Senior of the Ev. Luth. Ministerium of Ohio and pastor of the Lutheran congregation in Greensburg and vicinity departed this life July 14, 1830, aged 73 years, 9 months and 8 days. He had been truly a faithful and useful laborer in the vineyard of the divine Savior: and in consequence of his departure the Church has sustained a very serious loss. Without the fear of man he unreservedly reproved vice; he devoted much time to the instruction of the youth; he was a loving companion, an affectionate father and a friend to the poor and needy.

Rev. N. P. Hacke delivered the funeral discourse from Heb. 13:7: "Remember them which have the rule over you, who have spoken unto you the word of God: whose faith follow considering the end of their conversation," followed by remarks from the Rev. Jonas Mechling from the same passage. A sorrowing widow, thirteen children, one of whom

---

[4]List of Congregations served by Pastors, in 1826. Senior Steck (7 cong.) Greensburg, Brush Creek, Zehners, Herolds, Manor, Ritsch and Youngstown in Westmoreland County, Pa. History of the Ev. Luth. Joint Synod of Ohio.

followed his father into the ministry and sixty-six grandchildren, together with the members of his congregations were left to mourn his departure.

"The Gospel was his joy and song
E'en to his latest breath;
The truth he had proclaimed so long
Was his support in death."

Rev. Michael John Steck, 1831-1848

Rev. Michael John Steck was born in Greensburg, Pa., May 1, 1793. From early youth, he aspired to the ministry. He received his theological training under his father and the Rev. Jacob Schnee, of Pittsburgh. At the 69th Convention of the Ministerium of Pennsylvania, at Philadelphia, June, 1816, it was "Resolved that a candidate license be filled out for Mr. Steck."[5]

In December, 1816, he was called to Lancaster, Ohio, where he labored successfully for 13 years, from whence he was called in the Fall of 1829, to assist his father and in 1830 became pastor upon the death of his father.

It is difficult to form adequate estimate of his services to the Church. For many years, he served from eight to ten congregations, traveling to preaching points from ten to thirty miles distant.

"It is estimated that during his ministry of 32 years he preached 8,000 sermons, baptized 5,000 children, and confirmed over 2,000 adults, performed over 1,000 marriages, and pronounced the burial services over hundreds of his members."

He was eminently practical and gripped the affections of his people. They thought he did everything just right. For years afterward, "So hat es der Pfahrer Steck gemacht" was a by-word among the people.

---

[5]Minutes, etc.

"In his preaching he was always evangelical and scriptural. He united the qualities of a good preacher and a successful pastor in a high degree. He had a commanding presence, a strong and musical voice and distinct articulation. His manner in the pulpit was natural, his style simple, and his delivery earnest and impressive." In his early years, he was very timid, but he was always earnest and preached as if he believed in the efficacy of the Gospel.

Rev. Michael John Steck

Rev. Jonas Mechling

A Conference of Ohio Synod men was held at Greensburg, Pa., in 1831, just after Easter, and they prepared a memorial signed by ten ministers which they presented at Canton, Ohio and "in which they pray the Synod of Ohio to approve of their plan of forming a new synod between the Allegheny Mountains and the line of the state of Ohio."[6]

[6]History of the Ev. Luth. Joint Synod of Ohio, page 89.

The following is the Constitution of our first Domestic and Foreign Mission Society adopted October 18, 1837.

1. The name of this Union shall be: The Domestic and Foreign Missionary Society of the Eastern District of the Ev. Luth. Synod of Ohio.

2. The object of this Society shall be to preach the Gospel to the heathen and especially to assist those brethren of our household of faith, the German missionaries Rhenius, Schaffter, Mueller and Lechler in Palamcottah, East India.

3. Its officers shall be one President, one Secretary and one Treasurer. The officers of the District shall be its officers.

4. The Society shall choose at its yearly meeting (at the time when Synod sits) seven directors who in connection with the officers shall form the Executive Committee, six of which shall be a quorum.

5. Every person who contributes something can become a member. The amount of the yearly contribution shall be optional.

6. Whoever pays ten dollars shall be a member for life.

Upon the formation of the Pittsburg Synod of the Evangelical Lutheran Church, Rev. Steck became its first president.

Of the 26 congregations and 2255 members, constituting the Pittsburg Synod, Rev. Steck and his parish constituted 7 congregations and 1,005 members. Just about one-half of the membership of the Pittsburg Synod at its foundation was from Rev. Steck's parish. Jacob S. Steck was the layman representing the parish at the formation of the Synod.

The Synodical "Plan of Union" involved little more than a federation of independent churches for the purpose of supplying vacant places. It furnished no Confession of faith beyond the name "Lutheran" and no basis of co-operation.

It is as follows:

"We, the undersigned ministers and delegates of the Evangelical Lutheran Churches in the western counties of

Pennsylvania, being painfully sensible of the great destitution of the preached word and the ordinances of the gospel in our midst, and fully persuaded of the necessity of uniting our efforts for their supply, hereby form ourselves into a Synodical body, with the express understanding that each minister and church or churches shall be at perfect liberty to support such literary, theological or benevolent institutions, without the limits of our Synod, as may best accord with their own views of duty; and also that, as a Synodical body, we recognize no such distinctions among us as those commonly known by the terms of old and new measures, the Synod to be known by the name of The Pittsburgh Synod of the Evangelical Lutheran Church."

This "Plan of Union" was regarded only as a starting point. Beyond the words Lutheran and Evangelical there is no statement of faith or doctrinal position; in fact, faith in Christ or dependence upon the Bible is not stated, but the whole conception of the Christian faith and doctrine as held and taught by the Lutheran Church is implied and indeed is the incentive and spirit of action.

The founders may have had varying conception of what the Lutheran Church really did stand for, and this may be implied in the determination to not recognize old and new measures, but there was no doubt of the doctrinal position of the first president. He was soundly Lutheran according to the Lutheran Confessions.

The "old measures" named in the Plan of Union referred, principally, to catechetical instruction and the doctrine of regeneration in Infant Baptism. The "new measures" referred to "revivals" and the use of the "mourners' bench" in some Lutheran Churches, to the consequent neglect and omission of infant baptism, catechization, and confirmation.

Many English Lutheran Churches of that day were forsaking the ways of the old historic Lutheran faith and practice and were introducing revivals and the mourners' bench with their fanatical extremes.

The new Synod was not prepared to take up this question at this time. We shall see how it solved the problem later.

In the midst of his usefulness Rev. Steck, departed this life September 1, 1848, at the age of 57 years.

Rev. W. A. Passavant, D.D., preached the funeral sermon in the German church, Greensburg, from Acts 8: 2. The burial was made in the Church Cemetery, Greensburg. Dr. Passavant had this to say of Rev. Steck in the "Missionary:"

Pastor Michael J. Steck

"**The first President of the Pittsburg Synod,** born in Greensburg, Pa., May 1, 1791, and died at the same place September 1, 1848. He was an extraordinary gifted man. During his time of service he won for himself the title of the most distinguished pastor in Western Pennsylvania. Without him, the Pittsburg Synod could hardly have been founded."

Rev. Jonas Mechling, 1849-1868

In the spring of 1849, Rev. Jonas Mechling was called to be pastor. He labored here until his death in 1868.

Rev. Jonas Mechling, son of Philip Mechling, was born in Hempfield Township, Westmoreland County, on the 14th of August 1798. He was baptized in infancy by Rev. Wm. Weber, and confirmed by pastor John M. Steck. He received his early education in the church schools of Westmoreland County and studied theology under Rev. J. Schnee of Pittsburg and Rev. John M. Steck. He was licensed to preach by the Evangelical Lutheran Synod of Ohio on September 19th, 1820.

He then took charge of a number of congregations of Father Steck's parish; St. James and Hankeys, Hope, Zion's and St. John's and the Churches of Ligonier Valley. Later he served St. Paul's Ridge St. James, Youngstown, and Christ Church West Newton. Upon the death of Father Steck he was called to the Herold-Greensburg parish, which consisted then of the following congregations: Herold's, Brush-Creek, Greensburg, Manor, Hill's and several other preaching stations. He also preached in the Churches on this side of the Ridge until 1855. He died on the 2nd day of April, 1868 in the 70th year of his age and the 48th of his ministry.[7]

"Rev. Mechling was a man of persevering energy and remarkable endurance. As a testimony to his earnestness and fidelity as a minister of Christ, we need only to give a few items of the record of his ministerial acts. During his ministry of 48 years, he preached 6,327 sermons, baptized 6,286 children, confirmed 2,039 adults, married 890 couples, and buried thousands."[8]

---

[7]List of congregations served by pastors in 1826—Pastor Mechling (8 cong.) Kintigo, Henkes, Jacobs, Schwobs, Hoffmans, Salems, Brandts and Donegals in Westmoreland County, Pa. History of the Ev. Luth. Joint Synod of Ohio.

[8]Ullery, History of Southern Conference.

CHAPTER X

Property Affairs and Relations with the Reformed Church

During the pastorate of Rev. Luetge, Michael Rugh and Anthony Altman, trustees of the congregation procured a warrant for the tract known as "Good Purpose" on the twenty-second of August, 1785, and on the twenty-third of May, 1789, a patent was granted. In 1793 the trustees, by the advice, and with the approbation of the leading members of the congregation, sold 100 acres and allowances of said land, granted them by patent, to Rev. A. Ulrich Luetge for the benefit of the congregation. No deed was made for this land until several years after the death of Rev. Luetge, as the trustees had no authority to sell or give title for this land, for they held it in trust for the congregation. Hence, they applied to the legislature for power to sell and convey said land to the heirs of Rev. Luetge. In February, 1801, an act was passed authorizing them to sell and make a deed to the executors of Rev. Luetge, for the benefit of his heirs; the deed was made in 1805. The price agreed on was 60 pounds.[1]

"The remaining fifty-eight acres, with Church and Schoolhouse, by agreement mutually signed September. 24th, 1791, between the two denominations, was to remain **from that day, forever,** the joint property of both the Lutheran and Reformed organizations, to be used for church and school purposes till the "end of the world."[2]

---

[1] Ullery, History of Southern Conference.
[2] History of the Reformed Church, 1877.

As we have seen, the title to the land was vested in the trustees for the Lutheran congregation alone. In an agreement on Nov. 29, 1793, it appears that the Lutheran trustees Valentine Steiner, William Altman, Anthony Altman, and Jacob Seanor gave a bond for three hundred pounds sterling, to Jacob Painter and Nicholas Alleman, in trust for the German Reformed Church. Under these bonds and agreements the property was held from November 29th, 1793, until November 28th, 1819, when the deed was executed for the half of the property, by Jacob Haines and Jacob Miller, to Barnet Thomas and Peter Baum, trustees for the Reformed Congregation.

The agreement on September 24th, 1791 also included certain relations between the two congregations. The officers of both congregations were to examine, every year, the state of the common funds in the hands of the "manager," and pass upon the receipts and bills for expenses. (See Appendix E).

Each congregation was free to choose its own pastor and officers, and change them when necessary, without interference from the other side. No one shall have the right to introduce a strange minister without the consent of the officers of the Church to which he belongs. The minister of either side has power to baptize all such children as may be presented, without distinction of religion,—except only when the officers object.

The officers of both congregations unite in the choosing of a school-master; who shall instruct the children in such Catechism as the parents desire, whether Lutheran or Reformed.

This agreement involved no internal change in either congregation but formed a written working basis between the two. It was kept for nearly a century, until the property interests were divided, and now, as then, each congregation attends to its own internal affairs.

We might inquire what was the chief distinguishing factor that preserved these congregations as distinctive denominational Churches? It is conceded that in the earlier times, especially during the days of the German language, the two congregations used the same church building, alternately; they attended the services of both congregations; used the same hymns; often, where the family was divided, they communed at both communions, the husband communing with the wife and the wife with the husband; often some of the children of a family would attend the Reformed "Kinderlehre," and others, the Lutheran; children were baptized by either pastor; the whole settlement attended funerals; and all alike were buried in the same "God's acre," with almost identical burial service.

Having so many things in common, one would think there would be a confusion and mixture, but such was not the result, although the denominational consciousness was dulled and almost deadened; the missionary fires burned low; and in some cases "custom" had as much force as "thus saith the Lord." Those were good old days,—but-not-all-good. During the period of about 1820 to 1860 the spiritual life burned low. The children were no longer gathered in "Kinderlehre" on the Lord's Day regularly nor were there Sunday schools of much consequence.

Education was not supported as diligently as by the earlier pioneers. We do not know of a single normal adult among the early pioneers that could not read and write, but we have known many of their descendants who were illiterate; and only recently have some awakened to the importance of education.

The main factor in preserving the two denominations intact was and is the **Catechetical System.** A child might be baptized by either the Lutheran or Reformed minister; and not change its denomination; but when catechized and confirmed, then the child became a member of the denomination whose minister catechized and confirmed the child. The ministers of both the Reformed and Lutheran Churches have been great Catechists. The great sweep of frontier Revivalism never abated the regular Catechetical instruction in this settlement. However, in the anglisizing movement, before the English denominational hymn books were introduced, the congregations used to sing many of the "Gospel Hymns," but the more intelligent members always realized the emptiness of these jingles and when the worshipful service and hymns of the denominational hymn books came to them in the English language, they forsook the empty straw and chaff of the "Gospel Hymn" and fed upon the rich wheat of worship according to God's Word, as given in the authorized hymn books.

CHAPTER XI

Synodical Relations

This period was the time of storm and stress within the nation and within the church. The passions of the Civil War were reflected in the church for years afterward.

We have spoken of the formation of the Pittsburg Synod and the "Plan of Union" which, being a union of Evangelical Lutherans, did not state a definite confession of faith; as we have said before, it was little more than a loose federation to supply vacant preaching places. There was no basis of co-operation; besides, it was definitely stated that each Pastor and Congregation was at liberty to support institutions and missions anywhere they saw fit to do so. But it is evident that such a loose federation could not do the work of a Synod.

New congregations were being formed and in 1847 the Synod adopted the following in the Preamble for the "Form of Constitution for the Government and Discipline of Churches," "we receive the Augsburg Confession, the great Symbol of the Reformation, as the bond of union."

In 1852 when the Pittsburg Synod united with the General Synod, there was a hesitancy on the part of many (the vote standing 17 to 12) because they did not regard the General Synod's position as a clear confession of the Lutheran faith. Many leaders in the General Synod had repudiated parts of the Augsburg Confession. Whereupon the Pittsburg Synod resolved "that—the above action be in no wise regarded as an approval of the construction which has been put upon any of its writings (i. e., of the General Synod) recommendations or acts, as though it had rejected any part of the faith of the Church as contained in the Augsburg Confession."

In 1855 a proposition called the "Definite Platform" commonly ascribed to Rev. S. S. Schmucker, D. D., made its appearance.[1] This "Definite Platform" was intended as a substitute for the Augsburg Confession. In place of the Augsburg Confession, the "Definite Platform" should be the standard of the Lutheran Church, and all ministers entering Conference and Synod, must receive it before becoming members.

Now, what was this "Definite Platform?" "The 'Definite Platform' was offered as a more specific expression of the General Synod's doctrinal basis, being surrounded by German Churches, which profess the entire mass of former symbols." The thought underlying it was that confessions of faith should declare with such explicitness the faith of those who subscribe them, that all ambiguity and room for variety of interpretations should be excluded; and that the General Synod, **no longer holding to certain articles in the Augsburg Confession in the sense in which they were understood by its authors,** should, without hesitation or reservation, say so. It charges the Augsburg Confession with **five errors,** viz.: "Approval of the Ceremonies of the Mass; Private Confession and Absolution; Denial of the Divine Obligation of the Christian

[1]"The errors are not on the side of the Augsburg Confession, but on the side of those who agitate our Lutheran Church with the introduction of a fatherless and motherless child, the Definite Platform, Rev. W. J. Mann."

"To this we reply, the Platform was publically adopted by three or four Synods in the West within a few weeks after its publication. As to its authorship, we never denied having prepared it, at the urgent request of some of those brethren on the plan agreed on by them, and some Eastern brethren of the very first respectability. It was carefully revised by ourselves and Dr. B. Kurtz, and we have not yet found a single one of its positions refuted." Dr. S. S. Schmucker in Lutheran Symbols or American Lutheranism Vindicated, page 26.

Sabbath; Baptismal Regeneration; and the Real Presence (in the Lord's Supper)."[2]

Dr. Schmucker had personally advised that the "Platform" be adopted by the Conferences, preliminary to its adoption by the Synod.[3] Accordingly, it was presented for adoption, by Rev. George F. Ehrenfeld at the meeting of the Middle Conference Synod at the Worthington Church. After a hot debate, the "Platform" was adopted by this Conference.

In the fall of 1855, in the same Conference the "Platform" failed of adoption because the vote was made a tie vote by the vote of the president.

Accordingly, the action of the Conference came before the Pittsburg Synod at its next meeting, whereupon Dr. Charles Porterfield Krauth presented his famous "Testimony of the Pittsburg Synod" at Zelienople, 1856.

"Whereas, Our Church has been agitated by proposed changes in the Augsburg Confession—changes whose necessity has been predicted upon alleged errors of that Confession; and

Whereas, These changes and the charges connected with them, though set forth by individual authority, have been endorsed by some Synods of the Lutheran Church, are urged upon others for approval, and have been noticed by most of the Synods which have met since they have been brought before the Church; and

Whereas, Amid conflicting statements, many, who are sincerely desirous of knowing the truth, are distracted, knowing not what to believe, and the danger of internal conflict and of schism is incurred, etc.

1—Resolved, That by the Augsburg Confession, we mean that document which was framed by Melancthon, with the

---

[2]Lutheran Cyclopaedia. Lutheran Symbols or American Lutheranism Vindicated. Schmucker, page 5.

[3]Burgess, etc.

advice, aid and concurrence of Luther and the other great evangelical theologians, and presented by the Protestant Princes and Free Cities of Germany at the Diet of Augsburg in 1530.

5—Resolved, That now, **as we have ever done,** we regard the Augsburg Confession lovingly and reverently as the good confession of our Fathers witnessed before heaven, earth, and hell."

As this action was taken just eleven years after the formation of the Synod, it throws light upon the attitude of the fathers in regard to the confessions. Nearly all of the founders of the Synod were alive and they voted for this resolution **"That now, as we have ever done, we regard the Augsburg Confession lovingly and reverently as the good confession of our Fathers, etc.** This shows, then, that the Pittsburg Synod always received and acknowledged the unaltered Augsburg Confession.

In 1853 when the Pittsburg Synod entered the General Synod, other Synods were received also, namely, the Ministerium of Pennsylvania, Texas and Northern Illinois. These Synods were conservative and it is to these that Dr. Schmucker refers above when he states concerning the "Definite Platform" in 1855. It was offered "as a more specific expression of the General Synod's doctrinal basis, **being surrounded** by German churches, which profess the entire mass of former symbols."

This accession of conservative Synods to the General Synod alarmed the adherents of a loose Lutheranism, hence, the "Definite Platform" was put forth, but it failed to stem the tide of growing adherence to the Augsburg Confession.

"It could no longer be doubted that there were two parties in the General Synod, the one siding with and acting in the spirit of the Platform, the other strongly and persistently defending the pure faith of the Confession.

"When, therefore, the Platform party endeavored to strengthen their side by receiving, in 1859, the Melanchthon Synod—an extremely radical body—the conservative party solemnly protested and tried to prevent the action by voting against the reception of the Synod.

"The same spirit was again manifested, as that of 1859, in the action of the General Synod in regard to the admission of the Frankean Synod, at the convention at York in 1864. This was an un-Lutheran Synod, which not only did not endeavor to hide its variance with the Confession of the Lutheran Church, but openly boasted of it.

Article 5 of the Charter of the Western Conference of the Frankean Synod, contains the following "— — therefore, no minister or candidate for the ministry who advocates a subscription to the Augsburg Confession as a test of ministerial office, or church membership, shall be received into our connection" — — — . Notwithstanding all this, known to many, if not to all the members of the General Synod, the Frankean Synod was received, in 1864, as an integral part of the General Synod."[4]

When the Frankean Synod was admitted, the delegates of the Ministerium of Pennsylvania protested and withdrew to report to their Synod.

At the Fort Wayne Convention in May, 1866, the delegates of the Ministerium were present and presented their credentials but the president, Rev. Dr. S. Sprecher ruled as follows: "The Chair regards the acts of the delegates of the Pennsylvania Synod, by which they severed their practical relations with the General Synod, and withdrew from the partnership of the Synods in the governing functions of the General Synod, as an act of the Synod of Pennsylvania." Therefore, it would be necessary for this Synod to be received anew.

---

[4]Documentary History of the General Council.

After much debate, the delegation withdrew and Dr. W. A. Passavant read a protest against the action of the General Synod, signed by 28 delegates belonging to eight Synods.

Dr. Walther of the Missouri Synod said, "Scarcely any event within the bounds of the Lutheran Church of North America has ever afforded us greater joy than the withdrawal of the Synod of Pennsylvania from the unionistic so-called General Synod. — — They (the General Synodists) know right well what a blow it would give them if it were known that the oldest and largest Synod of their connection withdrew **because the General Synod had departed from the true doctrine of the Lutheran Church.**"

In 1866, the Ministerium of Pennsylvania instructed a committee "to prepare and issue a fraternal address to all Evangelical Lutheran Synods, ministers and congregations in the United States and Canadas, which confess the Unaltered Augsburg Confession, inviting them to unite in a convention for the purpose of forming a union of Lutheran Synods."

On Dec. 11, 1866, delegates from thirteen Synods met in Reading, Pa., and organized the General Council. The Pittsburg Synod was represented by Revs. G. Bassler, W. A. Passavant, G. A. Wenzel, and H. W. Roth; Laymen A. L. Thiel, John F. Duff. Rev. Bassler became the first president and Rev. H. W. Roth the first English Secretary of the General Council.

The call for a convention of all Synods which confess the Unaltered Augsburg Confession was laid before the Pittsburg Synod at Rochester, Pa., in 1866 and it was

Resolved 3—That we cordially accept the invitation extended through the "Fraternal Address" of the Synod of Pennsylvania, and during the present convention, elect delegates to represent this body in the proposed Convention.

Resolved 5—And inasmuch as a trial of thirteen years fully satisfied us that the object sought in our connection with the General Synod have not been and cannot be accomplished through that organization; and, inasmuch as your committee is **firmly persuaded that the General Synod, by its recent and previous actions, has shown itself unfaithful both to its own Constitution and also to the Confession of the Church of our Fathers;**

Resolved 6—That the action which, in 1852, resulted in our connection with the General Synod, be, and hereby is revoked.

At the following convention at Greenville, Pa., in October, 1867, "The Fundamental Principles of Faith and Church Polity" of the General Council were adopted by an overwhelming majority of 63 to 21.

Whereupon 10 ministers and 7 laymen withdrew and later formed the Pittsburg Synod of the General Synod. We find among their number those who had advocated the "Definite Platform." At a meeting at Worthington, Pa., Dec. 1867, they organized their Synod, styling it the Pittsburg Synod. "Legally, the minority party was not entitled to the name of 'The Pittsburg Synod of the Evangelical Lutheran Church.' The fact that they had withdrawn from the convention of the majority party and elected new officers, deprived them of all legal rights to the name of the incorporated body."[5]

Judge Trunkey, of Crawford County ruled that "The Pittsburg Synod had a right to connect itself with whatever general body of the Lutheran Church it chose, provided it did not make a radical change in points of doctrine.

"The General Council is strictly a Lutheran organization and the connection of the Synod with a general body could in no way affect the question of the rights of property in the Church.

---

[5]Burgess History of the Pittsburg Synod, General Synod.

"In 1867 the Pittsburg Synod divided, ten of its members withdrawing from its session at Greenville, Pa., because the majority of the Synod had decided to withdraw from the General Synod and connect themselves with the General Council. The officers, official seal, and records remaining with the majority.

"From what appears in the testimony concerning this division of the Synod, it is the opinion of the Master that the majority constitute the Pittsburg Synod proper. That the action of the majority in withdrawing from the General Synod and joining the new body was not inconsistent with Lutheran methods and regulations. All the testimony there is on the subject proves that the Synod had the right to withdraw in an orderly manner and join whatever Lutheran body it wished to, and the will of the majority must prevail, **and that majority is the Pittsburg Synod."**[6]

Notwithstanding such clear testimony, the secessionists of Greenville issued a "pastoral address" in which they say, "In view of these facts we, though in the minority, claim to be the Pittsburg Synod." And thus the strife was carried into Congregations. We may safely say that the ministers were the aggressive leaders and that where congregations were divided, it was generally because of pastoral interference. It is only too sad that ministers were busy trying to stir up trouble in neighboring congregations and to undermine the local pastor's influence.

We shall see how this conflict at length broke in upon the peaceful Zion.

When Rev. Jonas Mechling became Pastor in 1849 the Herold's Church, with the entire parish, united with the Joint Synod of Ohio and adjacent states. We see that the Synodical relationship of the Parish depended largely upon the Synodical relationship of the Pastor. We find no formal action of

[6] Ullery, History of Southern Conference.

the congregation in regard to this matter since 1796 and 1845. It was determined largely by the Pastor, the congregations concurring by electing delegates as is shown by the action of the Pittsburg Synod.

"First Church, Rev. Kunzmann, pastor, John Rugh Delegate. 40½ Annual Convention 1882 Wheeling, W. Va. Minutes page 20.—The Committee on business of congregations reported an application for membership with the Synod from First German Lutheran Church, Greensburg, Pa., and offered this action, which was passed.

"Resolved: that the 1st Lutheran Church, Greensburg, Pa., having been one of the original congregations, which took part in the organization of the Pittsburg Synod, and having never been dismissed to unite with any body, be cordially welcomed back to its former relation to this Synod."

Against this action, the Ev. Lutheran District Synod of Ohio protested in 1886, and a committee reported the following, which was adopted:

"Inasmuch as it appears that the reception of the 1st Church, Greensburg, under the care of Rev. J. C. Kunzmann, by the Pittsburg Synod, was not exactly **in accord with the compact** entered into by the Ev. Lutheran District Synod of Ohio, and the Pittsburg Synod, therefore, be it resolved that we hereby rescind our action receiving said congregation, and recommend that it apply to the Evangelical Lutheran District Synod of Ohio for dismission to the Pittsburg Synod. Resolved, that as soon as such dismissal shall be placed in the hands of the officers of the Synod, it shall become an integral part of this body."

This action was complied with on March 11, 1887, and the congregation re-entered the Pittsburg Synod.

What was true of the Synodical relationship of the 1st Church was true of Herold's Church also. That the Herold—Brushcreek—Greensburg parish was actually a part of the

Joint Synod of Ohio and Adjacent States is shown by the entertainment of "The ninth convention of the Joint Synod, the first Delegate—Synod, from the 9th to the 14th of November, 1854 at Greensburg, Pa. At this convention Synod discussed the "unaltered Augsburg Confession and Luther's Small Catechism."

The English District of the Joint Synod of Ohio and Adjacent States met at the Brush Church in 1859.[7]

There was no question as to the Synodical connection of the parish at this time; it belonged to the Joint Synod of Ohio.

We might inquire, How did Old Zion's or Herold's Church come to be a member of the Ev. Lutheran District Synod of Ohio?

At first as we have seen, the Congregations west of the Alleghenies belonged to the Pennsylvania Ministerium, but as the congregations grew in number, they felt the need of closer union, hence we read, "A report of a Special Conference held in Washington County in Pennsylvania, in the month of December, 1812. It was a matter of real gratification to the Synod to see that our brethren on the frontier show themselves so active in the spread of the Kingdom of God."[8]

The work prospered and the bonds of union grew stronger, hence, in 1817, this "Special Conference" petitioned the Ministerium of Pennsylvania "that they might be granted permission to form their own Ministerium in the State of Ohio." This permission was refused, but later tacitly granted. In 1818, at Somerset, Ohio, the first general conference was held and the "Evangelical Lutheran Synod of Ohio and Adjacent States" was founded. It consisted of fifteen ministers and about 3500 communicants. One of the most prominent

---

[7]History of the Joint Ev. Lutheran Synod of Ohio and Adjacent States, Peter & Schmidt, pages 134 and 181.

[8]Minutes Ministerium of Pennsylvania, 1813.

founders was John Michael Steck. His parish henceforth belonged to this Synod.

In 1833 the Synod was divided into districts and the name "Joint Synod of Ohio and Other States" was assumed. Old Zion or Herold's Church belonged to this Synod until the organization of the Pittsburg Synod in 1845. In 1849 under the pastorate of Rev. Jonas Mechling the parish again united with the Joint Synod.

In 1857 "The English District of the Ev. Lutheran Joint Synod of Ohio and Adjacent States" was organized. This District Synod participated in the founding of the General Council and was in entire harmony with the confessional position of the same. In 1872, its relation to the Joint Synod was severed and it assumed the name "The Ev. Lutheran District Synod of Ohio, formerly known as the English Ev. Lutheran District Synod, in connection with the Ev. Lutheran Joint Synod of Ohio and Adjacent States."

To this Synod, Old Zion or Herold's Church belonged until March 11, 1887, when it was again received into membership with the Pittsburg Synod.

CHAPTER XII

Contending for the Faith

Rev. George A. Bruegel—1868-1872

Rev. George A. Bruegel succeeded Rev. Mechling as pastor.

Rev. Bruegel was born on the 13th of June, 1837, in Goettenberg, Wuertemberg, Germany. He was baptized in infancy and confirmed by his father, Rev. Christopher J. Bruegel. He received his early training in the home and parochial school. He studied four years in the Gymnasium of Tuebingen and graduated from the Theological Seminary at Columbus, Ohio. He served parishes at Zanesville and Canton, Ohio before assuming the local pastorate. In 1872 he resigned and served parishes at Warren, Mauch Chunk and Cherryville in Pennsylvania and at Utica, N. Y. He also served as German Professor in Thiel College, then as pastor in Erie, Pa. and Philipsburg, N. J.

Rev. Bruegel was a man of talent and liberal education and an able pulpit orator.

He was the first pastor after the large parish had been divided and became pastor of the Herold's and Greensburg Congregations. He resigned in 1872 and was succeeded by Rev. Enoch Smith.

During Rev. Bruegel's pastorate, the congregation was a member of the Ev. Lutheran District Synod of Ohio, now connected with the General Council. Accordingly, the new Hymn Book of the General Council was introduced. Only a very few members opposed its introduction. This Hymn Book

Rev. Enoch Smith

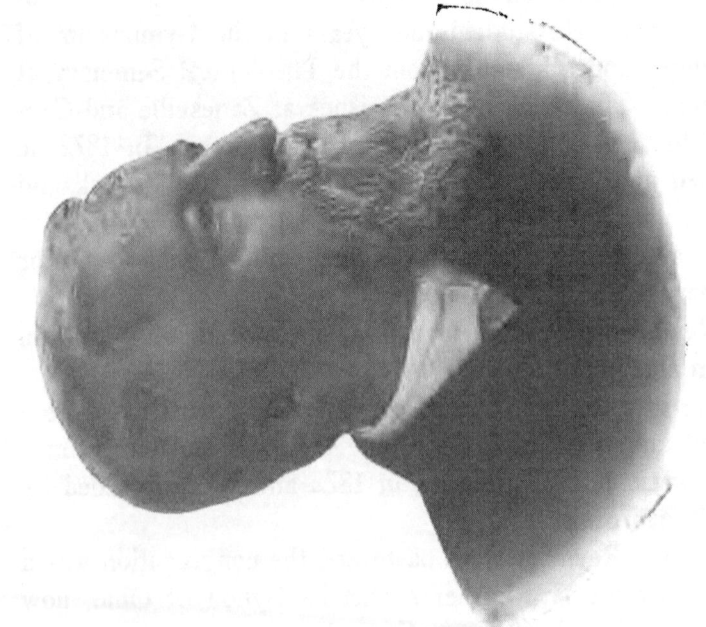

Rev. G. A. Bruegel

was the forerunner of the new Hymnal, which is the joint production of the General Council, General Synod, and the United Synod of the South—now adopted by the United Lutheran Church in America.

Rev. Enoch Smith—1873-1877

Rev. Enoch Smith became pastor early in 1873.

Rev. Smith was born, March 31st, 1839, in Delaware County, Ohio. He received his training in the College and Seminary of Capital University, Columbus, Ohio. He was ordained December 21, 1860. He served pastorates at Bellefontaine, Paris, and Carroll county, Ohio, and at Mt. Pleasant, Pa., before assuming the local pastorate, which he resigned in 1877. He later served parishes in Bethlehem and in Butler, Pa., where he died May 22, 1894.

"Rev. Smith was a good man, full of faith, and the spirit of the gospel. He was an earnest and effective preacher, a conscientious and faithful pastor, whom many will call blessed.."

During his pastorate, the congregation was chartered and a constitution was adopted. This was the first formal constitution the congregation ever had. It is clear that in these modern times, a church could not be well governed without a constitution. But, this was **new** and some members opposed it on that account. Again, it was Lutheran and recognized the Unaltered Augsburg Confession. There was also a lack of tact in its introduction that strengthened the opposition. It is claimed that few of the members really knew what it contained. In substance, this constitution is the Constitution of Old Zion today and it agrees doctrinally and substantially with the Model Constitution of the United Lutheran Church for Congregations.

This opposition, fanned to a flame by the opposing factions, largely by outsiders, finally led to the division of the congregation.

Rev. William F. Ulery—1880-1881

Rev. William F. Ulery was born in Westphalia, Germany. He received his education at the Connoquenessing Academy, Zelienople; Muehlenberg Institute, Greensburg; and Gettysburg College and Seminary. He was ordained in June, 1855, by the Pittsburg Synod. He has served parishes at the following places: Greensburg and Adamsburg; Greenville; Zion's Church, Greensburg; Fargo, N. D.; Allegheny and Hoffman's. Rev. Ulery did faithful service, adding about fifty persons to the membership of the congregation. He resigned in order that Zion's Church and Seanor's might be formed into a new parish.

Rev. W. F. Ulery

Before his resignation took effect, the disaffected persons invited Rev. A. C. Ehrenfeldt of the General Synod, to preach for them, and were by him organized as an independent congregation. Both congregations now held services in the old stone church.

"Rev. W. F. Ulery was called in 1880 and served about one year, when difficulty arose. Correspondence was carried on with ministers of a rival Synod, and a General Synod minister called, against the protest of many. A meeting was called by the General Synod party Aug. 22, 1880, to determine the Synodical relation of the congregation; tellers were appointed, and papers read excluding several members from voting. After some argument the General Synod party moved to adjourn, the majority voted in the negative; a division was called for but not granted. Rev. Ehrenfeld declared the meeting adjourned sine die. Litigation followed and the church was divided."[1]

On October 2, 1880 the General Synod division voted unanimously to unite with the Pittsburg Synod, General Synod.

It is noteworthy that the regular congregation, now connected with the General Council, continued its uninterrupted services and, under the injunction granted by Judge Hunter, had control of the records and property. It was during this time that Rev. A. C. Ehrenfeld organized The General Synod adherents into another congregation. The General Synod congregation, therefore, withdrew from the Old Zion's Church and from the "Evangelical Lutheran District Synod of Ohio, and from the General Council to which Synod and Council Old Zion Church had belonged for more than a decade, since 1866. Old Zion never belonged to the General Synod. Nor did the new congregation, until it joined the Pittsburg Synod of the General Synod, October 2, 1880.

Old Zion's did send delegates to the Ministerium of Pennsylvania and asked to be continued in membership with

---

[1]From Preface to Old Zion Constitution written July 31, 1889.

that body. Old Zion's parish did send a delegate to the organization of the Pittsburg Synod in 1845.

The parish entertained the Ninth Convention of the Joint Synod of Ohio and Adjacent States at Greensburg, in 1855 and the English District at Brush Creek in 1859.

There is no evidence denying that the parish sent delegates from time to time to the Ev. Lutheran District Synod of Ohio. Since this was customary, there surely was no opposition before 1875.

Since custom had much authority at Herold's, and the custom was, from the earliest times, to send delegates to Synod with the Pastor, we must infer that Herold's-Church-parish sent such delegates from time to time, thus acknowledging the Synodical relation, and that Synodical relation was, for more than a decade, to the Ev. Lutheran District Synod of Ohio, and the General Council.

The General Synod Congregation never applied to the Ev. Lutheran District Synod of Ohio for a dismissal to the Pittsburg Synod of the General Synod.

The decision of Judge Sharswood of the Supreme Court of Pennsylvania did not occur until after the General Synod congregation had been organized and the change of property rights did not change the preceding facts.

"Zion congregation secured an injunction against Rev. Ehrenfelt and his new congregation; Judge Hunter tried the case and granted the injunction; "but an appeal was taken to the Supreme Court and Justice Sharswood reversed the decision of the court below. This unjust decision robbed our church of all the property which rightly belonged to it. The decision was secured by misrepresentation on the part of the General Synod people, and by our neglect, as we made no statement of facts in the case before the Supreme Court, namely, that Old Zion never was in the General Synod, as was claimed."[2]

Three months after Rev. Ehrenfelt took charge of the General Synod congregation, "at a regular meeting of the (General Synod) congregation, it was unanimously resolved to unite with the Pittsburg Synod of the General Synod."[3]

We may inquire if the General Synod congregation was so afraid of change when a hymn book and constitution were introduced into the old church, why did they almost immediately join **a new and strange Synod,** and adopt a constitution and charter, which were **new.**

After all, we are inclined to believe that the hymn book and constitution were occasions for dissatisfaction and not the real cause.

Since that time, great changes have come about within the General Synod; (in 1866 there was a nucleus of conservative men left in the General Synod, who never ceased to labor and pray for a better confession of the old faith), there has been a growing appreciation of true Lutheranism, so that the General Synod itself felt constrained to give expression to this change, when at the Convention at Washington, D. C., 1911, the General Synod submitted the following for the ratification of the District Synods:

"Article 2. **Doctrinal Basis"**

"With the Evangelical Lutheran Church of the fathers, the General Synod receives and holds the Canonical Scriptures of the Old and New Testaments as the Word of God and the only infallible rule of faith and of practice; and it receives

---

[2]Ullery History.

[3](Burgess). When the Ohio Synod was formed 1818, application was made for the dismissal of the congregations west of the mountains. Again application was made to the Ohio Synod in 1831 for dismissal to form a synod in Western Pennsylvania. The General Synod Congregation at Herold's was not regularly transferred from the Ohio Synod to the Pittsburg Synod.

and holds the **Unaltered Augsburg Confession** as a correct exhibition of the faith and doctrine of our Church as founded upon that Word."

"Article 3. **The Secondary Symbols"**

"While the General Synod regards the Augsburg Confession as a suffcient and altogether adequate doctrinal basis for the co-operation of Lutheran Synods, it also recognizes the Apology of the Augsburg Confession, the Smalkald Articles, the Small Catechism of Luther, the Large Catechism of Luther, and the Formula of Concord, as expositions of Lutheran doctrine of great historical and interpretative value, and especially commends the Small Catechism as a book of instruction."

"Article 4. **Section 3."**

"Any properly organized Lutheran Synod may be received into the General Synod at any meeting, provided it shall have adopted this Constitution with its Doctrinal Basis as set forth in Article 2."

Now, compare the foregoing with the following which is condemned by the pastoral letter, published by a committee of the General Synod party. The pastoral letter analyzes the "Fundamental Principles of Faith" of the General Council as follows: "Certain 'Fundamental Principles of Faith' were proposed to district Synods by which all who adopt them agree:

1. To embrace from the heart and use the articles of faith and sacraments as they were held and administered when the (Lutheran) Church **came into distinctive being** and received a distinctive name.

2. To accept the Confessions in every statement of doctrine "in their own true, native, original, and only sense," agreeing not only to use the same words, but to use them in one and the same sense.

3. To receive not only the Unaltered Augsburg Confession, but also all the other Symbolical Books, as in perfect harmony with the Confession "of one and the same Scriptural faith." (Condemned by pastoral letter of Pittsburg Synod of General Synod, 1867).

"In explaining how the Committee came to the proposed new amended basis, Dr. Singmaster says:

1. The present form very awkwardly accepts the Confessional attitude of "Synods not now in connection with the General Synod." The amendment makes the Doctrinal Basis that of the General Synod itself, expressed in one plain sentence."[4]

Had the General Synod always maintained this Doctrinal Basis, there would have been no rupture at Ft. Wayne, no General Council, no two Pittsburg Synods, no rupture in Old Zion Congregation, with its resultant two congregations.

From the "Definite Platform" of 1855, which charged the Augsburg Confession with **five errors,** and rejected the Symbolical Books, from the admission of the Melanchthon Synod in 1859 and the Frankean Synod in 1864, which latter Synod repudiated the Augsburg Confession and boasted of it, from the "pastoral address" of the Pittsburg Synod of the General Synod in 1867, to the amendments of 1911 and 1913, was a far-reaching change in the attitude of the General Synod. Consequently there was a re-approachment of the General Council and the General Synod. They have co-operated in Sunday school work and in bringing out a common Service and Hymnal.

As the great conflict of 1866-1880 recedes and the personalities and bitterness die away, we can see more plainly the great central principles of the contest, and we all rejoice in the growing Lutheran consciousness among our people.

---

[4]Lutheran Church Review, July, 1912.

The four hundredth anniversary of the beginning of the Protestant Reformation by Luther, witnessed the reunion of the General Synod, General Council, and United Synod of the South in one organization, Nov. 10—18, 1918, entitled "The United Lutheran Church in America." The stress of war and the great work of helping soldiers and sailors and aiding suffering Europe, has brought about the organization (1918) of the "National Lutheran Council." The National Lutheran Council is composed of the following general Lutheran bodies: The United Lutheran Church in America, Joint Synod of Ohio, Synod of Iowa and Other States, Augustana Synod, Norwegian Lutheran Church, Danish Lutheran Church, and practically all Lutheran bodies except the Synodical Conference (Missouri Synod, etc).

May the four hundredth anniversary of the unaltered Augsburg Confession (1530-1930) witness a world-wide Federation of Lutherans.

The breach between the General Council and the General Synod has been closed. The two Pittsburg Synods have merged. Why should the two Herold congregations stand apart?

Upon the basis of the doctrinal position of the United Lutheran Church, which both congregations sanction, Article 2, Section 1: "The United Lutheran Church in America receives and holds the Canonical Scriptures of the Old and New Testaments as the inspired Word of God, and as the only infallible rule and standard of faith and practice, according to which all doctrines and teachers are to be judged.

Section 2: "The United Lutheran Church in America accepts the ecumenical creeds: namely, the Apostles', the Nicene, and the Athanasian, as important testimonies drawn from the Holy Scriptures, and rejects all errors which they condemn.

Section 3: "The United Lutheran Church in America receives and holds the Unaltered Augsburg Confession as a correct exhibition of the faith and doctrine of the Evangelical Lutheran Church, founded upon the Word of God; and acknowledges all churches that sincerely hold and faithfully confess the doctrines of the Unaltered Augsburg Confession to be entitled to the name of Evangelical Lutheran.

Section 4: "The United Lutheran Church in America recognizes the Apology of the Augsburg Confession, the Smalkald Articles, the Large and Small Catechisms of Luther, and the Formula of Concord, as in the harmony of one and the same pure Scriptural faith."

How closely this doctrinal position coincides with the "revers" signed by Mr. Anton Ulrich Luetge, the first preacher at Herolds.

"Section 1: To preach the Word of God in its purity, according to Law and Gospel, as it is explained in its chief points in the Augsburg Confession and the other Symbolical Books." (See Chapter 4).

Not only have both congregations the same identical faith and doctrines, but also the same Hymn Book. "Whereas, the General Synod, the General Council and the United Synod in the South have by resolution assigned their respective rights in the Common Service Book, prepared by the Joint Committee representing these three bodies, and adopted by these three bodies, to the United Lutheran Church, and have authorized the latter to publish the Common Service Book under its own imprint, be it

Resolved 1—That the United Lutheran Church hereby formally adopts the Common Service Book and approves and directs the use of the words "Authorized by The United Lutheran Church in America on the title page of all editions."[5]

"The United Lutheran Church in America shall provide books of devotion and instruction, such as Liturgies, Hymn

---

[5]Minutes of U. L. C., 1918.

Books and Catechisms, and no Synod without its sanction shall publish or recommend books of this kind other than those provided by the general body."[6]

Also the Sunday School Literature is issued by the U. L. C. Board; there is one church paper: The Lutheran; one Women's Missionary Society, one Brotherhood. With the same United Lutheran Church in America; the same Pittsburg Synod; the same faith; the same Common Service Book; the same Sunday School Literature; the same auxiliary organizations, it should be the duty of the two Congregations to unite into the one old historic "Herold's oder Zion's Kirche." The cause of separation was outside the congregation itself, brought in by the agitation of Synodical strife; now that the Synods have united, may Zion unite in peace and concord.

---

[6] Constitution U. L. C., Article 8, Section 7.

CHAPTER XIII

Rebuilding

Rev. J. C. Kunzman—1882-1887

Rev. Jacob C. Kunzman, D. D. was born in the Grand Duchy, Baden, Germany, on the 31st of December, 1852. In 1860, his parents emigrated to America and settled in Pittsburg. He received his education in the public schools of Pittsburg, Thiel College, and the Theological Seminary at Mt. Airy, Philadelphia. He was ordained by the Pittsburg Synod and served the following parishes: At Kitanning, Pa.; Greensburg and Harrold's; and Pittsburg. In 1899 he resigned Grace Church, Pittsburg, Pa., to accept the appointment of Superintendent of English Home Missions in the General Council. He later, under the United Board of Home Missions, became Western District Superintendent, which position he soon resigned to assume the presidency of the Pacific Lutheran Theological Seminary at Seattle, Washington.

Although Old Zion had lost her property by the decision of Justice Sharswood, she went right ahead and purchased a property for a location of a Church and Cemetery.

Law Courts can speak with authority in civil matters, but they have no jurisdiction or binding force in spiritual and ecclesiastical affairs.

While the property went to the General Synod party, the succession of spiritual and ecclesiastical affairs remained with Old Zion.

Rev. and Mrs. Alonzo Yount

Rev. J. C. Kunzmann, D.D.

Old Zion has always been true to the fathers from the beginning and she has always cherished the inheritance of historic Lutheranism, the Unaltered Augsburg Confession, and the Symbolical Books, and, hence, is true heir to the inheritance of "Herold's, oder Zion's Kirche."

The new church was built in 1884-1885, being dedicated June 14, 1885. Rev. Edmund Belfour, D. D. assisted the pastor. The church is built of brick, 32x64 feet in size and is well finished and furnished. The cost was $8,000.00, which was all provided for.

During the Pastorate of Rev. Kunzman, a good work was done. The congregation recovered from the shock of the division and was more firmly established. In the spring of 1887, Rev. Kunzman resigned Old Zion Congregation in order that it might unite with St. Paul's (Seanor's) to form a parish.

Rev. W. H. Zuber—1887-1894

Rev. William H. Zuber was born July 8, 1859, at Collegeville, Montgomery Co., Pa. He received his education at Muehlenberg College and the Seminary at Mt. Airy, Philadelphia. He was ordained in June, 1887. He has served pastorates at the following places: Harold's and Seanor's; St. Paul, Minn. He taught for a number of years in the Greensburg Seminary and Thiel College, and later served a parish in Chehalis, Washington. During Rev. Zuber's pastorate, a new cemetery was laid out and fenced. During his pastorate, here he also filled a professorship in the Greensburg Seminary. The entire parish increased 20 per cent in membership. Rev. Zuber was faithful and persevering and made a host of friends. He is also noted as a scholar in natural science.

Rev. Jonathan Sarver, D.D.—1895-1903

Rev. Jonathan Sarver, D.D., was born Nov. 2, 1837, in Hempfield Township, Westmoreland County, Pa. He received his education at Pennsylvania College and the theological

Rev. W. H. Zuber

Rev. Jonathan Sarver

Rev. E. H. Kohn

Rev. Isaac K. Wismer

Seminary at Gettysburg, Pa., and was licensed to preach by the Pittsburg Synod in 1864. He served pastorates at the following places: Zelienople; Leechburg; Mt. Pleasant, Pa.; Hazelton, Kansas; Jewett, Ohio; Beaver Falls; Allegheny; Harold's and Seanor's; and at Derry, Pa. Dr. Sarver was an eloquent preacher and has been successful in his several pastorates. He was in the ministry more than fifty years. In later years, though serving no regular pastorate, he still preached as supply in the various congregations. He died in Washington, Pa., 1922. During his pastorate the parsonage at New Stanton was built.

Rev. J. A. Yount—1904-1904

Rev. J. Alonzo Yount was born Dec. 17, 1864, in Catawba, Co., North Carolina. He received his education at Concordia College, Conover, North Carolina, and at Lenoir College, Hickory, North Carolina. He began his pastorate April 17, 1904 and, owing to ill health, resigned Oct. 16, 1904. Rev. Yount endeared himself to the people during his short pastorate. He resigned to resume his pastorate at Conover, N. Carolina.

Rev. J .O. Glenn—1904-1910

Rev. J. O. Glenn was born Oct. 18, 1862, at Singleton, Winston County, Miss. He received his education at Roanoke College and the Theological Seminary at Philadelphia. He was ordained June 3, 1901 by the Ministerium of Pennsylvania, and has served pastorates at the following places: Donegal, Harrold's and Seanor's, Irwin, and Scottdale.

During the pastorate of six years, Rev. Glenn rendered faithful service and was beloved by all. A congregation was organized at New Stanton and a new Church edifice built there.

Rev. E. H. Kohn, Ph.D.—1911-1913

Rev. E. H. Kohn was born at Little Mountain, Newberry County, South Carolina, Nov. 7, 1863. He graduated from Newberry College in 1886. After teaching in Texas and Virginia, he entered the Theological Seminary at Philadelphia. He was ordained by the Ministerium of Pennsylvania May 23, 1893.

He has served since ordination at Philadelphia, Pa.; Cherryville, North Carolina 1903-1909; Sumpter 1909-1911; at Harold's-Seanor's 1911-1913, and now is pastor at Mt. Holly, North Carolina.

Rev. Kohn was energetic and did good work during his brief pastorate. A new steam heating plant was installed and other improvements made.

Rev. I. K. Wismer—1913——

Rev. Isaac K. Wismer was born Sept. 24, 1853, in Bucks County, Pa. He received his education in the Select High School, Philadelphia, the University, and Mt. Airy Seminary. He was ordained in June, 1885, by the Ministerium of Pennsylvania. He has served pastorates at Dubois, Pa.; Latrobe and Youngstown, Uniontown, and on Oct. 1, 1913, became pastor of the Harrold—Seanor parish. In 1914 the Duplex Envelope System was introduced and in 1915, extensive improvements were made to the interior of the church and a piano secured.

These improvements make the church more churchly and better adapted to the Lutheran service, an enlarged Sunday school room and an inside stairway make for efficiency and comfort.

The following are the statistics for the church, 1922:

Members enrolled—179.

Sunday School enrollment—150.

Ladies' Mission and Aid Society—32.

The congregation pays its full apportionment to Synod and is liberal toward the general causes of beneficience.

The Sunday school is noted for the faithful attendance of its members. In fact, in the past, the Sunday school has been a great power of the church.

The church membership, 1922 is as follows:

Members of Old Zion

Allshouse, Etta
Allshouse, George M.
Allshouse, Emma
Allshouse, Mrs. Alice E.
Altman, Mrs. Susanna
Atcheson, Albert
Atcheson, Hannah
Bailey, Mrs. Mary
Baughman, Francis J.
Baughman, Annie M.
Baughman, Ward F.
Baughman, Cyrus F.
Baughman, Lydia A.
Baughman William J.
Baughman, Leah C.
Baughman, Mary Irene
Baughman, John
Baughman, Daniel H.
Baughman, Annie
Baughman, Lawrence J.
Baughman, Clarence J.
Baughman, Mary L.
Baughman, James Luther
Benson, Harry G.
Benson, Bessie C.
Benson, Arthur
Benson, William C.
Benson, Emma Martina
Beyer, Charles H.
Beyer, Sadie
Beyer, Dewey
Blank, Mrs. Edna
Cope, James E.
Cope, Susan
Cope, Lucy
Cope, Ella
Cope, John H.
Cope, Mrs. Edith
Eisaman, Solomon
Eisaman, Lucinda
Eisaman, Cyrus D.
Eisaman, Agnes
Eisaman, Charles H.
Eisaman, Cyrus Clark
Eisaman, Margaret J.
Eisaman, Martha Agnes
Eisaman, Ethel Leah
Eisaman, William P.
Eisaman, Phebe
Eisaman, Robert C.
Eisaman, Lyda
Eisaman, Mrs. Elizabeth C.
Erickson, Mrs. Sarah A.
Errett, Mrs. Mary E.
Errett, Mary
Errett, Lulu
Earhart, Mrs. Laura
Fischer, Carl
Fischer, Mary
Frye, David W.
Frye, Druella
Goodlin, Mrs. Elizabeth
Haines, Mrs. Myrtle
Harrold, Albert
Harrold, Hetty J.
Harrold, Walter A.
Harrold, William Humphrey
Harrold Frank M.

Rev. J. O. Glenn

Harrold, Mrs. Sarah
Harrold, Harry E.
Harrold, Emma J.
Harrold, Henry O.
Harrold, Thomas C.
Harrold, Lewis P.
Harrold, Florence M.
Henry, Daniel
Henry, Rachel
Henry, Jacob
Henry, Joseph
Henry, Elma
Henry, Thomas A.
Henry, James W.
Henry, Alberta E.
Henry, Russel E.
Henry, Olive M.
Henry, Mrs. Hannah
Henry John H.
Henry, May
Henry, Paul F.
Henry, Amos F.
Henry, Bertha
Henry, John W.
Henry, Maria J.
Herrod, James T.
Herrod, Mary
Herrod, Lawrence E.
Herrod, Edna O.
Herrod, Roy T.
Herrod, Idella M.
Herrod Edna L.
Herrod, Irene May
Holtzer, Mrs. Alice
Holtzer, Mrs. Lucy
Holtzer, Kathleen M.
Holtzer, Garnet Romayne
Jordan, Edgar W.
Kaylor, Mrs. Nellie M.
Landis, Mrs. Elizabeth V.
McGraw, Mrs. Leah
Miller, Mrs. Sarah
Miller, Mrs. Gertrude
Miller, Albert C.
Miller, J. Herman
Miller, Celia
Miller, William J.
Miller, Mary
Miller, Mrs. Alice T.
Moore, Peter A.
Orczeck, Mrs. Catherine
Orczeck, Cyrus Carl
Plischke, Charles
Plischke, Mabel
Plischke, Mary Dorothy
Plischke, Minnie
Ruff, John G.
Ruff, Urilla
Ruff, Samuel, M.
Ruff, Amanda M.
Ruff, John P.
Ruff, Sabilla E.
Rosensteel, Mrs. Ethel M.
Sindorf, Mrs. Margaret
Snyder, Cyrus A.
Snyder, Bessie
Steiner, Mrs. Alice
Smeltzer, Mrs. Margaret
Silvis, Jacob H.
Silvis, Anna M.
Silvis, Mabel
Silvis, John M.
Silvis, Anna Margaret
Silvis Charles O.
Silvis, L. V.
Silvis, Mary Ruth
Silvis, Myrtle E.
Silvis, Earl F.
Smeltzer, William
Smeltzer, Lucien
Smeltzer, Anna
Smeltzer, Logan

Stroble, Henry O.
Stroble, Francis M.
Stroble, William H.
Taylor, Thomas Earl
Taylor, Edna L,
Truxel, Mrs. Charlotte
Walthour, William W.
Walthour, Archibald
Walthour, Mary
Walthour, Calvin
Weightman, Mrs. Agnes
Wertz, Carl S.
Wertz, Mary
Wertz, C. Luther
Wertz, Naomi C.
Wertz, David, G.
Wertz, Mirram F.
Wertz, Martha E.
Wineman, Jacob E.
Wineman, Rebecca
Wineman, Mary J.
Wineman, George
Woodward, Mrs. Daniel
Zundel, Mary Martha
Zundel, Hermie Idella
Zundel, Albert Martin
Zundel, Emma May
Zundel, Martin L.
Zundel, Paul W.
Zundel Robert M.
Zundel, Ray A.

CHAPTER XIV

Our Sister Church

Zion Evangelical Lutheran Church emerged from the contest of the eighties victorious in property rights according to Justice Sharswood's decision. Rev. W. F. Ulery was the last pastor of the united church. Rev. Ulery states the issue as follows: "He resigned in order that Zion's Church and Seanor's might be formed into a new parish, but for the time being, this arrangement was not effected. Not all were ready.

During this vacancy, the disaffected persons invited Rev. A. C. Ehrenfeldt, of the General Synod, to preach for them, and were by him organized as an independent congregation. Both congregations now held services in the old stone church. The congregation of our synod had secured an injunction in our courts, under Judge Hunter, against Rev. Ehrenfelt, but an appeal was taken to the Supreme Court and Justice Sharswood reversed the decision of the court below."

We now give the General Synod view as recorded in Dr. Burgess' History of the Pittsburg Synod, General Synod.

"On April 30, 1878, nine days before Rev. Ulery's resignation took effect, the church council addressed a letter to the president of the Pittsburg Synod of the General Synod, asking for a pastor. Rev. A. C. Ehrenfeld, a retired minister of the Allegheny Synod, was secured for them, who served them as a stated supply from July 11, 1880 to Nov. 15, 1882. Rev. P. G. Bell also served them in the same capacity from 1882 to 1883. Three months after Rev. Ehrenfeld took charge, "at a regular meeting of the congregation, it was **unanimously** resolved to unite with the Pittsburg Synod of the General Synod." This meeting was held October 2, 1880. It was the first time in the history of the old Harold's Church that it had ever regularly united with any synodical body. They preferred to remain independent, fearing, as many of the older members said, "the tyranny of Synod." A few weeks after this action, on the 18th day of October, the party that favored the constitution of Rev. Smith began legal proceedings to dispossess the General Synod party of the church property. The case was tried in the Court of Westmoreland County before Judge Hunter, who decided in favor of the plaintiffs. An appeal was taken to the Supreme Court, and Justice Sharswood, before whom the case was heard, reversed the decision of the lower court and decided that the General Synod party constituted the original historic Harold's Church. The congregation continued to worship in the old stone church with the Reformed until July 8, 1884, when a new and beautiful brick church was dedicated some distance west of the old location, on land donated by Daniel Altman." (Compare Chapter 12).

The new church cost about $6,000.00, $3,500.00 of which was paid in cash, and the remainder in labor and material.

The sermons at the dedication were preached by Revs. A. C. Ehrenfeld and Rev. G. W. Leisher. The pastor, Rev. Isaiah Irvine performing the act of consecration.

During Rev. Irvine's pastorate, a lot was purchased from Daniel Altmann for fifty dollars and a commodious and beautiful parsonage built at a cost of one thousand dollars.

Rev. J. H. Wright served as pastor from April 1, 1888 to April 1, 1897. He received a salary of $500.00 and parsonage. It was during his pastorate that the half-interest of the congregation in the old property was sold to the Reformed, July 30, 1888, for $2,000.00, the money being invested for the use of the congregation. The congregation was also chartered January, 1884.

Rev. Charles L. Streamer began his pastorate September 1, 1897, and resigned January 15, 1903, because of ill health. Rev. J. E. F. Hassinger accepted a call and assumed the pastorate June 16, 1903 and served until 1912.

Rev. T. M. Daubenspeck became pastor Oct. 1912 and served until his death, May 28, 1913. Rev. Elmer Kahl served the congregation from 1913 to 1919. Rev. G. L. Courtney became pastor 1919 and served until 1921. Rev. J. L. Marvin of Bittinger, Md., assumed the pastorate in 1921 and continues to serve the congregation.

CHAPTER XV

The Fruitage

Old Zion has now closed one hundred fifty years of organized life, and one hundred fifty-seven years since her members, gathered together in the first rude log cabins, began to pray and plan for her welfare.

During these years, Old Zion has been a constant blessing to thousands of her members. We can count the pastorates and note somewhat of the pastoral labors, but who can count the hundreds of souls, in glory now, who were fed upon the bread of life within this fold.

To the great multitude, from the tiny babe to the aged saint, now sleeping beneath the sod in "God's Acre," Old Zion, with her ministrations of Word and Sacrament, was the only agency that offered to them values that they may still prize,

From her sacred precincts, the aged parson would go forth into the wilds of nature, through heat of summer and cold of winter, and minister to some departing soul. From Old Zion as a center, there went forth the ministrations of the Word and Sacraments throughout the territory west of the Alleghenies. The pastors of Old Zion traveled far and near to settlements in the woods and ministered to them until more ministers were secured and the field divided.

The influence of Old Zion is not, therefore, confined to those who attended services in her sanctuary at Herold's Church. It is interesting to note the large territory covered by this congregation.

Rev. John Allen Zundel

John Allen Zundel, son of Albert M. and Susannah Baughman Zundel, was born on the Aultman farm. Hempfield Township, Westmoreland County, Pennsylvania, February sixth 1854. He was baptized by the Rev. G. W. Mechling, on April twenty ninth following. Peter Baughman and his wife Anne Catherina, nee Wentzel, maternal grandparents, were the sponsors. He attended the Harrold's school and the Greensburg Seminary, fitting himself for teaching. After teaching many years in the grade schools of Hempfield Township he returned to the Greensburg Seminary and took the classical course. He entered Thiel College at Greenville, Pa., and graduated in 1895. He then entered the Chicago Lutheran Seminary, and graduated in 1898.

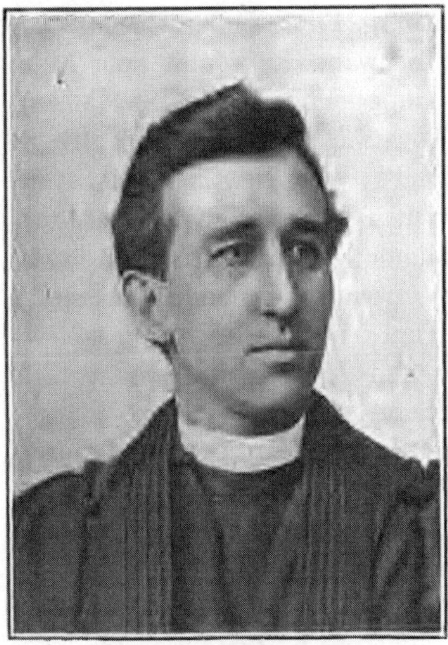

Rev. John Allen Zundel

He received a call to the mission at Beaver Falls, Pa. and was ordained in the First Lutheran Church, Greensburg, Pa., May 19, 1898.

After serving at Beaver Falls for about five years he accepted a call to Fargo, North Dakota. Later he served as Field Missionary for Minnesota under the Home Mission Board of the General Council.

He died, at the old Zundel homestead at 6-10 P. M., September 20, 1910, and was buried in the Old Zion Cemetery, September 23. Twenty ministers and a large concourse of friends attended the funeral.

He was married in 1900, to Miss Sophia Catherine Richter of Beaver Falls, Pa., who with three children; Ruth, Paul, and John, survive him.

His zeal for the Master's cause consumed him. Although he spent but twelve years in the ministry, those twelve years were at the battle-front of Home Missions.

The Master called him while preaching to his congregation in Minneapolis, Minn. He was truly a child of Old Zion's Church, identified with her life and development, giving freely of his time and talent for her welfare and advancement. He loved his church and gave his life for her.

The center of Protestant influence among the Germans was undoubtedly at Herold's or Zion Church. The early records contain the names of settlers on the Brush Creek, beyond Harrison City, Greensburg, Mt. Pleasant, and Pleasant Unity, showing that all the German Lutheran settlers were at first embraced within her fold.

Gradually other places of worship were formed; this was determined more likely because of school facilities than for church attendance; Brush Creek Church was the first, then followed Pleasant Unity; Greensburg, First; Indian Head, Good Hope; Kintig's, St. John's; Schwabs, Ruffsdale; Four Mile Run, Donegal; Hoffman's, Hope; Youngstown, St. James; Yockey's, St. James; Bell Township; Klingensmith's; Denmark Manor; Zehner's, St. Paul's; West Newton, Christ's; in later times Zion's, Greensburg; Holy Trinity, Jeannette; Penn, Penn Station; Unity, Manor; Zion's, Harrison City; St. John's Bouquet; Holy Trinity, Irwin; Salem and Emmanuel's Delmont; Mt. Zion's and St. Paul's, Donegal; St. Mark's, New Stanton; Trinity, St. John's and Zion's, Mt. Pleasant; St. Paul's, Scottdale; Bethel, Youngstown, St. Luke's, Youngwood, and St. Matthew's, Hunker; St. Paul's; Holy Trinity, Connellsville; Christ's, Chalk Hill; St. John's New Florence, and Memorial; Smithton, Jacobs, Smithfield, Trinity, Latrobe; Zion, Cribbs; St. Mark's, Arona, and St. Mark's Jeannette.

There are now forty-six Lutheran congregations upon the territory once embraced in the parish of Old Zion Church. Practically the South East Conference of the Pittsburg Synod. In these congregations are now 15,000 baptized, and 11,000 communicants, served by thirty pastors.

In the larger field, served by the Stecks' and Mechling, at various times as opportunity presented; on this field, embracing almost the entire western part of the state, excepting Erie, there are now approximately seventy-five thousand communicant members and about 150,000 baptized members.

Other influences helped to accomplish this great work, but before Passavant's pastorate in Pittsburg, the elder and younger Stecks were the Bishops of Western Pennsylvania.

While the pastors since Luetge, up to recent times, lived in Greensburg, Old Zion continued to be the principle congregation of the parish until about 1880. It is only within the last forty years that she has been surpassed by her daughter, the First Church, and her granddaughter, Zion Church, Greensburg.

The whole history of the church has been missionary. This missionary activity did not consist so much in giving money as in giving self. As congregation after congregation was formed in some portion of the parish territory, the mother church gave her parental blessing until at the present time, her territory is limited and her membership reduced.

Although, in addition to giving territory, she has continually enriched her daughter churches in the cities and towns by the migration of her people, young and old, still she maintains her vigor and activity. In some respects, as in interest in the general work of the church, such as Missions and works of Mercy, she is more interested and active now than ever before. All the good works of the church are remembered at proper times.

Among the young men of the parish who entered the ministry, we note the following:

Revs. Michael J. Steck, Jonas Mechling, Isaac O. P. Baker, G. W. Mechling, Edward L. Baker, Jonathan Sarver, W. F. Ulery, Isaac O. Baker, John A. L. Mench, John A. Zundel, William A. Zundel. So far as we know, only the last two were members of Old Zion Church at Herold's.

Rev. William Arter Zundel, M.A., B.D.

CHAPTER XVI

The Sunday School

When the Church Schools were superseded by State controlled schools (1820-1830), the fathers were not slow to make some provision for religious instruction under the new order.

In 1828, the Ohio Synod, to which Old Zion then belonged, adopted the following Sunday school plan and recommended that it be announced from the pulpit by every pastor. It shows how the fathers stressed the fundamentals. The plan: "The pastor with the advice of the church council shall appoint a capable person to act as superintendent, and as many male and female teachers as conditions require. (Boys and girls may come to the same school, although lady teachers should instruct the girls).

"When these arrangements have been made, the time and place for beginning the school should be determined, and where at all possible, the pastor, and at least some members of the church council, as well as the parents of the children should be present to lend the work as much gravity and importance as possible.

"The pupils should be separated into classes of 8 to 10 members. And here age should not be a determining factor, but the ability and progress of the pupil. Each class should retain its own teacher and it shall not be permitted the teacher to leave his **own** class and take up another without the consent of the superintendent and the other teachers.

"The school should be held in the church, school house or some suitable building and, where possible, every Sunday; it should begin at a definite time and continue at least two hours.

"The superintendent and teachers should see to it that Christian order, so necessary to the instruction and edification of the pupils, be maintained.

"The duties of the superintendent are, among others, the following: To open and close the school with singing and prayer, or at least to see that this is done.

"He shall keep a record of the names of all pupils, giving time of entry and withdrawal and all other data of importance.

"The teachers, male and female, should not remain away from school except from good reasons, and should they be prevented from coming, they shall make it their duty to have a capable person take their place, or at least notify the superintendent, the teachers shall make it their special duty to see that their pupils learn to spell, commit to memory and get hold of the fundamentals of our precious religion."[1]

Thus we see there is a gradual development of the Sunday school idea out of the original parish school. Doubtless this plan was used at Herold's from its adoption by Synod.

The earlier records of the Sunday school have not been preserved.

The first records of a Sunday school preserved to date are from the year 1859, when David A. Altman was elected Superintendent of the Union Sunday School, with George Eisaman and Abraham Altman as assistants. These officers all happened to be Lutherans, and, no doubt were selected because of their scholastic training, as all had been teachers.

After the erection of the new church, 1884-85), on the 29th of March, 1885, the Old Zion Lutheran Sunday school

[1]History of the Ev. Luth. Joint Synod of Ohio.

was organized by Henry M. Zundel, who became its first superintendent. The school began with 50 scholars which was soon increased to 79. At the earnest solicitation of the elder members, of both the Lutheran and Reformed Congre-

Henry M. Zundel
Sunday School Superintendent, 1885.

gations, this school was reorganized into a Union Sunday school, in the fall, November 15, of the same year. H. M. Zundel continued as Superintendent, with E. E. Wible of the Reformed Church as assistant. It continued as a Union Sunday school until January 1, 1888, when it was dissolved by a unanimous vote, and on the following Lord's Day the present

Lutheran Sunday school was organized, with 48 scholars and 17 officers and teachers, with Jno. A. Zundel as superintendent.

From the beginning, this school has observed the principal Festivals of the Church Year. Shortly after its beginning, during the Union period, an exceptionally good program was carried out at the Christmas-tide, in connection with which, there was a monster revolving Christmas tree, about 25 feet high, in the Old Stone Church, laden with gifts for the school.

Another Christmas a year later, when the school rendered "Ogden's Birth of Christ," a religious cantata containing bright carols, the congregation was delighted with the development of talent of the community. The expense of the cantata for those days, over $125, was considered quite an undertaking. So well were the Pastors, Rev. Dr. J. C. Kunzman and Rev. Dr. Cyrus Dieffenbacher, pleased, that from their seats in the audience, they arose and requested that it be repeated within a week, which was done, a crowded house again being present. These exercises were held in the Old Zion Lutheran Church.

Congregational reunions, then termed "Sunday School Celebrations," were begun in 1886, and have continued annually ever since, and increased in number and popularity. More recently the Old Zion's and Zion's Lutheran Sunday school and St. John's Reformed Sunday school, have joined their efforts, and the annual Church and Sunday school reunions have proven very successful, and productive of a splendid spirit in the community.

Memorial Day from 1886 and 87, and some years thereafter was also observed and occasionally since, when opportunity affords. At times the Sunday schools united in big patriotic parades, either from Old Zion's or from the Cross-road to the Old cemetery. Prominent speakers were secured and special patriotic music rendered by the large chorus choirs. Some years there were more flowers than could be used. Such participations in special Patriotic and Religious observances have been the means of fostering a spirit of earnest and successful co-operation.

The Old Zion's Sunday school has now 142 scholars and 12 officers and teachers, and is progressing nicely in its work.

The different superintendents of this school since its organization in 1885, have been, in turn; Henry M. Zundel, John A. Zundel, Cyrus D. Eisaman, A. M. Zundel, Jr., Robert M. Zundel, A. M. Zundel, Jr., James E. Cope and R. M. Zundel, (1922).

The Cemeteries

When the location for the new church was secured, provision was also made for a cemetery. Even before the erection of the church, and before the woods across the road from the school house was all cleared, a burial ground was needed.

Daniel Baughman, Sr., who died before the first cemetery plot was laid out, was buried in the extreme southwest corner, so as not to interfere in plotting the lots.

When it came to selling lots considerable discussion ensued. The fathers, who were really the bone and sinue of the congregation, with a very few exceptions, favored "free lots," the same as had been the custom in the Old Union Grave Yard. At one of the first meetings, a motion to sell the cemetery lots was discussed for a long time without a decision being reached. Those who favored "selling the lots," discovered that the motion would be overwhelmingly lost, so a postponement of two weeks was finally agreed upon. In the meantime, a person of the community, not a member, died, and was granted a lot. This was used as an argument at the next meeting, and the motion carried to sell the lots. This shows how difficult it was to establish a fund for the future care of the cemetery.

The first cemetery proved a success, financially, although the prices of lots were very low. Realizing the need of more burial ground for the future generations, more ground opposite the church was purchased, and laid out in lots. This second effort proving even more popular than the first, and the third tract was purchased. Now Old Zion's, with its combined plots has indeed a beautiful burial place, a veritable "God's Acre," and also has a fund which will provide proper care of the cemetery.

The first church and cemetery ground, of two acres, was donated by Mother Eisaman in 1883-84.

The second cemetery plot of three and one half acres, and one half acre for hitching place, was purchased from the Eisaman Estate, during Rev. W. H. Zuber's pastorate.

The third and last cemetery plot of five acres, was purchased from Cyrus D. Eisaman in 1907. The three parts thus, contain over ten acres for burial purposes. The ground is well located and well adapted for the purpose. This is now one of the most attractive cemeteries of the county.

Church Music

Years ago when books were very scarce, the pioneer pastor was accustomed, to announce the hymns, line by line, and especially so, at the grave, during the burial of the dead. Those who sang then joined in or closely followed the pastor or "fore singer."

The gallery in the Old Stone Church, forming the three sides of a square, with the "wine-glass shaped pulpit" against the wall, in the middle of the open space, was the place for the singers. Grandfather Eisaman, in his day, and later I. W. Wentzel, David B. Wentzel, Reuben Eisaman and others served as "fore-singers," or leaders in the music. The singers when out in number, were lined all around the three sides in

Rev. L. D. Steckel ---------------1904-1909
Rev. E. D. Bright ---------------1910——

Zion Settlement and Patriotism

The people of Zion Church Settlement have always been patriotic. They took their full share in defending their country's flag. They were among the most skillful and daring Indian fighters. They did their full share in the several wars of our country, as the following report will show. We need to note, however, that not all who fought with the colors are buried here. In the Indian wars, he who fell was fortunate if he was buried at all, and in the earlier wars those who fell in battle or succumbed to disease,, were not sent home, but buried where they died. Many names on the early rolls of this Church were extinguished in this way.

The Annual Memorial Roster of Adjutant S. P. Feightner of Capt. George A. Cribbs, Post, No. 276 G. A. R. for May 30, 1922, shows the following summary of the soldier dead in the Herold Cemeteries.

Indian War, 1; Revolutionary War, 6; War of 1812, 1; Mexican War, 3; Civil War, 45; Spanish American War, 4; World War, 4; a total of 64.

In all the cemeteries closely connected with the Herold Settlement the totals are Indian War, 1; Revolutionary War, 15; War of 1812, 11; Mexican War, 23; Civil War, 323; Spanish American War, 19; World War, 38; Regular Army, 2; Mexican Border, 1; total 433. The Post No. 276 has 59 survivers of the Civil War and there are hundreds of survivers of the later wars. The Herold cemeteries contain the dead of every American War.

Fort Allen was built in 1774 during Connolly's War. The Herold Settlement stood solidly for Pennsylvania's rights west of the mountains.

The fact that the great west was peopled through Pennsylvania has meant more to our country than many suppose.

Pennsylvania developed the first true type of Americanism. The great west followed the Pennsylvania type of civilization and government.

The celebrated Historian, Woodrow Wilson, twice president of the United States, a Virginian by birth, governor of New Jersey and president of Princeton University, says; "However mortifying it may be to them or to us, America did not come out of the South and it did not come out of New England. The characteristic part of America originated in the middle states of Pennsylvania, New York, and New Jersey, because there, from the first, was that mixture of populations, that mixture of racial stocks, that mixture of antecedents, which is the singular and distinguishing mark of the United States."

In helping to maintain Pennsylvania's rights west of the Alleghenies the Herold Settlement contributed to the influence that Pennsylvania, New York and New Jersey exerted even the western states.

Bancroft says: "The Germans who composed a large part of the inhabitants of Pennsylvania were all on the side of liberty."

CHAPTER XVII

Education among the German Elements in Western Pennsylvania

For the history of the settlements and the problems of the early settlers see the preceeding first eight chapters.

It required several years for these hardy pioneers to build necessary cabins for shelter against the cold of winter, and to clear sufficient ground for the necessary crops; hence school work had to wait until the work necessary to existance was accomplished. However, the historical interest of the German for education was shown when, in 1772, three years after the settlement at Zion Church or Herold's a school-house was erected and a teacher secured. This school-house also served for church purposes until a suitable church was built.

Balthasar Meyer, who settled in Zion Church Settlement in 1779, was the first schoolmaster in the settlement and, perhaps, the first in Western Pennsylvania. There being no minister in the settlement as yet, the schoolmaster was called upon to read sermons, baptize infants, and children, and to bury the dead.

The early records of the school are mingled with the church records of the time, hence we read in the old Lutheran Parish Register at Herold's: "Register of all children in Zion Church Settlement baptized by Balthasar Meyer, schoolmaster, from the second of August, 1772, until ——." The last entry in the handwriting of Balthasar Meyer is in the year 1792, the fourth of June. The record indicates, in the year 1782, the advent of a regular Lutheran Minister, Rev. Anton Ulrich

Luetge, but owing to the vastness of the field schoolmaster Meyer still continued to baptize children, though in limited number, and to enter the baptisms on the record, up until the fourth of June, 1792; hence we may believe that Balthasar Meyer served as schoolmaster from August 2, 1772, until June 4, 1792.

It is difficult to give an estimate of the life and work of this pioneer educator. The only knowledge we have of him is the records that he left. Judging from the neatness, style and content of these writings, he was a man of no mean ability. His standing in the community is attested by the fact that they made him their pastor de facto, and when the congregation called Anton Ulrich Luetge to become their pastor, it was schoolmaster Balthasar Meyer who ordained him to the ministry and installed him as Pastor.

The intelligence of these early pioneers may be gauged from their acts and writings. In 1774 the settlers met at Fort Allen at Zion Church Settlement and signed a petition to the governor. Of the seventy-seven signers every one could read, and write his own name legibly; which was not a general attainment among pioneers of other nationalities of that day. It is a mark of intelligence and progressiveness that they so early made provision for schools and churches. Because they spoke German and many did not speak English fluently, they were generally rated as "dumb Dutch" by many of their illiterate contemporaries.

The personnel of the early county officialdom is no indication of the relative qualities and worth of the early settlers. In the first place the German settlers took up farms and did not seek political preferment as did their Irish, Scotch-Irish and English neighbors.

Secondly, during the reign of the Penn heirs, many of the first officials of the county were appointed; consequently the better known English speaking men received the lion's share of the best political jobs. That the officials were not always the best men is shown by the following instances: "John Smith was charged with stealing and pleaded guilty. He was sentenced to receive thirty-nine lashes on the bare back, well laid on, and his ears were then to be cut off and nailed to the pillory: and he was to stand one hour in the pillory."

"In October, 1775, Elizabeth Smith was ordered to receive fifteen lashes on the bare back, well laid on. She was furthermore an indentured servant of James Kinkaid, who had a right to her uninterrupted services. Four days after she was whipped, James Kinkaid presented a petition to our courts setting forth that he had been unjustly deprived of her services while she was in prison, and while she was recovering from the effects of the sentence. He therefore asked a redress for this loss. Judges Hanna, Lochry, Sloan and Cavett were on the bench and they deliberately considered his request and decreed that she should serve Kinkaid for a period of two years after the expiration of her indenture."

"James McGill was found guilty of a felony in 1782, and was sentenced to a public whipping, then to the pillory, after which his right ear was cut off, and he was to be branded on the forehead with a hot iron."[1]

Such revolting incidents as the above speak volumes in the fact that not a German is mentioned in these crimes. While the English, Irish, and Scotch-Irish were thus extending the "blessings" of English laws and customs to Western Pennsylvania, the German settlers were building schools, supporting schoolmasters and Ministers of the Gospel.

Boucher in his history of Westmoreland County says: "A people are not generally better than their laws. Many who came from England and Ireland and settled in Western Pennsylvania purchased large tracts of land and at once regarded

[1]History of Westmoreland County, by John W. Boucher.

themselves as nabobs, owners of large landed estates, like the nobles of England. They tried to emulate and imitate the weaker rather than the stronger characteristics of the landed gentry of Great Britain. Hugh Henry Brackenridge, afterwards justice of the supreme court, says in "Modern Chivalry," that we had men in Westmoreland County who held and abused slaves and Redemptioneers, who would not for a fine cow have shaved their beards on Sunday."

As a rule the Germans settled on moderately sized farms, and owned no slaves or Redemptioneers, although quite a number of Germans were brought here as Redemptioneers; choosing to sell their services for a period of years in order to gain transportation to America.

In 1780 there were two hundred and three slave holders, including George Washington, in Westmoreland County, and six hundred ninety-five slaves. In 1798 there were only twelve slaves in Hempfield township, which then embraced Greensburg, the county seat. Hempfield Township was settled mainly by Germans, and this small number of slaves in this large township, is proof of the general attitude of the German toward slavery.

Mr. Boucher pays the following tribute to their peaceableness and self-governing ability: "They had an unwritten law among themselves which in effect worked out the spirit of all law as defined by Justinian, the great Roman law-giver, viz.: 'To live honestly, hurt nobody, and render to everyone his due.' One in that community who habitually violated this precept, was very soon ostracised from the society of his neighbors; the ordinary field hand would not work for or associate with him. He was not invited to the barn raisings or log rollings so common in the sparsely settled country; and this unwritten law of social ostracism was carried out so thoroughly against the offending dishonest or unworthy neighbor, that families thus ostracised have abhorrently left the fields they had cleared with great labor, never to return to them.

"These principles of right living were brought with them and thoroughly implanted in the new country, for most of them had been brought up under the English law and knew thoroughly their inherent rights as citizens of a community. The very absence of courts or convenient tribunals before which to redress their grievances, helped them in a great measure, to give a high moral tone to their rural communities in their personal relations with each other."

This brief survey of the community life will give some insight into the aims and objects toward which they desired their schools to function in those pioneer days.

A record of the financial settlement of the church council, dated the fifteenth day of February, 1793, is signed by (Rev.) John Michael Steck, President, and Karl Sheibeler, schoolmaster, which indicates that Karl Sheibeler succeeded Balthasar Meyer as schoolmaster in the Zion or Herold's Settlement.

The writer is in possession of a Getaufschein (Baptismal Certificate)[1] of John George Eisenmann, a great great grandfather of the writer. This Getaufschein names as parents the honorable Peter Eisenmann and Justina, nee Altmann, his beloved wife. The sponsors were John Peter Eisenmann and Anna Barbara his wife. This certificate was "made by Karl Sheibeler, schoolmaster, Hempfield Township, Westmoreland County, 1788." It is a work of art. The penmanship is beautiful. The body of the certificate consists of a poem concerning Baptism and its meaning, then follows the names of child, parents and sponsors, then another poem or hymn. About this body there is a border of fine workmanship done in mosaics and flowers in three colors. After one hundred twenty-four years the colors are bright and the writing legible.

---

[1]See cut page—also Appendix D.

Schoolmaster Sheibeler was a pen artist of no mean ability, in his day. He was also a veteran of the Revolutionary War and the first schoolmaster in Greensburg. In 1788 the German settlement in Hempfield Township had at least two schoolmasters, Balthasar Meyer and Karl Sheibeler.

To show that even the life of a schoolmaster has its perils and also to show the devotion of the early schoolmasters we append the following story.

To this early period belongs the Massacre of Schoolmaster Brown and his ten scholars. We quote from Col. Henry Bouquet and his Campaigns, by Cort:

"In 1764, July 26, three miles northwest of Greencastle, Franklin County, Pa., was perpetrated what Parkman, the great historian of Colonial times, pronounces 'an outrage unmatched in fiend-like atrocity through all the annals of the war.' This was the massacre of Enoch Brown, a kindhearted exemplary Christian schoolmaster, and ten scholars, eight boys and two girls. Ruth Hart and Ruth Hale were the names of the girls. Among the boys were Eben Taylor, George Dustan and Archie McCullough. All were knocked down like so many beeves and scalped by the merciless savages. Mourning and desolation came to many homes in the valley, for each of the slaughtered innocents belonged to a different family. The last named boy, indeed, survived the effects of the scalping knife, but in somewhat demented condition.

The teacher offered his life and scalp in a spirit of self-sacrificing devotion if the savages would only spare the lives of the little ones under his charge and care. But no! the tender mercies of the heathen are cruel, and so a perfect holocaust was made to the Moloch of war by the relentless fiends in human form. The schoolhouse was located on the farm now occupied by Mr. Henry Diehl, and formerly owned by Mr. Christian Koser. It stood in a cleared field, at the head of a deep ravine, surrounded by a dense forrest. Down this ravine the savages fled a mile or two until they struck Conococheague Creek, along the bed of which, to conceal their tracks, they traveled to the mouth of Path Valley, up which and across the mountains they made good their escape to their village, near the Ohio.

It is some relief to know that this diabolical deed, whose recital makes us shudder even at this late date, was disapproved by the old warriors when the marauding party of young Indians came back with their horrid trophies. Neephaughwhese, or Night Walker, an old chief or half-king, denounced them as a pack of cowards for killing and scalping so many children.

But who can describe the agony of those parents in the Conococheague settlement weeping like Rachel for her children and refused to be comforted? Or who can describe the horror of the scene in that lonely log school house, when one of the settlers chanced to look in at the door to ascertain the cause of the unusual quietness?

In the center lay the faithful Brown, scalped and lifeless, with a Bible clasped in his hand. Around the room were strewn the dead and mangled bodies of seven boys and two girls, while little Archie, stunned, scalped and bleeding, was creeping around among his dead companions, rubbing his hands over their faces and trying to gain some token of recognition.

A few days later the innocent victims of savage atrocity received a common sepulchre. All were buried in one large rough box at the border of the ravine, a few rods from the school house where they had been so ruthlessly slaughtered. Side by side, with head and feet alternately, the little ones were laid with their master, just as they were clad at the time of the massacre."

This story shows the perils as well as the devotion of the frontier schoolmaster.

How long Karl Sheibeler served as schoolmaster in the Zion's or Herold's school, the records do not reveal, but the records of the annual settlements of the Lutheran and Reformed Congregations indicate that the school was continued without interruption.

In September, 1810, we have the first record of the schoolmastership of John Michael Zundel. He served continuously in this settlement and neighboring settlements until May, 1827. After considerable search we located his grave in a little neglected cemetery near Mt. Pleasant, Pa. The inscription on the tomb stone is as follows: "Hier ruhet Johan Michael Zundel. Er ward geboren den 25ten Julius 1757 und starb den 14ten August 1844. Sein ganzes Alter war 87 Yahren und 19 tagen." "Selig sind die reines herzens sind, denn sie werden Gott schauen."

We were told the following incidents relating to Michael Zundel and his work by Mrs. Salome Miller, nee Leasure, of Armburst, Pa., in the year 1912. Mrs. Miller was then in her ninety-third year but was well preserved in health and had a remarkably clear memory. She was born March 31, 1819, and as a little girl was a pupil of "Grandpap" Zundel, as his pupils affectionately called him. She remembered him as a little old man with side whiskers who was a "Vorsteher" (Deacon) in Herold's Church. He lived at that time (probably 1829) on the "Yar" Adam Schneider's place, later the Goodlin farm.

When not busy teaching at Herold's he would organize schools at various places wherever scholars could be assembled and a room secured for their comfort. While teaching such a school at Keppels near Feightner's school house, he boarded with Mrs. Leasure, a widow, mother of Mrs. Miller, who lived on the Heckler farm. The term of school was three months. Tuition was fifty cents a month per pupil, and there were generally about twelve pupils; making a monthly salary of six dollars: and eighteen dollars per term.

Mrs. Miller also related how her own tuition was remitted because her mother was very poor. The Bible and Luther's Catechism were the text books. All instruction was in German. The curriculum comprised the four R's: Reading, 'Riting, 'Rithmetic, and Religion. The schoolmaster found means out of his "liberal" salary to offer prizes and ofttimes to remit part of the tuition for work well done.

Granted that the schoolmaster could arrange two such terms in a year, we find his total money income to be about $36.00 per year. Schoolmaster Zundel supported his wife and four children upon his salary and by working for the farmers in harvest time. This work was paid for largely in produce.

We must remember that during these times there were no state public schools. The schools were under church influence or were conducted by individuals and societies.

Mrs. Miller remembered the old school house at Herold's. It was first built as a one-room log house. There was one door facing the east and one window opposite the door. The floor was of puncheon, the seats of hewn logs made into benches. At first the window lights were of greased paper; later we read in the Annual settlement of the Church, of an item of expenditure "for glass in schoolhouse, 8 shillings." This was in 1792. As glass was then an imported novelty this item shows how highly these settlers rated their school and how progressive they were to improve the equipment of their school. It is probable that this was the only school house west of the Alleghenies that had a glass window.

About the time Michael Zundel became schoolmaster, probably in order to furnish him a house, a second story was added to the school house. This second story extended beyond the main building in order to afford protection to the doorway to the schoolroom and also to give room for an entrance to the second story. This entrance to the second story was not very elaborate. It consisted of a trap door in the floor of the extended story and a ladder which could be drawn up at night. There was no provision for a stove or fireplace in the second story; the only heat obtainable was from the fireplace in the schoolroom below. The cooking for the family was done outside the house in an open fireplace. Thus in winter and summer it was necessary for the schoolmaster and his good helpmeet, upon arising in the morning, to open the trap door, let down the ladder, then descend to the ground outside the school house, clear away the snow, if it be winter, then build a fire from the glowing embers secured in the school house fireplace, or start the fire anew with flint and steel and punk, and finally prepare the morning meal.

In this second story of the school house, schoolmaster Zundel lived many years. Here his children were born and reared until the eldest was probably fourteen years of age. Notwithstanding such hardships, Michael Zundel lived to see his eighty-seventh year and he became the progenitor of a long line of schoolteacher, some of whom have succeeded him in the Herold's school.

After moving from the school house in 1827, he lived for a time on the "Yar" Adam Schneider farm and later lived with his daughter near Mt. Pleasant, Pa., and was buried in the private cemetery on the Schneider farm.

In the year 1828 George Eisenmann moved into the school house and in 1829 he built a tenant house on the Church farm and removed thither. This log house stood until the present generation. George Eisenmann taught the school and led the congregational singing for many years.

Herold's school has had a continuous history since 1772, a period of one hundred and fifty years. When the state schools were authorized Herold's school became a district school and continues as such to the present in Hempfield Township, Westmoreland County.

List of Teachers

Balthasar Meyer	1772-1792	Art A. Keener	1891-1892
Karl Scheibeler	1793——	Art A. Keener	1892-1893
John Michael Zundel	1810?-1827	(Dr.) A. N. Pershing	1893-1894
George Eisenmann	1828——	Art A. Keener	1894-1895
Mr. Lemke		Art A. Keener	1895-1896
Mr. Thompson		Albert M. Zundel, Jr.	1896-1897
Mr. Kemp		Albert M. Zundel, Jr.	1897-1898
Michael Keener		W. W. Henry	1898-1899
William Sullenberger		Albert M. Zundel, Jr.	1899-1900
Abram Altman		J. E. Ferguson	1900-1901
David Altman		Robert M. Zundel	1901-1902
H. C. Harrold		Robert M. Zundel	1902-1903
Andrew Guffey		Jennie E. Bailey	1903-1904
Irving Tarr		Mack Reed	1904-1905
W. F. Scheibler		H. J. Holtzer	1905-1906
Malinda Algire		H. J. Holtzer	1906-1907
John Sweeney	1875-1876	Robert M. Zundel	1907-1908
James Sweeney	1876-1877	Carrie Kennedy	1908-1909
Mattie Shields	1877-1878	Carrie Kennedy	1909-1910
Abe Musick	1878-1879	Robert M. Zundel	1910-1911
(Dr.) George Miller	1879-1880	Robert M. Zundel	1911-1912
David Bush	1880-1881	F. Wayland Bailey	1912-1913
H. A. King (Esq.)	1881-1882	Edna Tyler	1913-1914
H. A. King (Esq.)	1882-1883	Lyda Ruhe	1914-1915
G. M. Allshouse	1883-1884	Lulu Felters	1915-1916
(Rev.) John A. Zundel	1884-1885	Ethel Fink	1916-1917
(Rev.) John A. Zundel	1885-1886	Ethel Fink	1917-1918
(Dr.) Elmer E. Wible	1886-1887	Miss Whitehill	1918-1919
(Dr.) Elmer E. Wible	1887-1888	Rev. G. L. Courtney	1919-1920
John F. Wright	1888-1889	Prof. R. M. Zundel	1920-1921
(Rev.) John A. Zundel	1889-1890	Prof. H. J. Holtzer	1921-1922
John F. Goodlin	1890-1891	Miss Devit	1921-1922

In 1824 when the state first tried to assert its authority over the education of the children of the state, the German settlers protested. Many have criticised the German settlers unjustly because they protested against the state taking away from them the right to oversee the education of their own children. Such an eminent authority as Wickersham does not do them justice.

We must understand that the province and state for nearly one hundred fifty years was indifferent to education; and the German settlers, realizing the need, established schools in connection with their churches and maintained them effectually during all these years. The state laws of 1824 and 1834 almost amounted to confiscation of property and rights.

Another basis of protest was on account of the banishment of religion from the schools. These intelligent settlers clearly saw that religion could not be continued in schools suported by the state. The religions of the German settlers required education as the basis of communicant membership in their churches. They always insisted that the candidate have an intelligent grasp of the fundamental doctrines of the Christian religion and the Confessions of their church before he was admitted to communicant membership.

The two leading denominations among the German element were the Lutheran and German Reformed. These two churches have always maintained an educated ministry, requiring the regular college course and three years of special training in a theological seminary before the candidate was ordained to the ministry: for example, Rev. Henry Melchior Muehlenberg sent his three sons to Halle University for their education. Exceptions were made to this rule during the early colonial period, but the standard was always maintained.

The laity of these churches have always ranked high in intelligent grasp of the principles of their religion. The reason their early contemporaries spoke of them as the "dumb Dutch" was because the education of the German settlers was in German and not in English, and many of their contemporaries were too ignorant to appreciate and too bigoted to admit that the German settlers were educated. Illiteracy, then common among the pioneers, was almost unknown among the early

German settlers. We have read their documents and have seen their signatures and know whereof we speak. So far as we know it has never been necessary for the early German settler to make his mark in signing a document.

Thus we see that the new school laws deprived them of the control of their schools and of their German culture and language, and also of the religious educational basis for their church development.

The opposition of the German to the laws of 1824 and 1834 was not against education, as some have wrongly interpreted it, but it was against the assumption of a new power by the state. This question is not yet settled satisfactorily and is the greatest problem before our state and national school systems. The church needs education as well as the state. The church founded the schools, the state has assumed supreme authority. That the church and the home have rights in the education of the children but few will deny, but the problem remains to be solved as to how these rights are to be recognized and granted by the state. This problem could have been solved, probably more easily a century ago than now. It is a mark of the intelligent foresight of the German settlers that they realized the problems before them and protested against this unwarranted action of the state.

In order to have a religious educational basis for their church work and to preserve the German culture and language, a number of the German congregations maintain parochial schools today. These schools fulfill the requirements of the school laws and teach religion and the German language in addition. They are supported entirely by the local congregation. Almost every German congregation, when financially able, maintains a parochial school. There are probably twenty-five such schools among the Protestants and a greater number among the Roman Catholics in Western Pennsylvania.

Our histories of the present give scant attention to things other than politics and legislation. In the future when histories properly evaluate the social, religious, educational and economical as well as the political elements that function in society and the state, then will the quiet, peace-loving, genial, honest, industrious German receive proper recognition for what he has done to build up our Commonwealth west of the Alleghenies.

Brush Creek School

The settlement at Brush Creek, Hempfield Township, Westmoreland County, was made about 1770. This community was closely connected with Zion settlement at Herold's, and probably teachers were interchanged and when a vacancy existed in one settlement it was temporarily filled by the schoolmaster from the other settlement. Here in Brush Creek the schoolmaster was both teacher and pastor until the arrival of Rev. Luetge in 1782 and Rev. Weber in 1783.

There were several persons who filled this office in the Brush Creek church at different times, among whom were Michael Zundel and George Bushyager. Provision was made for the education of the children and youth, as well as for the worship of Almighty God, as soon as circumstances permitted. A house was erected to be used as a schoolhouse and also a place of divine worship. This house was built of rough logs, split logs for floor and hewn logs for seats, and was very primitive in all its appointments. It stood a few rods north of the present church. It served a good purpose for the time being till a more commodious building could be erected; but during one of those dreadful Indian raids which were then a frequent occurrence, it was burned, leaving the poor colony without a school or a church."[2]

After the schoolhouse was destroyed by the Indians, the school was conducted in private houses and at Fort Walthour,

---

[2]Ullery, Southern Conference History.

until a new church and schoolhouse could be built. The instruction was in German, the Bible and Catechism were the main textbooks. The curriculum consisted of the four R's: Reading, 'Riting, 'Rithmetic, and Religion. During the transition from the German to the English language, English was introduced and upon the formation of the State school system, the school became a township school and continues to this day.

Fayette County School

In German Township, Fayette County, Mr. Johannes Stauch was schoolmaster from 1791 to 1793, when he was ordained a minister of the Lutheran Church. This settlement was made about 1775 and a school was established at an early date.

Greensburg Schools

After the burning of Hannastown (1782) a state road was laid out from Fort Ligonier to Pittsburgh by way of Newtown, now called Greensburg. In December, 1785, Newtown was made the county seat of Westmoreland County, and in the spring of 1786 a court house was built by Anthony Altman, a German. In fact there was a sharp competition at first as to whether the courts of the county should be held at Pittsburgh, at Hannastown, or at Newtown. Pittsburgh was eliminated by legislative enactment; then the contest was between Hannastown and Newtown. Now the Germans had settled mainly south of or near to the new state road, hence they favored Newtown. Among those most influential in bringing the courts to Greensburg, were Michael Ruch, commissioner, Christopher Truby, Ludwig Otterman, citizens of Newtown and land owners, and John Miller, Justice of the Peace. All these were Germans. The name of the town was changed from Newtown to Greensburg in 1786.

In 1784 a schoolhouse was built by general subscription in St. Clair cemetery near a spring. Here Schoolmaster Karl

Sheibeler, a Revolutionary War veteran, taught school. This German school, later changed to English, is continued in the splendid school system of Greensburg today.

We see the influence of the German element in Greensburg when we note that a large part of the site of Greensburg was owned by Germans. The first court house was built by a German. The first school was conducted by Germans, and the first church was built by the Germans. The first bank was conducted by Sheibeler, a German.

As we have seen from the foregoing illustrations, it was a settled policy of the German settlers to erect school houses and support schools. These schools were for the children of the entire settlement and were free schools to all the children, although supported by the subscriptions of those able to pay. We note also, in many cases, the use of the gentle art of persuasion instead of the rod, as the incentive to study. We nowhere note the brutality in the early German schools that existed in the English schools of later date. The German "Schulmeister" was a father to his pupils, their protector in danger, their counsellor and friend.

Academies, Colleges

In higher education we know of no schools established and supported upon this territory by the strictly German settlers. The earlier settlers, as soon as organized into churches, supported colleges in Eastern Pennsylvania, such as Franklin College, founded 1787, which was largely governed by the German element in Eastern Pennsylvania. They also supported Gettysburg Seminary, 1826, and College, 1832, when founded. Also Capital University, Columbus, Ohio.

The first attempt to establish an institution of higher learning in Western Pennsylvania by the German element, now rapidly becoming anglicised, was by the Pittsburgh Synod of the Evangelical Lutheran Church at Zelienople, Pa. Rev. Gottlieb Bassler was at the head of the school. In 1848 the school was moved to Greensburg and called "The Muehlenberg Collegiate Institute." Prof. W. P. Ruthrauff was principal and Mr. Asa H. Waters and Miss Mary A. Haft, assistant teachers. This school continued but two years and was then closed.[3]

The Westmoreland classes of the Reformed Church established a college at Mt. Pleasant, Pa., in 1861, under the presidency of Rev. F. K. Levan. This school was closed in 1868.[4]

Other schools were conducted for brief periods by Prof. J. R. Titzel at Zelienople, and by Prof. D. McKee at Leechburg.

In 1866 Thiel Hall was opened at Phillipsburg, now Monaca. In 1869 through the benefaction of Mr. Louis Thiel, the property of Thiel Hall was conveyed to the Pittsburgh Synod of the Evangelical Lutheran Church with the condition that the Academy be erected into a college. The gift was accepted; a Charter was secured from the State Legislature April 14, 1870, and Thiel Hall became Thiel College.

In 1870 the college was moved to Greenville, Pa., where it has since prospered. The college is co-educational and is equipped for high class work in the courses that are offered. The library contains 9,540 bound volumes and is being constantly enlarged. A new Administration building was opened for use in September, 1913, and a gymnasium in 1922. The campus consists of 34 acres of land, beautifully situated at the forks of the Big and Little Shenango rivers.

In 1874 Prof. Lucian Cort organized a school on Bunker Hill, Greensburg, Pa., known as a "Female Seminary." Later both sexes were admitted and the school was known as "Greensburg Seminary." Prof. Cort conducted this school under the control of the Pittsburgh Synod of the Reformed Church, for fourteen years, when the control passed into the

---

[3] Ullery, History Southern Conference.

[4] History of the Reformed Church within the bounds of the Westmoreland Classis.

hands of the Lutheran Pastors of Greensburg and vicinity. In 1889, "The Educational Society of Westmoreland County" was chartered and the property and control of the school passed to the society. This school had College Preparatory, Normal Training and Musical (instrumental and vocal) courses, and in its Business College filled a great need in its locality. In the days before the full development of the High School the Seminary flourished. Many professional men and school teachers received their early training here. Gradually the High Schools of the county became more efficient and the townships paid the tuition of the common school graduate in the nearest High School; thus free tuition in the High School began to attract students to these institutions. The Seminary had little endowment, hence could not meet the competition: so in the year 1908 the school closed, the property having been previously sold.

The Pennsylvania German Language

The language spoken by the German element in Western Pennsylvania erroneously called "Pennsylvania Dutch" is not Dutch, neither is it a mixture of High German and English, as many believe, but a German dialect derived from Southern Germany and Switzerland, where the people still speak a dialect closely resembling the Pennsylvania German. The word "Dutch" as applied to this German dialect probobly has its origin in the similarity between "Dutch" and "Deutsch," the former meaning Holandish and the latter German. The English colonists often made this mistake; sometimes because they knew no better and sometimes they used the word "Dutch" as a term of reproach and a mark of inferiority. The Dutch are a good people, but there is no more reason why the German should be called Dutch than the Englishman should be called French.

Dr. Henry W. Gehman, in an article in the Pennsylvania School Journal for September, 1915, shows that this German dialect consists of 5,500 words, exclusive of English words, and that it is very expressive in matters pertaining to everyday life. The Germans do not all speak the same dialect, neither do the English. The Englishman from Yorkshire has difficulty in being understood by other Englishmen. Many Englishmen coming to this country cannot be understood by Americans because of their peculiar dialect. The New Englander and the Southerner have each their peculiar dialect.

Dialects are no corruption of the literary language. The literary language is simply a certain dialect that happened to be chosen as a standard. Notwithstanding the literary form, dialects continue to exist in all languages, and Pennsylvania German is a good South German dialect.

The German language has two main divisions, the High German and the Low German. To the High German group belong such dialects as the Bavarian, Saxon, Swabian, Alemanic, and Pennslyvania German. The Low German group embraces the English and Dutch dialects. There never has been a universal German dialect or language. The modern High German, perhaps approaches nearest to it, yet, as we have seen, many dialects still flourish.

Therefore, to say, as some have said, that the Pennsylvania German is not a language, is aside from the facts. The function of a language is to express thought and the Pennsylvania German performs that function very well. We may say that in domestic affairs the Pennsylvania German performs this function better than the English, High German, or the classical languages, Greek and Latin. The only language familiar to us, that equals its expressiveness is the Hebrew language. A few illustrations will make this plain. Compare the following words; in Pennsylvania German, High German and English: Gaul, Pferd, Horse; Hutch, Fuellen, Colt; Hammei, Kalb, Calf; Biebi, Henne, Hen; Wutz, Schwein, Pig. The Pennsylvania German approaches more nearly to a nature language than the other languages.

With the early settlers, because of their German education and the reading of German books and newspapers, the dialect was preserved in relative purity. However, in later years when the schools became Anglicised, and English newspapers became the newscarriers, there was a decline in the purity of the language: many English words being introduced and sometimes the German grammatical construction was used with English words, which often produced an amusing result. This practice contributed largely to the ridicule that other nationalities heaped upon them.

The literature of the early German settler was of the High German dialect. Nearly every settler possessed Luther's German Bible, a catechism, a praper book, and a hymn book. Many had books of sermons and historical works. In fact the library of the early German settler, in quality and quantity, was vastly superior to that of his English contemporaries, and superior to the libraries in the homes of the farming and merchant class today, with a possible exception of cheap fiction, among the merchant class.

Their appreciation of art is shown in the prints of great paintings in the homes, by the pictorial editions of the Bible, and by the attempt to make their churches beautiful. Even in their first rude attempts to build churches, we find a laudable attempt to beautify them, and the churches of the Lutheran and German Reformed demominations were the most beautiful in the country, and in striking contrast, in their day, with the severely plain and homely church buildings of their contemporaries. We have already referred to the artistic penwork on the Baptismal Certificates.

How little is known concerning education among the Germans in Western Pennsylvania, is shown by the following extract from "The History of Westmoreland County, Pennsylvania," published in three volumes, 1906, by John W. Boucher. We read in Chapter 26, subject Common Schools, "Scarcely any record was kept of our early schools in Westmoreland County until about 1820, and even for thirty years after that they were very meager. Our early settlers, as we have said, were almost invariably either English, Scotch-Irish, or German. Of these the Germans, or Dutch, as they were called, were behind either of the others in their general education and in the establishment of schools. Many of the pioneer preachers tried to introduce schools in connection with their churches, but their efforts in this direction were crowned with a very meager measure of success. The Scotch Presbyterian clergy, always more bold and zealous in any cause than the Germans, had the better success in the founding of schools."

The Harold school in Hempfield Township, Westmoreland County, Pennsylvania, was founded in 1772, and has been instructing children ever since. It was founded by Germans.

The Greensburg schools were founded by Karl Scheibeler, a German, in 1784, and today Greensburg is among the foremost towns in education; supporting a High School, second to none in Western Pennsylvania.

We know of no English or Scotch-Irish schools in Western Pennsylvania before 1772. The country was only opened to settlers in 1769. Hence if they had brought portable schoolhouses with them, they could have preceeded the Germans by only three years at the most.

The work of the early Germans in education is notable. The reason they have not founded German higher schools and colleges is that by the time they became prosperous enough for such an enterprise their children were beginning to speak English—the official language of the country. The establishment of public schools by the state met their needs in elementary education and the eastern and western colleges received their bright boys and taught them in the two languages. As we have seen, secondary schools were founded to meet their needs until the High Schools, State Normal Schools and the various colleges developed and offered advantages with free tuition.

APPENDIX A.

Baptisms

Register of all the children in Zion Church Settlement baptized by Balthasar Meyer, Schoolmaster from the 2nd day of August, 1772 until ....

Children	Parents	God-Parents
John Peter	Anthony Walter	Frederick Reisz
Born Sept. 11, 1771, bapt. Aug. 2, 1772	Elizabeth, his wife	Susanna Elizabeth Altmann—single
Susannah Elizabeth	Jacob Stroh	Frederick Reisz
Born Nov. 25, 1771, bapt. Aug. 2, 1772	Maria Catherine	Susanna Altman—single
John Michael	John Peter Altmann	Michael Gondel
Born May 11, 1772, bapt. Aug. 2, 1772	Christiana, his wife	Margaret, his wife
Maria Catherine	Peter Laszner	Wendel Uhrig
Born Jan. 24, 1772, bapt. Aug. 16, 1772	Magdelena, his wife	Catherina, his wife
John Daniel	Philip Klingenschmitt	Peter Klingenschmitt
Born Jan. 16, 1770, bapt. Aug. 9, 1772	Christina, his wife	Elizabeth, his wife
Christina	Michael Gundel	Peter Altmann
Born Feb. 26, 1771, bapt. Feb. 13, 1772	Anna Margaretta, his wife	Christina, his wife
John	Adam Jerg	Wendel Uhrig
Born Feb. 18, 1771, bapt. Feb. 20, 1772	Elizabeth, his wife	Catherina, his wife
John	George Weidendoerfer	John Braeunig
Born Aug. 14, 1772, bapt. Oct. 18, 1772	Catherine, his wife	Susannah Elizabeth Altmann—single
Catherine	George Rau	Catherina, the wife of Peter Snyder
Born July 4, 1771, bapt. Feb. 18, 1772	Catherine, his wife	

Children	Parents	God-Parents
Christian Frederick	Jacob Kuemmel	Frederick Reisz
Born Jan. 8, 1772, bapt. Feb. 1, 1772	Margaretta, his wife	Ana Barbara Mayer, L. St.
		Xtina, Baltzer Mayer's wife
Jacob	Adam Kneiszle	George Koeltz
Born May 22, 1770, bapt. Nov. 16, 1772	Elizabeth, his wife	Anna Maria, his wife
Joseph	Joseph Sinterena	George Koeltz
Born Apr. 20, 1772, bapt. Nov. 16, 1772	Anna, his wife	Anna Maria, his wife
Magdelena	Daniel Madheis	Jacob Muehleisen
Born Nov. 14, 1772, bapt. Dec. 26, 1772	Catherine, his wife	Catherina Altmaenn—single
John	Christoph Truby	John Mustly
Born Oct. 18, 1772, bapt. Jan. 4, 1773	Sibella, his wife	Catherina, Ruch—single
	1773	
John	George Klein	John Bock
Born Nov. 21, 1772, bapt. Feb. 7, 1773	Susannah, his wife	Elizabeth, his wife
Anna Elizabeth	John Balthaser Mayer	Daniel William
Born Feb. 25, 1773, bapt. Apr. 11, 1773	Anna Maria, his wife	Miss Margaretta Steis
Elizabeth	Michael Horninger	Christian Rothenbach
Born Feb. 25, 1770, bapt. Apr. 4, 1773	Elizabeth, his wife	Elizabeth, his wife
Jacob	Jacob Schroeder	William Schroeder
Born Aug. 17, 1771, bapt. Apr. 12, 1773	Anna Maria, his wife	Susannah, his wife
John	Wendel Uhrig	Peter Uhrig
Born Feb. 8, 1772, bapt. Apr. 18, 1773	Catherina, his wife	Margaretta, his wife
Abraham	Abraham Loesher	Michael Starberger
Born Aug. 26, 1770, bapt. Apr. 24, 1773	Anna Margaretta, his wife	Charlotta, his wife

Children	Parents	God-Parents
Anna Margaret	Abraham Loesher	Anthony Walder
Born Feb. 31, 1772, bapt. Apr. 24, 1773	Anna Margaretta, his wife	Elizabeth, his wife
John	John Laydig	Michael Starberger
Born Nov. 30, 1770, bapt. May 16, 1773	Anna Maria	Charlotta, his wife
Abraham	John Stuetzel	Abraham Loesher
Born Feb. 18, 1772, bapt. May 16, 1773	Catherina, his wife	Anna Margaretta, his wife
Anna Maria	John Laeydig	Abraham Loesher
Born Feb. 24, 1773, bapt. May 16, 1773	Anna Maria, his wife	Anna Margaretta, his wife
Frederick	John Adam Brueder	Peter Klingelschmidt
Born Feb. 28, 1773, bapt. May 20, 1773	Anna Margaretta, his wife	Maria Elizabeth, his wife
John Peter	Philip Klingelschmidt	Peter Klingelschmidt
Born May 19, 1773, bapt. June 13, 1773	Christiana, his wife	Maria Elizabeth, his wife
William	Henry Reuth	Andrew Klingelschmmidt
Born Mar. 3, 1773, bapt. July 19, 1773	Christina, his wife	Anna Margaretta, Mauren Let. St.
Andrew Traffert, born out of wedlock		Reinhart Waldenbach
Born May 1, 1771, bapt. July 19, 1773		Elizabeth Catherina, his wife
Jacob	Peter Uber	Parents themselves
Born July 7, 1773, bapt. July 24, 1773	Maria, his wife	
Christian	Peter Ruch	Philip Koester
Born June 20, 1773, bapt. Aug. 1, 1773	Margaretta, his wife	Christina Ruch—single
John	John Splaengler	John Herold
Born Aug. 29, 1773, bapt. Feb. 5, ——	Salome, his wife	Barbara Altmann (in single state)
Maria Barbara	Christian Hermann	John Yundel
Born Feb. 9, 1773, bapt. Feb. 26, ——	Christina, his wife	Margaretta, his wife

Children	Parents	God-Parents
Elizabeth	Archibald Hanszhalter	Christoph Herold
Born Oct. 13, 1773, bapt. Oct. 24, ——	Elizabeth, his wife	Catherina, his wife
Catherina	Christian Jade	Adam Uhrig
Born Feb. 20, 1773, bapt. Nov. 14, 1773	Susannah, his wife	Catherina, his wife
Conrad	Conrad Haag	Parents
Born Apr. 20, 1771, bapt. Oct. 19, 1773	Sarah, his wife	
Catherina	Conrad Haag	John George Haag
Born Aug. 19, 1773, bapt. Oct. 19, 1773	Sarah, his wife	Catherina, his wife
	1774	
John	Peter Laszner	John Gundel
Born Oct. 29, 1773, bapt. Jan. 23, 1774	Magdelena, his wife	Margaretta, his wife
Margaretta	George Saltzer	
Born Jan. 16, 1774, bapt. Apr. 3, 1774	Catherine, his wife	
Susannah	Philip Schroedder	John Balthasar Duerr
Born Aug. 15, 1773, bapt. Apr. 4, 1774	Eva, his wife	Catherine, his wife
Maria Barbara	Jacob Stroh	William Altmann
Born Jan. 27, 1774, bapt. May 4, 1774	Maria Catherina, his wife	Maria Barbara, his wife
Maria	John Kulten	Christoph Urig
Born Mar. 31, 1774, bapt. May 12, 1774	Margaretta, his wife	Maria Ruch (in single state)
Jacob	Adam Mayer	Peter Hill
Born Nov. 30, 1773, bapt. May 22, 1774	Catherina, his wife	Catherina Kuntel (in single state)
Anna Magdelena	Gerhart Thomas	Adam Fridchmann
Born Mar. 27, 1774, bapt. May 22, 1774	Magdelena, his wife	Catherina, his wife

Children	Parents	God-Parents
Christina Born Jan. 13, 1774, bapt. May 22, 1774	John Peter Altmann Christina, his wife	Christoph Urig Christina Ruch (in single state)
Scharlodda Born Feb. 24, 1773, bapt. May 23, 1774	Conrad Jung Elizabeth, his wife	Michael Starberger Scharlodda, his wife
Elizabetha Born June 17, 1774, bapt. June 19, 1774	Frederich Werner Margaretta, his wife	Christian Ehret Elizabeth Miehleisen (in single state) Addillea, Jacob Miehleisen's wife
Maria Margaretta Born Apr. 17, 1774, bapt. July 13, 1774	John Adam Brueder Margaretta, his wife	Nicholaus Scheurer Anna Maria, his wife Margaretta, Jacob Kuemmel's wife
Maria Magdalena Born Feb. 14, 1773, bapt. July 3, 1774	John Kraushaar Maria Avolonia, his wife	George Bender Maria Susannah, his wife
Margaretta Born June 14, 1774, bapt. July 3, 1774	Jacob Kuemmel Margaretta, his wife	John Adam Brueder Margaretta, his wife
John Frederick Born Feb. 3, 1773, bapt. May 7, 1774	John Laidy Maria, his wife	Christoph Renner Eva Catherina, his wife
Christoph John Born July 25, 1774, bapt. Aug. 14, 1774	Nicholaus Schaeurer Maria, his wife	Christoph Truby Sibilla, his wife
John Christoph Born Sept. 7, 1771, bapt. Apr. 21, 1774	Martin Oberle Eva, his wife	Christoph Lawingays Elizabeth, his wife
Philip Henry Born Feb. 6, 1769, bapt. Aug. 21, 1774	Philip Hermann Barbara, his wife	Henry Schantz Barbara Dinnbald (in single state)

Children	Parents	God-Parents
Abraham	Michael Hoeh	Abraham Dumbald
Born Jan. 12, 1773, bapt. Aug. 21, 1774	Anna Elizabeth, his wife	Rosina Gerwin (in single state)
Elizabeth	John Heintz	Philip Hermann
Born Mar. 2, 1774, bapt. Aug. 21, 1774	Elizabeth, his wife	Barbara, his wife
John	Henry Weisz	Caspar Senft
Born Mar. 26, 1773, bapt. Aug. 21, 1774	Eva Maria, his wife	Catherina Maria, his wife
Eva Catherina	Caspar Senft	Henry Weisz
Born June 18, 1774, bapt. Aug. 21, 1774	Catherina Maria, his wife	Eva Catherina, his wife
Elizabeth	George Jann	Christoph Lawengayer
Born Mar. 23, 1774, bapt. Feb. 18	Margaretta, his wife	Elizabeth, his wife
Eva Margarett	George Rau	Jacob Stroh
Born July 21, 1774, bapt. Feb. 25	Catherina, his wife	Maria Catherina, his wife
William	Jacob Schroeder	Jacob Zehner
Born Feb. 1, 1774, bapt. Oct. 2, 1774	Anna Maria, his wife	Catherina, his wife
John Anthony	Jacob Miehleisen	John Anthony Altmann
Born Feb. 8, 1774, bapt. Oct. 2, 1774	Christina Oddilia	Maria, his wife
Maria Magdelena	Adam Joerg	Frederich Reisz
Born Feb. 16, 1774, bapt. Oct. 16, 1774	Elizabeth, his wife	Magdelena Joerg (in single state)
Catherina	Jacob Hauser	Philip Schmidt
Born Feb. 22, 1774, bapt. Oct. 23, 1774	Christina, his wife	Catherina Ruzz (in single state)
Susannah Catherina	Adam Uhrig	Christian Jade
Born Aug. 27, 1774, bapt. Oct. 30, 1774	Catherina, his wife	Susannah, his wife
Eva Christina	Peter Ruch	Daniel Williams
Born Aug. 11, 1774, bapt. Oct. 6, 1774	Margaretta, his wife	Christina, his wife

Children	Parents	God-Parents
John Jacob	John Conrad	Jacob Miehleisen
Born Feb. 3, 1774, bapt. Oct. 13, 1774	Anna Maria	Christina Oddellia, his wife
John	Adam Fritchmann	Balthasar Meyer
Born Feb. 25, 1774, bapt. Oct. 14, 1774	Catherina, his wife	Christina, his wife
Michael	Matthew Stoldberger	Michael Stoldberger
Born Feb. 4, 1774, bapt. Feb. 11, 1774		Scharlodda, his wife

1775

Children	Parents	God-Parents
Maria	William Altmann	John Anthony Altmann
Born Feb. 4, 1774, bapt. Jan. 1, 1775	Maria Barbara, his wife	Maria, his wife
Maria Susannah	George Medenndoerfer	William Altmann
Born Oct. 6, 1774, bapt. Jan. 1, 1775	Catherina, his wife	Maria Barbara, his wife
George	George Zehner	Christian Ehret
Born Jan. 5, 1775, bapt. Jan. 16, 1775	Anna Maria, his wife	Magdalena Zehner (in single state)
John	Jacob Watterson	John Herold
Born Oct. 5, 1774, bapt. Jan. 16, 1775.	Catherina, his wife	Barbara Altmann (in single state)
Jacob	Peter Keiger	Jacob Kerber
Born Nov. 4, 1774, bapt. Jan. 29, 1775	Anna Maria, his wife	Maria Darnig (in single state)
John Lorenz	Michael Rundel	Lorenz Rundel
Born Feb. 2, 1774, bapt. Jan. 29, 1775	Margaretta, his wife	Regina Stroh (in single state)
John George	Christoph Lawengayer	George Jan
Born Feb. 23, 1775, bapt. Mar. 5, 1775	Elizabeth, his wife	Margaretta, his wife
Samuel	Christoph Shad	Anthony Walder
Born Feb. 25, 1774, bapt. Mar. 5, 1775	Anna Maria, his wife	Elizabeth, his wife

Children	Parents	God-Parents
John David	Anthony Walder	George Saltzer
Born Aug. 24, 1774, bapt. Mar. 26, 1775	Elizabeth, his wife	Catherine, his wife
John Frederich	Anthony Walder	George Saltzer
Born Aug. 21, 1774, bapt. Mar. 26, 1775	Elizabeth, his wife	Catherina, his wife
Anna Elizabeth	John Reitmauer	Anthony Walder
Born Jan. 1, 1774, bapt. Mar. 26, 1775	Christina, his wife	Elizabeth, his wife
Elizabeth	John Stutzel	Anthony Walder
Born Feb. 14, 1775, bapt. Apr. 9, 1775	Catherina, his wife	Elizabeth, his wife
John Sebastian	John Gundel	Michael Gundel
Born Jan. 2, 1775, bapt. Apr. 16, 1775	Margaretta, his wife	Margaretta, his wife
Margaretta	Frederick Woerner	John Ehret
Born May 5, 1775, bapt. Oct. 14, 1775	Margaretta, his wife	Catherina, his wife
Jacob	Jacob Zehnor	Jacob Schroedder
Born Apr. 19, 1775, bapt. May 28, 1775	Catherina, his wife	Anna Maria, his wife
Daniel	Daniel Maddheis	George Maddheis
Born Apr. 27, 1775, bapt. May 28, 1775	Catherina, his wife	Magdalena, his wife
John Philip	John Reyt	Philip Klingenschmidt
Born Jan. 3, 1775, bapt. June 4, 1775	Christina, his wife	Christina, his wife
Jacob	John Hill	Peter Ruch
Born Oct. 1, 1774, bapt. June 4, 1775	Magdalena, his wife	Margaret, his wife
John Michael	John Wad	Michael Stadberger
Born July 16, 1774, bapt. June 5, 1775	Christina, his wife	Maria Magdalena, J. Alterman's wife
Philip	John Adam Brider	Philip Klingenschmidt
Born Apr. 14, 1775, bapt. June 25, 1775	Margaretta, his wife	Christina, his wife

Children	Parents	God-Parents
Maria Elizabeth Born Feb. 18, 1774, bapt. July 30, 1775	John Frederich Hauszer Elizabeth, his wife	Elizabeth John Reitenauer's wife
Maria Catherina Born Apr. 4, 1775, bapt. Aug. 10, 1775	Ludwig Stad Anna Elizabeth, his wife	Peter Dumbal Catherina Matheisen (in single state)
John Christian Born July 4, 1775, bapt. Aug. 27, 1775	John Christian Miller Barbara, his wife	Christian Salsmann Elizabeth, his wife
Elizabeth Barbara Born July 21, 1775, bapt. Aug. 27, 1775	Christian Salsmann Elizabeth, his wife	John Christian Miller Barbara, his wife
John Born July 9, 1775, bapt. Oct. 10, 1775	John Shram Eva Margaretta, his wife	John Ehret Barbara, his wife
John George Born Aug. 17, 1775, bapt. Feb. 10	John Staengler Salome, his wife	Bernard Reisz Magdalena, Nicholaus Allemann's wife
John Anthony Born Aug. 18, 1775, bapt. Oct. 15, 1775	Peter Altmann Catherina, his wife	John Anthony Altmann Maria, his wife
Catherine Born July 22, 1775, bapt. Oct. 22, 1775	George Loesher Catherina, his wife	Michael Stodberger Scharlodda, his wife
Julianna Born Aug. 17, 1775, bapt. Oct. 22, 1775	Abraham Loesher Margaretta, his wife	Rudolph Baer Catherina, his wife
Daniel Born June 4, 1774, bapt. Nov. 16, 1775	Jacob Husong Magdalena, his wife	Henry Hirsche Barbara, his wife
Anna Margaretta Born Nov. 5, 1775, bapt. Nov. 26, 1775	Peter Ruch Margaretta	Philip Kuntz Margaretta, his wife

Children	Parents	God-Parents
Thomas Born Oct. 16, 1775, bapt. Feb. 17	Daniel Williams Christina, his wife	Thomas Williams Margaretta Schmidt (in single state)
John Peter Born Nov. 12, 1775, bapt. Feb. 17	Ludwig Koester Margaretta, his wife	John Peter Altmann Christina, his wife
Conrad Born Feb. 3, 1775, bapt. Feb. 23, 1775	Jacob Gerber Anna Maria, his wife	Conrad Bayer Margaretta, his wife
Rudolph Bernhart Born Oct. 6, 1775, bapt. Oct. 25, 1775	William Bernhart Anna, his wife	Jacob Bernhart Catherina, his wife
Elizabeth Born Feb. 1, 1775, bapt. Oct. 25, 1775	Peter Loszner Magdalena, his wife	Ludwig Oddermann Francina, his wife
Jacob Born Nov. 23, 1775, bapt. Feb. 26	John Laster Catherina, his wife	Jacob Rauszer Catherina, his wife
	1776	
Elizabeth Born Oct. 31, 1775, bapt. Jan. 14, 1776	Adam Seib Thorodea, his wife	Peter Ferri Elizabeth, his wife
Susannah Born Nov. 12, 1775, bapt. Feb. 4, 1776	Peter Ferri Elizabeth, his wife	Adam Seib Thorodea, his wife
John Jacob Born Oct. 31, 1775, bapt. Feb. 25, 1776	Wendel Uhrig Catherina, his wife	Theobald Mechling Maria Rugh (in single state)
Jacob Born Mar. 15, 1775, bapt. Mar. 3, 1776	Lawrence Struder Barbara, his wife	Christoph Lawenjay Elizabeth, his wife
John Born Oct. 12, 1775, bapt. Mar. 3, 1776	Peter Ueber Maria, his wife	Abraham Frantz Catherina, his wife

Children	Parents	God-Parents
John George Born Feb. 7, 1776, bapt. Mar. 3, 1776	Ludwig Ottermann Franzina, his wife	Nicholas Speyrer Maria, his wife
Jacob Born Jan. 29, 1776, bapt. Mar. 3, 1776	John Herold Barbara, his wife	Jacob Debar Catherina Herold (in single state)
John George Born Feb. 7, 1776, bapt. Mar. 10, 1776	Andreas Rosenstiehl Catherina, his wife	Caspar Schneider Christina Bardy (in single state)
John Frederick Born Oct. 28, 1775, bapt. Mar. 10, 1776	Christian Jade Susannah, his wife	Frederich Reisz Barbara Jade (in single state)
Anna Maria Born Feb. 8, 1776, bapt. Mar. 17, 1776	Theobald Mechlin Sibilla, his wife	Michael Ruch Franzina, his wife
Anna Catherine Born Apr. 1, 1776, bapt. Apr. 10, 1776	Nicholas Weitzel Magdalena, his wife	John Stielman Catherina, his wife
Andrew Born Mar. 7, 1776, bapt. Apr. 13, 1776	Conrad Bayer Margaretta, his wife	Adam Fridshman Catherina, his wife
Michael Born Mar. 5, 1776, bapt. Apr. 14, 1776	Jacob Stroh Marie Catherina, his wife	Michael Gundel Margaretta, his wife
Anna Barbara Born Nov. 6, 1775, bapt. Apr. 21, 1776	John Dueringer Catherina, his wife	Rudolph Baehr Catherina, his wife
Christoph Born Nov. 15, 1775, bapt. May 12, 1776	Henry Weisz Eva, his wife	Christoph Lawengayer Elizabeth, his wife
Margaretta Born Aug. 1, 1775, bapt. May 27, 1776	Robertus Grastert Anna, his wife	Parents
John Born Oct. 11, 1772, bapt. May 27, 1776	Robertus Grastert Anna, his wife	Parents

Children	Parents	God-Parents
John George Born Nov. 29, 1775, bapt. May 27, 1776	Philip Klingenschmidt Christina, his wife	Peter Klingenschmidt Elizabeth, his wife
Christian Born Apr. 1, 1776, bapt. May 27, 1776	John Balthasar Meyer Maria, his wife	Christian Meyer Margaretta Rust (in single state)
Adam Born Jan. 7, 1776, bapt. June 27, 1776	George Jan Margaretta, his wife	Peter Uhrig Elizabeth, his wife
Peter Born Oct. 22, 1774, bapt. June 9, 1776	Adam Weber Maria Catherina, his wife	Peter Uhrig Margaretta, his wife
Christina Elizabeth Born June 14, bapt. June 30, 1776	Conrad Beis Anna Maria, his wife	Christoph Uhrig Catherina, his wife
John Born June 18, 1776, bapt. July 14, 1776	John Spielmann Catherina, his wife	Balthasar Mayer Christina, his wife
Catherine Born Feb. 22, 1776, bapt. Feb. 29, 1776	Caspar Schmidtle Christina, his wife	Nicholas Weisz Magdalena, his wife
Anna Margaretta Born Feb. 24, 1776, bapt. Oct. 20, 1776	Adam Uhrig Catherina, his wife	Peter Uhrig Anna Margaretta, his wife
Scharlodda Born Aug. 12, 1776, bapt. Oct. 13, 1776	Christoph Suesz Anna Maria, his wife	Michael Stodberger Scharlodda, his wife
Christoph Born Aug. 12, 1776, bapt. Nov. 3, 1776	Christoph Suesz Anna Maria, his wife	Christoph Lawengayer Elizabeth, his wife
George Frederich Born Nov. 18, 1776, bapt. Oct. 1, 1776	Mattheus Stadberger Saloma, his wife	George Stadberger Barbara, his wife
Maria Born Feb. 27, 1776, bapt. Apr. 15, 1776	Philip Kuntz Margaretta, his wife	Frederich Reisz Maria Ruch (in single state)

Children	Parents	God-Parents
Elizabeth Born Feb. 3, 1776, bapt. Oct. 15, 1776	Peter Ruch Margaretta, his wife	Philip Kaester Elizabeth, his wife
	1777	
Maria Christina Born Jan. 30, 1777, bapt. Mar. 30, 1777	Philip Miehleisen Barbara, his wife	Tobias Lang Christina, his wife
Maria Catherina Born 1776, bapt. Mar. 30, 1777	George Meidendoerfer Catherina, his wife	William Altmann Maria Barbara, his wife
Maria Catherina Born Oct. 22, 1776, bapt. Mar. 30, 1777	Michael Gundel Margaretta, his wife	Jacob Stroh Maria Catherina, his wife
Elizabeth Born Nov. 7, 1776, bapt. Mar. 31, 1777	John Guldan Margaretta, his wife	Conrad Lind Anna Maria, his wife
Christina Born Feb. 21, 1777, bapt. Apr. 27, 1777	Jacob Hauser Christina, his wife	Deideuch Walgenbach Catherina Mann (in single state)
Anna Maria Born Oct. 28, 1776, bapt. May 8, 1777	Christoph Renner Catherina, his wife	George Saldzer Catherina, his wife
Eva Catherina Born May 1, 1777, bapt. May 19, 1777	Nicholas Speyrer Anna Maria, his wife	George Ottermann Franzina, his wife
Margaretta Born Oct. 21, 1776, bapt. May 18, 1777	Daniel William Christina, his wife	Peter Ruch Margaretta, his wife
John Philip Born Mar. 19, 1777, bapt. May 18, 1777	Andrew Klingenschmidt Agnes	Philip Klingenschmidt Elizabeth Baum (in single state)
Sarah Born Jan. 9, 1777, bapt. May 18, 1777	Henry Reit Christina, his wife	John Jacob Klingenschmidt Catherina Wann (in single state)

Children	Parents	God-Parents
John Peter	Adam Jerg	Peter Herold
Born Jan. 1, 1777, bapt. May 25, 1777	Elizabeth, his wife	Elizabeth Baum (in single state)
Christoph	John Herold	Christoph Herold
Born Mar. 1, 1777, bapt. June 1, 1777	Barbara, his wife	Catherina, his wife
Maria Magdalena	Simon Drum	Nicholaus Allmann
Born Mar 2, 1777, bapt. June 12, 1777	Susannah, his wife	Magdalena, his wife
John Benjamin	Abraham Gardner	Christian Sachsmann
Born Feb. 16, 1776, bapt. June 15, 1777	Susannah, his wife	Anna Elizabeth, his wife
John Christian	Christian Sachsmann	Christian Miller
Born Apr. 22, 1777, bapt. June 15, 1777	Anna Elizabeth, his wife	Barbara, his wife
Maria Barbara	Michael Walter	Marx Braeunig
Born Feb. 11, 1777, bapt. June 15, 1777	Barbara, his wife	Maria Catherina, his wife
John	Christian Ehret	John Ehret
Born June 12, 1777, bapt. June 22, 1777	Maria Elizabeth, his wife	Barbara, his wife
Christina	Peter Braeunig	Michael Wentzel
Born Feb. 15, 1776, bapt. June 22, 1777	Catherina, his wife	Christina Braeunig (in single state)
Conrad	Adam Fritschmann	Conrad Bayer
Born May 12, 1777, bapt. June 1, 1777	Catherina, his wife	Margaretta, his wife
George Jacob	Jacob Kimmel	John George Stahr
Born Oct. 6, 1776, bapt. June 1, 1777	Anna Margaretta, his wife	Anna Margaretta, his wife
John	John Braeunig	Philip Wentzel
Born Feb. 26, 1776, bapt. July 13, 1777	Jmy, his wife	Margaretta Schmidt (in single state)
Elizabeth	John Laydi	George Suldzers
Born June 11, 1777, bapt. July 25, 1777	Maria, his wife	Maria Catherina, his wife

Children	Parents	God-Parents
John Christian Born June 12, 1777, bapt. Aug. 3, 1777	John Stutzel Catherina, his wife	Christian Sachsmann Elizabeth, his wife
Peter Born July 22, 1777, bapt. Aug. 31, 1777	John Hill Magdalena, his wife	Peter Ruch Margaretta, his wife
Peter Born Aug. 15, 1777, bapt. Aug. 31, 1777	Christoph Uhrig Catherina, his wife	Peter Uhrig Margaretta, his wife
Catherina Born Aug. 9, 1777, bapt. Aug. 31, 1777	Jacob Gerber Anna Maria, his wife	Jacob Mechling Catherina, his wife
Elizabeth Born May 15, 1776, bapt. Feb. 14, 1777	Conrad Jung Elizabeth, his wife	Christian Jade Susannah, his wife
Maria Magdalena Born Feb. 14, 1777, bapt. Dec. 17, 1777	Nicholas Rezwel Anna Maria, his wife	Adam Meyer Louisa Rezwel (in single state)
John Peter Born Oct. 26, 1776, bapt. Feb. 2, 1777	Peter Lenhart Catherine, his wife	Peter Klingenschmidt Catherina, his wife
Maria Elizabeth Born July 3, 1777, bapt. Oct. 24, 1777	Christian Maurer Anna Margaretta, his wife	Peter Klingelschmidt Catherina, his wife
Maria Born May 25, 1777, bapt. Oct. 24, 1777	William Bell Barbara, his wife	Daniel Klingenschmidt Anna Elizabeth, his wife
Margaretta Born Aug. 3, 1777, bapt. Oct. 24, 1777	Peter Klingenschmidt Margaretta, his wife	John George Staar Anna Margaretta, his wife
Susannah Born Aug. 30, 1776, bapt. Feb. 24, 1777	John Adam Brider Margaretta, his wife	Margaretta, Henry Kister's wife
Philip Born Apr. 10, 1776, bapt. Oct. 12, 1777	Philip Schwartz Elizabeth, his wife	Philip Drum Margaretta, his wife

Children	Parents	God-Parents
Magdalena Born Aug. 15, 1776, bapt. Oct. 12, 1777	Jacob Zehner Catherina, his wife	George Mathers Magdelena, his wife
Jacob Born Oct. 4, 1777, bapt. Oct. 12, 1777	Conrad Bayer Margaretta, his wife	Jacob Mechling Catherina, his wife
Catherine Born Feb. 3, 1777, bapt. Feb. 14, 1777	Philip Schmidt Catherina, his wife	Anna Maria Ruch (in single state)
Christina Born Aug. 8, 1777, bapt. Nov. 14, 1777	Frederich Werner Margaretta, his wife	Ludwig Lang Agnes, his wife
John Jacob Born Feb. 14, 1777, bapt. Feb. 17, 1777	Ludwig Koester Catherina, his wife	Jacob Stroh Maria Catherina, his wife
Susannah Margaretta Born June 18, 1777, bapt. Oct. 28, 1777	William Altmann Barbara, his wife	Adam Mayer Regina Stroh (in single state)
Adam Born Feb. 11, 1777, bapt. Feb. 28, 1777	John Gundel Margaretta, his wife	Parents
	1778	
John George Born Oct. 10, 1777, bapt. Feb. 9, 1778	Daniel Madheis Catherina, his wife	George Madheis Magdalena, his wife
John Born Feb. 17, 1774, bapt. Feb. 19, 1778	Andrew Wolf	Eva his wife
Elizabeth Born July 23, 1776, bapt. Feb. 9, 1778	Andrew Wolf Eva, his wife	Jacob Zehner Catherina, his wife
Anna Maria Born July 23, 1776, bapt. Feb. 9, 1778	Andrew Wolf Eva, his wife	George Zehner Anna Maria, his wife

Children	Parents	God-Parents
Catherine	Jacob Schroeder	Jacob Schnet
Born Feb. 2, 1777, bapt. Feb. 9, 1778	Anna Maria, his wife	Maria B. Schroeder (in single state)
Magdalena	George Matheis	Daniel Matheis
Born Oct. 10, 1776, bapt. Feb. 9, 1778	Magdalena, his wife	Catherina, his wife
Catherine	George Matheis	George Zehner
Born June 30, 1775, bapt. Feb. 14, 1778	Magdalena, his wife	Catherina, his wife
John	John Ermel	Christian Persing
Born Feb. 13, 1777, bapt. Feb. 22, 1778	Elizabeth, his wife	Elizabeth, his wife
Maria Magdalena	John Wad	Parents themselves
Born Feb. 13, 1777, bapt. Feb. 22, 1778	Christina, his wife	
John Peter	Andrew Hobach	Peter Wannenmager
Born Aug. 26, 1777, bapt. Aug. 4, 1778	Catherina Eliz. his wife	Christina, his wife
Magdalena	Peter Ruch	Jacob Ruch
Born Mar. 7, 1777, bapt. Apr. 19, 1778	Margaretta, his wife	Louisa Keppel (in single state)
Sarah	Frederich Hinrich	Adam Shaster
Born Oct. 24, 1777, bapt. Apr. 19, 1778	Catherina, his wife	Sarah Wegel (in single state)
Magdalena	Philip Drum	Michael Liszeman
Born Feb. 4, 1777, bapt. Apr. 19, 1778	Margaretta, his wife	Elizabeth Bandry (in single state)
Scharlodda	Nicholas Weitzel	Michael Stotberger
Born Apr. 18, 1778, bapt. May 17, 1778	Magdalena, his wife	Scharlodda, his wife
John Jacob	Carl fisgi Elizabeth	Jacob Bernhart
Born Apr. 3, 1778, bapt. May 17, 1778	Barbara (Illegitimate)	Catherina, his wife
John	John Reitenauer	John Reitenauer
Born Apr. 6, 1778, bapt. May 24, 1778	Christina, his wife	Elizabeth, his wife

Children	Parents	God-Parents
Isaac	Peter Miller	Christian Ehret
Born Apr. 4, 1778, bapt. May 28, 1778	Catherina, his wife	Maria Elizabeth, his wife
Maria Elizabeth	Nicholas Junt	Jacob Zehner
Born May 21, 1778, bapt. May 28, 1778	Anna Maria, his wife	Catherina, his wife
John	Andrew Rosenstiehl	Joseph Saufrit
Born May 9, 1778, bapt. June 14, 1778	Catherina, his wife	Rosina Barbara, his wife
Anna Margaretta	Nicholas Schmidt	Magdalena, Peter Laub's widow
Born Oct. 27, 1777, bapt. July 5, 1778	Anna Maria, his wife	
Joseph	Joseph Saufriet	Andrew Rosanstiehl
Born June 16, 1778, bapt. July 5, 1778	Rosina Barbara, his wife	Catherina, his wife
Abraham	Peter Ueber	Abraham Frandz
Born Apr. 6, 1778, bapt. July 5, 1778	Maria, his wife	Catherina, his wife
Catherina	George Bayer	Peter Ueber
Born Jan. 17, 1778, bapt. July 6, 1778	Susannah, his wife	Maria, his wife
Susannah	George Kliffinger	Christian Lauffer
Born Aug. 20, 1777, bapt. July 19, 1778	Anna Maria, his wife	Susannah, his wife
John Peter	John Balthasar Mayer	Peter Wannenmacher
Born July 8, 1778, bapt. Aug. 9, 1778	Maria, his wife	Christina, his wife
Maria Elizabeth	George Zehner	Adam Fritchman
Born July 31, 1778, bapt. Aug. 12, 1778	Anna Maria, his wife	Catherina, his wife
Sarah	Peter Dscherre	Conrad Hag
Born Nov. 27, 1777, bapt. Feb. 3, 1778	Elizabeth Bertha, his wife	Sarah, his wife
Maria Barbara	Christian Jade	Peter Jade
Born Feb. 7, 1778, bapt. Oct. 6, 1778	Susannah, his wife	Maria Barbara Meyer (in single state)

Children	Parents	God-Parents
Matthew Born Aug. 23, 1778, bapt. Feb. 13, 1778	Franz Weidel Elizabeth, his wife	Matthew Kaemel Anna Katherina, his wife
Catherine Born Feb. 11, 1773, bapt. Feb. 13, 1778	Etwardus Wackerd Margaretta, his wife	John Balthasar Duerr Catherina, his wife
Catherine Born Feb. 26, 1778, bapt. Oct. 13, 1778	George Sheid Eva, his wife	John Balthaser Duerr Catherina, his wife
Catherine Born Feb. 26, 1778, bapt. Oct. 13, 1778	George Metzler Anna Margaretta, his wife	Peter Creudzschwert Maria Catherina Livs (in single state)
Margaretta Born Feb. 13, 1777, bapt. Sept. 13, 1778	Edwartus Wadert Margaretta	John Balthaser Duerr Catherina, his wife
Helena Born Feb. 9, 1776, bapt. Feb. 13, 1778	George Metzler	Maria Elizabeth Creudzschwert (in single state)
Maria Christina Born Mar. 29, 1778, bapt. Oct. 20, 1778	Thomas Williams Magdalena, his wife	George Jan Margaretta
John Born Feb. 1, 1776, bapt. Oct. 4, 1778	Matthew Remes Elizabeth, his wife	John Conrad Anna Maria, his wife
Catherine Born Mar. 26, 1776, bapt. Oct. 4, 1778	Gerheart Remes Elizabeth, his wife	Matthew Remes Elizabeth, his wife
Christina Born Mar. 10, 1777, bapt. Oct. 4, 1778	Matthew Remes Elizabeth, his wife	Gerhartus Remes Elizabeth, his wife
Imma Born Jan. 9, 1776, bapt. Oct. 4, 1778	Thomas Redern Margaretta, his wife	John Balthasar Duerr Catherina, his wife
Elizabeth Born June 23, 1777, bapt. Oct. 4, 1778	Thomas Redern Margaretta, his wife	John Balthaser Duerr Catherina, his wife

Children	Parents	God-Parents
Henry	Thomas Tompson	John Balthasar Duerr
Born Feb. 14, 1778, bapt. Oct. 4, 1778	Catherina, his wife	Catherina, his wife
Magdalena	Thomas Tompson	John B. Duerr
Born Feb. 14, 1778, bapt. Oct. 4, 1778	Catherina, his wife	Catherina, his wife
Christoph	Jacob Rund	William Schroeter
Born May 2, 1773, bapt. Oct. 4, 1778	Emma Magdalena, his wife	Susannah, his wife
Andrew	Jacob Rund	Conrad Kohner
Born Mar. 24, 1775, bapt. Oct. 4, 1778	Emma Magdalena, his wife	Susannah, his wife
Maria Barbara	Jacob Rund	Arnold Schroeter
Born Feb. 27, 1778, bapt. Oct. 4, 1778	Emma Magdalena, his wife	Maria Barbara, his wife
Margaretta	Jacob Kerber	Christian Miller
Born Aug. 17, 1778, bapt. Oct. 11, 1778	Anna Maria, his wife	Barbara, his wife
Daniel	Daniel Wilhelm	Michael Kerwel
Born Aug. 11, 1778, bapt. Oct. 11, 1778	Christina, his wife	Catherina Eberhart (in single state)
Margaretta Elizabeth	Frederick Henrich	Isaac Wegele
Born Aug. 13, 1778, bapt. Oct. 25, 1778	Catherina, his wife	Margaretta Schmitt (in single state)
John Christoph	Wendel Uhrig	Christopher Truby
Born Aug. 13, 1778, bapt. Oct. 25, 1778	Catherina, his wife	Sibilla, his wife
John Phillip	William Bernhart	Philip Kuns
Born Feb. 27, 1778, bapt. Oct. 25, 1778	Anna	Margaretta, his wife
John	Thomas Semson	Parents
Born Aug. 14, 1776, bapt. Oct. 3, 1778	Margaretta, his wife	
Rudolph Suesz	Christoph Suesz	Rudolph Baehr
Born Oct. 13, 1778, bapt. Dec. 8, 1778	Margaretta, his wife	Catherina, his wife

Children	Parents	God-Parents
Abraham	Conrad Kolmer	Abraham Loecher
Born June 2, 1777, bapt. Feb. 8, 1778	Margaretta, his wife	Margaretta, his wife
Elizabeth	Abraham Loecher	Conrad Kolmer
Born Aug. 26, 1778, bapt. Oct. 8, 1778	Margaretta	Susannah, his wife
John William	Anthony Walter	William Gernhart
Born July 10, 1778, bapt. Oct. 8, 1778	Elizabeth	Anna, his wife
Isaac	Abraham Frantz	Conrad Hag
Born Oct. 25, 1778, bapt. Dec. 22, 1778	Catherina, his wife	Sarah
Maria Christina	Jacob Stroh	Ludwig Koester
Born Feb. 17, 1778, bapt. Oct. 26, 1778	Maria Catherina	Catherina, his wife
John Philip	Philip Schmidt	Joh Ermel
Born July 24, 1778, bapt. Dec. 20, 1778	Maria	Elizabeth, his wife

1779

Children	Parents	God-Parents
Adam	Peter Altmann	Adam Schaester
Born Oct. 10, 1778, bapt. Jan. 1, 1779	Catherina, his wife	Magdalena Bender (in single state)
Daniel	Adam Briker	Adam Seib
Born Feb. 1, 1778, bapt. Jan. 1, 1779	Margaretta, his wife	Dorothy, his wife
Michael	Philip Klingelschmidt	Peter Klingelschmidt
Born May 9, 1778, bapt. Jan. 1, 1779	Christina, his wife	Maria Elizabeth
Frederick	Christian Petersing	Frederick Petersing
Born Oct. 21, 1778, bapt. Jan. 10, 1779	Barbara, his wife	Elizabeth, his wife
Christina	John Spielmann	Rudolph Baehr
Born Feb. 10, 1778, bapt. Jan, 10, 1779	Catherine, his wife	Catherina, his wife

Children	Parents	God-Parents
Susannah Born Nov. 5, 1778, bapt. Jan. 17, 1779	John Herold Barbara, his wife	Anthony Altmann Maria, his wife
John Christian Born Feb. 20, 1778, bapt. Jan. 23, 1779	Andrew Wolff Eva, his wife	John Krebs Sophia Sebring (in single state)
Maria Christina Born Feb. 6, 1778, bapt. Jan. 23, 1779	Christian Miller Anna Barbara, his wife	Jacob Gerber Anna Maria, his wife
Theobold Born Feb. 6, 1778, bapt. June 24, 1779	Theobold Mechling Anna Maria	Theobold Mechling Sibilla Gross
John Born June 18, 1778, bapt. Feb. 14, 1779	John McManners Anna, his wife	George Heddenbach and the mother herself
John Ernst Frederick Born Feb. 15, 1778, bapt. Feb. 21, 1779	Matthew Strokberger Saloma, his wife	George Frederick Dumbal Elizabeth, his wife
John David Born Feb. 23, 1778, bapt. Feb. 28, 1779	Philip Miehleisen Barbara, his wife	William Altmann Eva Milhleisen (in single state)
John Michael Born Feb. 23, 1778, bapt. Feb. 28, 1779	George Stau Catherina, his wife	Jacob Stroh Maria Catherina, his wife
Anna Margaretta Born Feb. 17, 1778, bapt. Mar. 4, 1779	Anna Elizabeth Meyers (Illegitimate)	Anna Barbara Eisemaenn (in single state)
John Born Feb. 27, 1778, bapt. Mar. 7, 1779	Philip Koster Magdalena, his wife	Peter Hill Regina Stroh (in single state)
Hannah Born Jan. 12, 1779, bapt. Mar. 7, 1779	John Hill Magdalena, his wife	Ludwig Ottermann Franzina, his wife
John Born Oct. 1, 1773, bapt. Mar. 14, 1779	Joseph McMachen Salome, his wife	Matthew Strodberger Salome, his wife

Children	Parents	God-Parents
John William	John Peter Altmann	William Altmann
Born Feb. 7, 1778, bapt. Mar. 21, 1779	Christina, his wife	Barbara, his wife
Anna Magdalena	Jacob Keppel	Jacob Mechling
Born Feb. 16, 1778, bapt. Mar. 21, 1779	Eleanora, his wife	Catherina, his wife
Anna Maria	Peter Braeunig	Michael Wentzel
Born Jan. 11, 1779, bapt. Mar 21, 1779	Catherina, his wife	Catherina Bungel (in single state)
Joshua	Thomas Simpson	Sponsors parents
Born Oct. 20, 1771, bapt. Mar. 17, .779	Anna, his wife	
Sarah	Thomas Simpson	Parents
Born Feb. 30, 1772, bapt. Mar. 17, 1779	Anna, his wife	
William	Thomas Simpson	Parents
Born Oct. 20, 1775, bapt. Mar. 17, 1779	Anna, his wife	
John Christoph	Franz Rue	Christoph Uhrig
Born Mar. 3, 1779, bapt. Mar. 18, 1779	Margaretta, his wife	Margaretta—John Wilden's wife
Maria Catherina	Adam Uhrig	Adam Meyer
Born Mar. 1, 1779, bapt. Mar. 18, 1779	Catherina, his wife	Elizabeth Eisemann (in single state)
John George	Adam Brinker	John George Schaar
Born Mar. 10, 1779, bapt. Apr. 2, 1779	Margaretta, his wife	Margaretta, his wife
Susannah	Adam Seip	Abraham Frantz
Born Apr. 2, 1779, bapt. Oct. 2, 1779	Dorothy, his wife	Catherina, his wife
Felix	Adam Kaerdner	Parents
Born Mar. 23, 1779, bapt. Apr. 3, 1779	Susannah, his wife	
Anna	Casper Schmiddle	Magdalena, Peter Laup's widow
Born Feb. 8, 1779, bapt. Apr. 2, 1779	Christina, his wife	

Children	Parents	God-Parents
Catherine Born Oct. 2, 1778, bapt. Apr. 5, 1779	Adam Meyer Catherina, his wife	Frederick Hill Catherina Merkly (in single state)
Catherina Barbara Born Feb. 10, 1779, bapt. Apr. 5, 1779	John Kunkel Margaretta, his wife	Catherina Daering (in single state)
Jacob Born Apr. 15, 1779, bapt. Apr. 18, 1779	Philip Kuntz Margaretta, his wife	Jacob Ruch Sibilla Mechling (in single state)
William Born Jan. 9, 1779, bapt. Apr. 18, 1779	William Best Catherina, his wife	John Dorn Elizabeth Reisz (in single state)
Simon Born May 13, 1778, bapt. June 13, 1779	Philip Schmidt Catherina, his wife	Ludwig Otterman Franzina, his wife
Elizabeth Catherina Born Apr. 16, 1779, bapt. June 13, 1779	Jacob Bernhard Catherina, his wife	Peter Daherry Elizabeth, his wife
Catherine Born June 17, 1779, bapt. June 23, 1779	Theobold Mechling Sibilla, his wife	Michael Ruch Franzina, his wife
Michael Born Mar. 12, 1779, bapt. June 27, 1779	Jacob Zehner Catherina, his wife	Parents
Peter Born June 9, 1779, bapt. July 4, 1779	Peter Ruch Margaretta, his wife	Michael Mechling Catherina Uber (in single state)
John Born July 19, 1779, bapt. July 25, 1779	Jacob Hausser Christina, his wife	Ludwig Ottermann Franzina, his wife
Henry Born Mar. 1, 1779, bapt. Aug. 8, 1779	Henry Steit Christina, his wife	Peter Eiseman Barb. Klingelschmidt (in single state)
John Adam Born Oct. 8, 1777, bapt. Apr. 29, 1779	Adam Daerr Dorothea, his wife	Adam Fridshmann Catherina, his wife

Children	Parents	God-Parents
Christina	Jacob Heins	Adam Fridshmann
Born June 1, 1779, bapt. Aug. 23, 1779	Anna Elizabeth, his wife	Catherina, his wife
Sarah	Richard Bowman	Parents
Born Aug. 4, 1777, bapt. Feb. 15, 1779	Elizabeth, his wife	
Anna	Richard Bowman	Parents
Born Mar. 13, 1778, bapt. Feb. 15, 1779	Elizabeth, his wife	
Daniel	Thomas Rodhen	Parents
Born June 25, 1778, bapt. Feb. 15, 1779	Maria Catherina	
David	Gerhard Reineg	Parents
Born Mar. 14, 1778, bapt. Feb. 15, 1779	Elizabeth, his wife	
Anthony	Matthew Reineg	Parents
Born Mar. 14, 1778, bapt. Feb. 15, 1779	Catherina, his wife	
Magdalena	Michael Hablit	Gerhard Reineg
Born Oct. 25, 1778, bapt. Feb. 19, 1779	Anna Catherina	Elizabeth, his wife
Elizabeth	John Conrad	Matthew Reineg
Born Feb. 1, 1779, bapt. Feb. 19, 1779	Anna Maria, his wife	Catherina, his wife
Ludwig	Nicholas Keppel	Ludwig Ottermann
Born Aug. 14, 1779, bapt. Oct. 20, 1779	Anna Maria, his wife	Franzina, his wife
Catherine Elizabeth	Christoph Uhrig	Peter Schelhammer
Born Feb. 4, 1779, bapt. Feb. 20, 1779	Catherina, his wife	Elizabeth Friedle (in single state)
Michael	Michael Gunkel	Michael Mechling
Born June 29, 1779, bapt. Oct. 31, 1779	Margaretta, his wife	Catherina Gunkel (in single state)
Isaac	Frederick Pfersig	John Conrad
Born Oct. 2, 1779, bapt. Oct. 18, 1779	Maria Elizabeth, his wife	Anna Maria, his wife

Children	Parents	God-Parents
Michael	Michael Schmidd	Michael Ruch
Born Feb. 2, 1779, bapt. Oct. 4, 1779	Sarah	Franzina, his wife
Frederick	Archibald Hanszhalter	Frederick Reisz
Born Feb. 24, 1779, bapt. Oct. 24, 1779	Maria Elizabeth	Catherina, his wife
John Philip	Jacob Mechling	Michael Mechling
Born Nov. 18, 1779, bapt. Dec. 25, 1779	Catherina, his wife	Louise Keppel (in single state)
	1780	
Nicholas	Nicholas Sheyrer	Michael Truby
Born Dec. 20, 1779, bapt. Feb. 7, 1780	Anna Maria, his wife	Maria Eliz. Keppel (in single state)
Justina Magdalena	Conrad Aehrig	Barbara, William Altman's wife
Born Jan. 10, 1780, bapt. Feb. 2, 1780	Juliana, his wife	Justina Altmann (in single state)
Christoph	John Krebs	Christoph Herold
Born Feb. 10, 1780, bapt. Feb. 27, 1780	Catherina, his wife	Catherina, his wife
Scharlodda	John Ermel	Michael Stadberger
Born Feb. 18, 1780, bapt. Mar. 5, 1780	Elizabeth, his wife	Scharlodda, his wife
Elizabeth	Conrad Lint	Adam Joerg
Born Feb. 31, 1779, bapt. Mar. 12, 1780	Anna Maria, his wife	Elizabeth, his wife
Maria Catherina	Frederick Waernes	Daniel Madhes
Born Feb. 23, 1780, bapt. Mar. 19, 1780	Margaretta, his wife	Catherina, his wife
John	Jacob Klingenschmidt	Andreas Klingenschmidt
Born Oct. 10, 1779, bapt. Mar. 19, 1780	Margaretta	Agnes, his wife
John Peter	Peter Herold	Daniel Bug
Born Jan. 23, 1780, bapt. Mar. 19, 1780	Elizabeth, his wife	Catherina, his wife

Children	Parents	God-Parents
Christian	Andreas Wolff	George Haeddenbach
Born Feb. 23, 1780, bapt. Mar. 19, 1780	Eva, his wife	Anna Margaretta, his wife
Anna Catherina	Conrad Jung	Peter Jade
Born Oct. 17, 1779, bapt. Mar. 26, 1780	Elizabeth, his wife	Maria Barbara, his wife
Regina	Jacob Wolff	Nicholas Wentzel
Born Mar 26, 1780, bapt. Apr. 10, 1780	Christina, his wife	Magdalena, his wife
John	Thomas Simpson	Parents
Born Apr. 10, 1780, bapt. Apr. 23, 1780	Magdalena, his wife	
Maria Catherina	Christian Sachsmann	Christian Miller
Born Feb. 16, 1780, bapt. Apr. 23, 1780	Elizabeth, his wife	Barbara, his wife
Christian	George Zehner	Christian Ehrett
Born Apr. 30, 1780, bapt. May 21, 1780	Maria, his wife	Maria Elizabeth, his wife
Maria	Abraham Waegele	Isaac Waegele
Born Feb. 10, 1780, bapt. May 20, 1780	Maria Christina, his wife	Catherina, his wife
Anna Maria	John Nicholas Riehm	Philip Wentzel
Born Mar. 23, 1780, bapt. May 21, 1780	Maria Margaretta, his wife	Anna Maria, his wife
Elizabeth	George Bayer	Christoph Herold
Born May 15, 1780, bapt. May 21, 1780	Saloma, his wife	Elizabeth, his wife
John	Philip Klingenschmidd	Daniel Klingenschmidt
Born Jan. 21, 1780, bapt. May 28, 1780	Catherina, his wife	Elizabeth, his wife
Catherina Margaretta	Ludwig Koster	William Altman
Born Mar. 3, 1780, bapt. June 14, 1780	Catherina Margaretta	Regina Stroh (in single state)
John	Thomas Winter	Christian Pfersing
Born June 12, 1780, bapt. July 9, 1780	Anna Maria, his wife	Barbara, his wife

Children	Parents	God-Parents
Franzina Born Apr. 22, 1780, bapt. July 16, 1780	Ludwig Ottermann Franzina, his wife	Ludwig Schmidt Catherina, his wife
Henry Born Jan. 22, 1780, bapt. Aug., 1780	Jacob Schmidt Anna Maria, his wife	Henry Kaeuster Catherina Stahr (in single state)
Christian Born Nov. 30, 1779, bapt. Feb. 24, 1780	Jacob Schroedher Anna Maria, his wife	Adam Fritchmann Catherina, his wife
Peter Born Feb. 15, 1780, bapt. Oct. 8, 1780	Theobald Mechling Anna Maria, his wife	Peter Mechling Christina Ruch (in single state)
Thomas Born Aug. 14, 1780, bapt. Oct. 12, 1780	Thomas Roethen Maria Catherina, his wife	John Conrad Anna Maria, his wife
John Jacob Born Aug. 9, 1780, bapt. Oct. 29, 1780	Philip Schmidt Maria, his wife	Jacob Laydig Juliana, his wife
John Jacob Born Feb. 8, 1780, bapt. Oct. 5, 1780	Andrew Rosenstiehl Anna Catherina, his wife	Jacob Seyfried Anna Maria Uhrig (in single state)
Magdalena Born Feb. 11, 1780, bapt. Oct. 12, 1780	Bartholemew Laster Anna Maria, his wife	Simon Drum Susannah, his wife
Catherine Margaretta Born July 20, 1780, bapt. Oct. 12, 1780	Casper Altmann Susannah, his wife	Ludwig Koster Catherina Margaretta
Anna Maria Born Feb. 20, 1780, bapt. Oct. 19, 1780	Peter Ruch Margaretta, his wife	Theobold Mechling Maria, his wife
Maria Elizabeth Born Oct. 4, 1780, bapt. Oct. 26, 1780	Christian Miller Barbara, his wife	Christian Salsmann Elizabeth, his wife
Susannah Catherina Born Feb. 18, 1780, bapt. Oct. 3, 1780	Nicholas Weifel Magdalena, his wife	Christian Laszer Susannah, his wife

Children	Parents	God-Parents
Susannah Born Oct. 20, 1780, bapt. Dec. 17, 1780	Philip Wentzel Maria, his wife	Christian Laszer Susannah, his wife
Christiana Born Oct. 22, 1780, bapt. Dec. 17, 1780	Peter Braeunig Elizabeth, his wife	Abraham Waegele Christina, his wife
Maria Elizabeth Born Oct. 3, 1780, bapt. Dec. 24, 1780	Peter Klingenschmidt Margaretta, his wife	Peter Klingenschmidt Elizabeth, his wife
Maria Magdalena Born Dec. 18, 1780, bapt. Dec. 31, 1780	Michael Wentzel Elizabeth, his wife	John Kraushaar Maria, his wife
	1781	
Susannah Born Jan. 28, 1781, bapt. Feb. 18, 1781	Simon Drum Susannah, his wife	Christian Laffer Susannah, his wife
Anna Maria Born Jan. 3, 1781, bapt. Feb. 18, 1781	Jacob Kerber Anna Maria, his wife	Jacob Mechling Catherina, his wife
Maria Barbara Born Feb. 6, 1781, bapt. Feb. 19, 1781	Christian Pfersing Barbara, his wife	John Ermel Elizabeth, his wife
Simon Born Oct. 23, 1780, bapt. Mar. 4, 1781	John Braeunig Maria; his wife	Simon Braeunig Christina Reysz (in single state)
Michael Born Feb. 20, 1781, bapt. Mar. 18, 1781	Peter Uber Maria, his wife	Michael Ruch Franzina, his wife
John Philip Born Feb. 12, 1780, bapt. Mar. 18, 1781	Philip Koester Elizabeth	Philip Kuntz Margaretta, his wife
Magdalena Born Feb. 9, 1781, bapt. Mar. 18, 1781	Adam Schaeffer Dorothea, his wife	Christian Mannenschmidt Susannah, his wife

Children	Parents	God-Parents
Jacob	Michael Schmidt	Jacob Waegele
Born Jan. 22, 1781, bapt. Mar. 25, 1781	Sarah, his wife	Catherina Schneider (in single state)
Maria Magdalena	Christoph Herold	George Baender
Born July 18, 1780, bapt. Mar. 25, 1781	Elizabeth, his wife	Magdalena, his wife
John George	Jacob Zehner	George Zehner
Born Feb. 28, 1781, bapt. Mar. 25, 1781	Catherina, his wife	Anna Maria, his wife
John Henry	Christian Ehrett	John Henry Schmidt
Born Mar. 12, 1781, bapt. Mar. 25, 1781	Maria Elizabeth	Anna Catherina, his wife
Catherina	William Best	Catherina Dorn
Born Feb. 15, 1781, bapt. Apr. 8, 1781	Catherina, his wife	George Hag (in single state)
John	John Herold	Peter Wanenmacher
Born Feb. 6, 1781, bapt. Apr. 15, 1781	Barbara, his wife	Christina, his wife
Maria	Isaac Waegele	Abraham Waegele
Born Feb. 22, 1781, bapt. Apr. 15, 1781	Catherine, his wife	Christina, his wife
Maria Awolina	Peter Hill	Lawrence Gundel
Born Feb. 28, 1780, bapt. Apr. 15, 1781	Catherine, his wife	Maria Meyer (in single state)
John Philip	Philip Kuntz	Philip Koester
Born Feb. 5, 1781, bapt. Apr. 29, 1781	Margaretta, his wife	Elizabeth, his wife
William	Peter Shaerre	Wiliam Best
Born Mar. 9, 1781, bapt. Apr. 29, 1781	Elizabeth, his wife	Catherina, his wife
Anna Maria	John Peter Altmann	Peter Wanenmacher
Born Mar. 30, 1781, bapt. May 6, 1781	Christina, his wife	Christina, his wife
Susannah Magdalena	Philip Miehleisen	Peter Eismann
Born Apr. 22, 1781, bapt. May 6, 1781	Maria Barbara	Justina M. Altmann (in single state)

Children	Parents	God-Parents
Regina Born Apr. 9, 1781, bapt. May 13, 1781	John Spielmann Catherina	Nicholas Weidzel Magdalena, his wife
Michael Born Feb. 11, 1781, bapt. May 28, 1781	Jacob Ruch Sibilla, his wife	Michael Ruch Franzina, his wife
Margaret Born July 23, 1780, bapt. May 24, 1781	Benjamin Brauer Catherina Gertrude	George Metzler Anna Margaretta
George Born May 28, 1780, bapt. May 24, 1781	George Metzler Anna Margaretta	Parents
William Born Feb. 22, 1780, bapt. May 24, 1781	Peter Stoese Canna Catherina, his wife	Anna Maria, William Baertrum's wife
Elizabeth Born Feb. 20, 1781, bapt. May 24, 1781	Matthew Kaemmerer Catherina, his wife	Parents
William Born Feb. 11, 1779, bapt. May 24, 1781	Samuel Hitz Magdalena, his wife	John Balthasar Duerr Catherina, his wife
Anna Margaretta Born May 18, 1780, bapt. May 24, 1781	Andrew Stoebel Anna Maria, his wife	Gerhard Kanig Regina, his wife
Joseph Born Feb. 1, 1780, bapt. May 24, 1781	John Doeringer Maria Catherina	The mother herself alone.
Martin Born Aug. 8, 1780, bapt. May 24, 1781	John Doeringer Maria Catherina	Maria Mahnen
James Born Oct. 10, 1778, bapt. May 24, 1781	Patrick Merony Jany, his wife	George Fischer Catherina, his wife
Helena Born Feb. 9, 1778, bapt. May 24, 1781	Laban Kurwer Elizabeth, his wife	George Fischer Catherina, his wife

Children	Parents	God-Parents
Sarah Born Feb. 20, 1780, bapt. May 24, 1781	Laban Kurwer Elizabeth, his wife	George Fischer Catherina, his wife
Theodora Born Jan. 15, 1778, bapt. May 24, 1781	George Fischer Catherina, his wife	Parents
Elizabeth Born Apr. 1, 1781, bapt. May 24, 1781	George Fischer Catherina, his wife	Parents
Rachel Born Feb. 10, 1780, bapt. May 24, 1781	Patrick Merony Jany, his wife	George Fischer Catherina, his wife
Lydia Born Feb. 28, 1777, bapt. May 24, 1781	Peter Eisle Esther, his wife	George Metzler Margaretta, his wife
Ephraim Born Dec. 14, 1780, bapt. May 24, 1781	Peter Eisle Esther, his wife	George Metzler Margaretta, his wife
Margaretta Born Mar. 7, 1781, bapt. June 3, 1781	Andrew Bernges Gertrude, his wife	Conrad Bauer Margaretta, his wife
Anna Margaretta Born June 20, 1780, bapt. June 3, 1781	John M. Kraechen Elizabeth Barbara	Jacob Walter Maria, his wife
Joseph Born June 7, 1781, bapt. June 17, 1781	Jacob Bender Sophia, his wife	Christoph Herold Elizabeth, his wife
James Born Feb. 10, 1781, bapt. June 24, 1781	John Swift Sarah, his wife	John Balthaser Duerr Catherina, his wife
John Born Apr. 3, 1778, bapt. June 24, 1781	John Swift Sarah, his wife	George Metzler Maria, his wife
Hannah Born Apr. 28, 1781, bapt. July 1, 1781	Peter Altmann Catherina, his wife	Jacob Stroh Maria Catherina, his wife

Children	Parents	God-Parents
Maria Catherina	Philip Klingenschmidt	Jacob Mechling
Born Feb. 17, 1780, bapt. July 16, 1781	Christina, his wife	Catherina, his wife
William	William Bernhard	Christoph Truby
Born June 5, 1781, bapt. July 22, 1781	Anna, his wife	Sibilla, his wife
William	Patrick Lerkan	John Balthaser Duerr
Born May 14, 1780, bapt. Aug. 5, 1781	Catherina, his wife	Catherina, his wife
David	Valentine Sychrist	Aaron Schroedher
Born Dec. 24, 1780, bapt. Aug. 5, 1781	Susannah, his wife	(in single state)
Anna Martha	Valentine Hobach	Andrew Hobach
Born Dec. 15, 1780, bapt. Aug. 5, 1781	Elizabeth Cath. his wife	Catherina Elizabeth, his wife
Elizabeth	William Schmidd	Parents
Born Mar. 2, 1779, bapt. Aug. 5, 1781	Johanetta, his wife	
Elizabeth	Jacob Kimmel	Parents
Born July 3, 1780, bapt. Aug. 27, 1781	Margaretta, his wife	
Maria	Philip Schmidt	Theobold Mechling
Born July 11, 1781, bapt. Aug. 12, 1781	Catherina, his wife	Maria, his wife
John	John George Lutz	John Shrum
Born July 27, 1781, bapt. Aug. 19, 1781	Anna, his wife	Eva Maria
Jacob	George Mathes	Jacob Zehner
Born July 20, 1781, bapt. Aug. 22, 1781	Magdalena, his wife	Catherina, his wife
Elizabeth	Henry Reuth	Jacob Keppel
Born May 20, 1781, bapt. Aug. 26, 1781	Christina, his wife	Elizabeth, his wife
Anna Elizabeth	Adam Meyer	William Altmann
Born July 22, 1781, bapt. Feb. 9, 1781	Catherina, his wife	Barbara, his wife

Children	Parents	God-Parents
Anna Maria Born Aug. 22, 1781, bapt. Aug. 9, 1781	William Van Dyke Anna Barbara, his wife	Peter Eisamann Barbara, his wife
John George Born Aug. 13, 1778, bapt. Oct. 16, 1781	John Michael Bernard Anna Maria, his wife	Henry Weisz Eva, his wife
John Born Oct. 14, 1777, bapt. Feb. 16, 1781	Patrick Lerken Catherina, his wife	John Balthaser Duerr Catherina, his wife
Elizabeth Born Oct. 7, 1775, bapt. Feb. 16, 1781	Patrick Lerken Catherina, his wife	John Balthaser Duerr Catherina, his wife
John George Born Feb. 24, 1781, bapt. Oct. 16, 1781	George Shilling Elizabeth	Parents
Sarah Born Apr. 24, 1771, bapt. Feb. 16, 1781	Valentine Hobach Catherina, his wife	Andrew Hobach Catherina Elizabeth, his wife
Catherina Elizabeth Born Oct. 16, 1775, bapt. Feb. 16, 1781	Valentine Hobach Catherina, his wife	Andrew Hobach Catherina Elizabeth, his wife
Christina Born May 10, 1778, bapt. Feb. 16, 1781	Michael Miller Margaretta, his wife	John Balthaser Duerr Catherina, his wife
Thomas Born Aug. 17, 1776, bapt. Feb. 16, 1781	John Swift Sarah	Parents
Juliana Born Feb. 18, 1781, bapt. Dec. 16, 1781	Michael Zehner Barbara, his wife	John Ruch Juliana Shrother (in single state)
Anna Born July 5, 1781, bapt. Oct. 16, 1781	Abraham Gartner Susannah, his wife	Parents
John George Born Feb. 1, 1781, bapt. Feb. 18, 1781	Adam Mayer Elizabeth, his wife	John Wentzel Christina, his wife

Children	Parents	God-Parents
Adam	Christoph Uhrig	Adam Uhrig
Born Feb. 8, 1781, bapt. Feb. 23, 1781	Catherina, his wife	Catherina, his wife
Anna Catherina	Peter Schollhammer	Diederich Walgenbach
Born Feb. 19, 1781, bapt. Feb. 23, 1781	Catherina, his wife	Margaret, his wife
John George	Jacob Klingenschmidt	Jacob Mechling
Born Aug. 19, 1781, bapt. Oct. 7, 1781	Margaretta, his wife	Catherina, his wife
John Peter	John Krebs	Peter Herold
Born Aug. 18, 1781, bapt. Oct. 21, 1781	Catherina, his wife	Elizabeth, his wife
Jacob	Daniel Mathes	Jacob Schroeder
Born Feb. 3, 1781, bapt. Oct. 21, 1781	Catherina, his wife	Maria, his wife
John	Michael Hablitz	John Conrad
Born Mar. 22, 1781, bapt. Dec. 28, 1781	Catherina, his wife	Maria, his wife
Anna	Enoch Rosz	Christina Catherina Berden
Born Apr. 12, 1781, bapt. Oct. 28, 1781	Maria	(In single state)
Maria	Patrick Lerden	Maria Catherina Thoeringer
Born Mar. 1, 1773, bapt. Oct. 28, 1781	Catherina, his wife	(in single state)
Catherina	Frederick Henrich	George Altman
Born Feb. 6, 1781, bapt. Oct. 11, 1781	Margaretta, his wife	Catherina Schmidt (in single state)
Anna Margaretta	Philip Walter	John George Stahr
Born Oct. 9, 1781, bapt. Oct. 18, 1781	Maria Catherina, his wife	Anna Margaretta, his wife
John George	John Jost Schneider	John George Haeddenbach
Born Oct. 28, 1780, bapt. Feb. 28, 1781	Catherina, his wife	Anna Margaretta, his wife
Michael	George Haeddenbach	Michael Truby
Born Feb. 5, 1781, bapt. Feb. 18, 1781	Anna Margaretta, his wife	Anna Marg. Baum (in single state)

Children	Parents	God-Parents
John	Sadrach Davis	William Altmann
Born Feb. 3, 1780, bapt. Feb. 18, 1781	Susannah, his wife	Tillina Rundel (in single state)
John Jacob	Andrew Keppel	Jacob Keppel
Born Aug. 26, 1781, bapt. Dec. 25, 1781	Anna Maria, his wife	Eleanora, his wife
Catherina	Jacob Mechling	Theobold Mechling
Born Oct. 4, 1781, bapt. Dec. 25, 1781	Catherina, his wife	Sibilla, his wife
	1782	
Elizabeth	Abraham Waegele	John Braeunig
Born Oct. 26, 1781, bapt. Feb. 17, 1782	Christina, his wife	Christina, his wife
Peter	Peter Kuntz	Peter Ruch
Born Jan. 26, 1782, bapt. Mar. 3, 1782	Saloma Koestern	Margaretta, his wife
	(Illegitimate)	
John Henry	George Zehner	Christian Ehret
Born Feb. 10, 1782, bapt. Mar. 10, 1782	Anna Maria, his wife	Elizabeth, his wife
Maria Elizabeth	Nicholas Keppel	Jacob Keppel
Born Feb. 17, 1781, bapt. Mar. 24, 1782	Anna Maria, his wife	Anna M. Ottermann (in single state)
Catherine	Jacob Schmidt	William Altman
Born Feb. 14, 1781, bapt. Mar. 31, 1782	Anna Maria	Barbara, his wife
Maria Barbara	Michael Waelger	William Altmann
Born Jan. 28, 1782, bapt. Mar. 31, 1782	Elizabeth, his wife	Barbara, his wife
Susannah	Peter Braeunig	Michael Waelger
Born Feb. 9, 1782, bapt. Mar. 31, 1782	Catherina, his wife	Elizabeth, his wife
Maria Catherina	Christian Rothenbach	Caspar Altman
Born July 25, 1781, bapt. Mar. 31, 1782	Barbara, his wife	Susannah, his wife

Children	Parents	God-Parents
Anna Catherina Born Feb. 4, 1782, bapt. Apr. 28, 1782	John Balthaser Meyer Maria, his wife	Michael Fritchman Christina Meyer (in single state)
Anna Catherina Born Feb. 24, 1782, bapt. May 2, 1782	Andrew Klingenschmidt Agnes, his wife	Jacob Keppel Elenora, his wife
Christina Born Feb. 28, 1782, bapt. May 12, 1782	Philip Wentzel Anna Maria, his wife	John Wentzel Christina, his wife
Philip Born Apr. 14, 1782, bapt. May 12, 1782	John Wentzel Christina, his wife	Philip Wentzel Anna Maria, his wife
John Peter Born Jan. 23, 1782, bapt. May 19, 1782	Philip Klingenschmidt Catherina, his wife	John Peter Altman Christina, his wife
Catherina Bor Jan. 26, 1782, bapt. May 19, 1782	William Bell Catherina Barbara, his wife	Peter Klingenschmidt Margaretta, his wife
John Born Oct. 21, 1781, bapt. May 19, 1782	Simon Hicks Magdalena, his wife	Gerhard Keniv Regina, his wife
Benjamin Born Mar. 15, 1782, bapt. May 20, 1782	Benjamin Brauer Catherina, Gert., his wife	John Balthaser Duerr Catherina, his wife
Catherine Gertrude Born May 20, 1782	Benjamin Brauer	Magdalena, his wife
Magdalena Born 1782	Simon Hicks	Magdalena, his wife
Isaac Born Apr. 10, 1781, bapt. May 20, 1782	David Hertzog Christina, his wife	Peter Wannenmacher Christina, his wife
Catherine Born Apr. 7, 1782, bapt. May 20, 1782	Peter Ruch Margaretta	Philip Schmidt Catherina, his wife

Children	Parents	God-Parents
Peter	Thomas Boyd	Henry Shrum
Born Jan. 6, 1782, bapt. June 2, 1782	Catherina, his wife	Margaretta Lang (in single state)
Emma Maria	Frederich Werner	Adam Fritchman
Born Aug. 5, 1782, bapt. Aug. 25, 1782	Margaretta, his wife	Catherina, his wife
Thomas	Joseph Broenig	George Fischer
Born Apr. 19, 1779, bapt. June 30, 1782	Elizabeth, his wife	Thorodea, his wife
Thomas	John Conrad Miller	Parents
Born Mar. 27, 1780, bapt. June 3, 1782	Anna Maria, his wife	
Elizabeth	Joseph Braeunig's wife	
Born 1760, bapt. June 30, 1782		
Philip	George Bayer	Philip Schmidt and the mother
Born June 13, 1782, bapt. July 7, 1782	Susannah, his wife	
Anna Maria	Jacob Runt	Christian Salsman
Born Feb. 4, 1780, bapt. July 7, 1782	Anna Maria, his wife	Elizabeth, his wife
Catherina Margaretta	Christian Salsman	Christian Miller
Born Aug. 9, 1781, bapt. July 21, 1782	Elizabeth, his wife	Elizabeth, his wife
John	Nicholas Scheurer	Jacob Stroh
Born June 24, 1782, bapt. July 28, 1782	Anna Maria, his wife	Anna M. Ottermann (in single state)
Christoph	Peter Herold	Christoph Herold
Born Apr. 30, 1782, bapt. July 28, 1782	Elizabeth, his wife	Catherina, his wife
John Henry	Isaac Stimmel	Henry Hoffman
Born June 1, 1782, bapt. Aug. 4, 1782	Elizabeth, his wife	Eleanora, his wife
Saloma	Solomon Druschel	Peter Breitschwert
Born Jan. 20, 1782, bapt. Aug. 11, 1782	Anna Maria	Elizabeth, his wife

Grbg. 8

Children	Parents	God-Parents
Anna Maria Born Mar 15, 1776, bapt. Aug. 11, 1782	Valentine Hobach Elizabeth, his wife	Hannah, Christian Waller's wife
Maria Born Mar. 20, 1781, bapt. Aug. 11, 1782	Joseph Brauen Elizabeth, his wife	Theodore George Fisher and his wife
Elizabeth Baptized Aug. 11, 1782	Isaac Stimmel and his wife	Parents
Maria Born Jan. 13, 1782, bapt. Aug. 4, 1782	Isaac Stiehl Maria, his wife	The mother alone
John Born Aug. 16, 1782, bapt. Oct. 22, 1782	Thomas Arten Nelle, his wife	Annie Arten
Christian Born Oct. 17, 1782, bapt. Oct. 18, 1782	Daniel Ermel Christina, his wife	Christian Pfersich Maria Barbara, his wife
William Born Apr. 10, 1782, bapt. Oct. 20, 1782	Conrad Hag Sarah, his wife	William Best Catherina, his wife
Elizabeth Born Feb. 22, 1782, bapt. Oct. 20, 1782	Daniel William Christina, his wife	Jacob Stroh Maria Catherina, his wife
John Peter Born Aug. 24, 1782, bapt. Dec. 7, 1782	Caspar Altman Susannah, his wife	Andrew Klingenschmidt Regina Barbara (Rodenbach's wife)
Elizabeth Born Oct. 1, 1782, bapt. Dec. 15, 1782	Jacob Ruch Sibilla, his wife	Peter Ruch Margaretta, his wife
Jacob Born Feb. 21, 1781, bapt. Dec. 25, 1782	Thomas Johns Magdalena, his wife	Jacob Erb Catherina, his wife
Catherine Born Feb. 24, 1782, bapt. Dec. 25, 1782	Jacob Esbi Catherina, his wife	Anthony Ruff Anna Maria, his wife

Children	Parents	God-Parents
Anna Catherina Born Oct. 23, 1782, bapt. Dec. 26, 1782	Christian Ehret Maria Elizabeth	Adam Fritchman Catherina, his wife
Christina Born Oct. 29 1782, bapt. Dec. 29, 1782	Adam Uhrig Catherina, his wife	Christoph Uhrig Catherina, his wife
	1783	
John Born Oct. 18, 1782, bapt. Jan. 31, 1783	Jacob Heinsz Anna Elizabeth	Adam Damsom Catherina, his wife
Simon Born Dec. 5, 1782, bapt. Feb. 2, 1783	Simon Drum Susannah	Bartholemew Laster Anna Maria, his wife
John George Born Jan. 6, 1783, bapt. Feb. 16, 1783	Michael Wentzel Elizabeth, his wife	Christian Miller Anna Barbara, his wife
John George Born Feb. 10, 1782, bapt. Feb. 23, 1783	Jacob Kerber Anna Maria, his wife	Jacob Esbi Catherina, his wife
John Born Jan. 19, 1783, bapt. Mar. 9, 1783	William von Dyke Anna Barbara	Adam Meyer Elizabeth, his wife
George Peter Born Oct. 7, 1782, bapt. Mar. 12, 1783	Christian Stiehl Christina, his wife	George Walter Catherina Kokler (in single state) and Elizabeth, Anthony Walter's wife).
Susannah Born Feb. 3, 1783, bapt. Mar. 12, 1783	Archibald Hausshalter Elizabeth, his wife	Simon Drum Susannah, his wife
Christina Born Jan. 27, 1783, bapt. Apr. 1, 1783	Peter Lassner Magdalena, his wife	Michael Ruch and mother of child
Christoph Born June 14, 1782, bapt. Apr. 6, 1783	Adam Damm Thorodea, his wife	Christoph Lawengayer Elizabeth, his wife

Children	Parents	God-Parents
Anna Maria Born Feb. 30, 1782, bapt. Apr. 18, 1783	John Conrad Anna Maria, his wife	Elizabeth Matthew Keniv's wife
Philip Born Jan. 1, 1783, bapt. Apr. 20, 1783	Jacob Zehner Catherina, his wife	Daniel Mathes Catherina, his wife
Anna Elizabeth Born Feb. 26, 1783, bapt. Apr. 20, 1783	Peter Hill Catherina, his wife	John Gundel Margaretta, his wife
	1784	
Sophia Born Apr. 15, 1784, bapt. Apr. 19, 1784	George Haetzenbach Anna Margaretta, his wife	Jacob Bender Sophia, his wife
Susannah Born Mar. 6, 1784, bapt. May 31, 1784	Caspar Altmann Susannah, his wife	William Beit Eva Elizabeth
John Peter Born June 20, 1784, bapt. June 21, 1784	John Peter Wannenmacher Margaretta, his wife	Christina, Peter Wannenmacher's wife
William Born May 2, 1784, bapt. June 27, 1784	Daniel McCannel Magdalena, his wife	Parents sponsors
Philip Born May 5, 1784, bapt. July 11, 1784	William Bell Barbara, his wife	John Peter Wannenmacher Margaretta, his wife
Daniel Born Apr. 22, 1784, bapt. Oct. 26, 1784	Philip Koester Elizabeth, his wife	Jacob Berlin Magdalena, his wife
John Born Apr. 22, 1784, bapt. Oct. 26, 1784	Jacob Berlin Magdalena, his wife	Philip Koester Elizabeth, his wife
Magdalena Born Mar. 13, bapt. Apr. 4, 1785	Saloma Koestern (Illegitimate)	Elizabeth Philip Koester's wife

Children	Parents	God-Parents
Elizabeth Born Feb. 2, 1786, bapt. Mar. 30, 1786	William Bell Barbara, his wife	John Peter Wannenmacher Margaretta, his wife
Michael Born May 23, 1788, bapt. May 23, 1788	Michael Bayerle Anna, his wife	Jacob Bayerle Elizabeth, his wife
David Born Jan. 26, 1790, bapt. Jan. 28, 1790	Michael Bayerle Anna, his wife	Parents Sponsors
Christina Born Feb. 24, 1789, bapt. Mar. 8, 1790	Conrad Hermann Christina, his wife	George Ament Esther, his wife
Michael Born May 9, 1790, bapt. June 29, 1790	Christoph Walthauer Dorothea, his wife	Conrad Schueddler Elizabeth, his wife
Susannah Born Aug. 22, 1790, bapt. Oct. 25, 1790	Andrew Bayerle Christina, his wife	Elizabeth, Jacob Bayerle's wife
Elizabeth Born Aug. 20, 1790, bapt. Oct. 11, 1790	Christoph Artmann Elizabeth Barbara, his wife	John Koch Magdalena, Frederick Wujart's wife
Anna Maria Born Feb. 14, 1790, bapt. Oct. 11, 1790	Adam Walgenbach Rosina, his wife	Peter Schoellhammer Catherine, his wife
Abraham Born June 14, 1790, bapt. Oct. 31, 1790	John Rudolph Christina, his wife	Nicholaus Mayer Ester Walthauer (in single state)
Elizabeth Born Oct. 23, 1790, bapt. Dec. 25, 1790	Henry Braeuling Margaretta, his wife	Catherina Braulinger, widow
Susannah Born Jan. 19, 1790, bapt. Dec. 26, 1790	Christian Rodenbach Barbara, his wife	Parents themselves
Daniel Born Dec. 10, 1790, bapt. Dec. 20, 1790	Peter Schoellhammer Catherina, his wife	Adam Waldenbach Rosina, his wife

Children	Parents	God-Parents
Anna Maria	Peter Klingenschmidt	Vallentin Stahr
Born Dec. 28, 1790, bapt. Jan. 25, 1791	Margaretta, his wife	Anna Maria Klingenschmidt
		(in single state)
Andrew	Caspar Klingenschmidt	Andrew Keppel
Born Jan. 6, 1791, bapt. Jan. 30, 1791	Anna Margaretta, his wife	Maria, his wife
John Jacob	John Balthaser Meyer	Jacob Berlin
Born, Dec. 12, 1790, bapt. Feb. 20, 1791	Maria, his wife	Magdalena, his wife
Andrew	Peter Schmidt	John Balthaser Meyer
Born Dec. 10, 1790, bapt. Mar. 13, 1791	Christina, his wife	Maria, his wife
Christina	Michael Berlin	Christina, Frederick Marschang's wife
Born Mar. 29, 1791, bapt. Mar. 31, 1791	Anna Maria	
John	Jacob Kimmel	John Hauszer
Born Apr. 31, 1789, hapt. Apr. 24, 1791	Margaretta, his wife	
George Jacob	Moses Decart	Parents sponsors
Born May 14, 1790, bapt. June 12, 1791	Maria, his wife	
John George	Conrad Hermann	George Anthony
Born Jan. 26, 1791, bapt. Aug. 7, 1791	Christina	Margaretta, his wife
John Peter	Peter Hill	John Gundel
Born June 10, 1791, bapt. Aug. 21, 1791	Catherina, his wife	Margaretta, his wife
Tobias	Tobias Bender	Peter Braeling
Born Apr. 6, 1791, bapt. Oct. 18, 1791	Elizabeth Scholl	Catherina, his wife
(Illegitimate)		
William	Conrad Knappenberger	John Moser
Born Feb. 16, 1791, bapt. Feb. 18, 1791	Eva Barbara	Catherina, his wife

Children	Parents	God-Parents
Catherina Elizabeth	Moses Decart	Parents sponsors
Born Oct. 19, 1791, bapt. May 16 1792	Maria, his wife	
Susannah	John Rudolph	Parents sponsors
Born May 30, 1792, bapt. June 4, 1792	Christina, his wife	

Note:—Here ends Balthasar Meyer's list of Baptisms. A new list of Baptisms was begun by Karl Sheibeler, the schoolmaster who succeeded Meyer at Herolds, Rev. Anton Ulrich Luetge being pastor. The list of baptisms indicates that Balthasar Meyer moved to the Brush Creek valley about 1784 as the latter baptisms of his list are from this region.

APPENDIX B
Communicants
Selected Lists, 1791-1862)

Record of Communicants in Herold's or Zion's Church in Hempfield Township, Westmoreland County in the year of our Lord and Savior, Jesus Christ, October 11, 1791.

1 Jacob Stroh and wife
2 Maria Catherina
3 Susannah Stroh
4 Maria Barbara Stroh
5 Michael Stroh
6 Christoph Amelang and wife
7 Anna Catherina
8 Anna Elizabeth Amelang
9 Ludwig Staudengauer and
10 wife Elizabeth Margaretta
11 Ludwig Ottermann
12 Maria Esther
13 George Keit and wife
14 Anna Catherina
15 Peter Keit
16 Joseph Keit
17 Jacob Stroh and wife
18 Sarah
19 Andreas Altmann and wife
20 Anna Elizabeth
21 Anna Maria Mechling
22 Anna Maria Rab
23 Anna Maria Traeg
24 Peter Huber and wife
25 Anna Maria
26 William Altmann and wife
27 Barbara
28 Susannah Altmann
29 Barbara Altmann
30 Peter Huber
31 George Jacob Altmann
32 Magdalena Dorn
33 Jacob Weller
34 Philip Kuntz and wife
35 Margaretta
36 Catherina Kuntz
37 Nicholaus Mueller and wife
38 Catherina
39 Simon Huber
40 Jacob Mueller and wife
41 Anna Maria
42 Anna Maria Herold
43 Peter Eisenman and wife
44 Anna Barbara
45 Elizabeth Ehrbach
46 John Kuntz
47 Jacob Ruch
48 Jacob Steinmetz
49 Susannah Steinmetz
50 Michael Ruch and wife
51 Lucia
52 Catherina Zehner
53 Catherina Schneider
54 Valentine Steiner and wife
55 Catherina
56 Adam Steiner
57 Jacob Steiner and wife
58 Catherina
59 Catherina Zehner
60 Peter Ruch and wife
61 Anna Margaretta
62 Peter Fuchs and wife
63 Anna Margaretta
64 Catherina Schneider
65 Anna Maria Sheur
66 Maria Barbara Sheur
67 Sibylla Drubin
68 Philip Keck

69 Samuel Richard and wife
70 Juliana Richard
71 Margaretta Seitgerten
72 Matthias Bratschwert and
73 wife Maria Barbara
74 Christina Duner
75 Sarah Haakin
76 Maria Brucker
77 Margaretta Bayer
78 Catherina Kestin
79 Veronica Summisen
80 Christian Benus

Communicants, May 27, 1792, by Pastor Steck

1 Henry Schatz and wife
2 Eva
3 Jacob Stroh and wife
4 Maria Catherina
5 Regina Kempf
6 George Peter Altmann
7 Andrew Altman and wife
8 Elizabeth
9 John Kunkel
10 Christian Eisenmann and
11 wife Susannah
12 William Altman
13 Peter Eisenmann
14 Anna Margaretta Scheibel
15 Catherina Thomas
16 Frederich Koch
17 Adam Steiner
18 Valentine Steiner
19 Samuel Ritscher and wife
20 Juliana
21 David Mechling
22 John Peter Miller and wife
23 Catherina
24 Adam Meyer and wife
25 Catherina
26 Christian Ruch
27 Peter Ruch and wife
28 Margaretta
29 George Franz
30 Christian Hartman and wife
31 Barbara
32 Abraham Hermann and wife
33 Sibilla
34 Philip Beyer and wife
35 Margaretta
36 Christian Beyer
37 Daniel William and wife
38 Christina
39 William William
40 Nicholaus Keppel and wife
41 Anna Maria
42 George Dormeyer and wife
43 Catherina
44 George Suens and wife
45 Anna Maria
46 William Best and wife
47 Catherina
48 John Stingler and wife
49 Anna Maria
50 Magdalena Stingler
51 John Stingler
52 George Stingler
53 Adam Uhrig and wife
54 Catherina
55 Jacob Schmeltzer
56 Henry Eisenmann and wife
57 Christina
58 David Altmann
59 John Hartmann
60 Susannah Steinmetz
61 Daniel Keppel
62 Frederich Mechling
63 George Keppel
64 John Mechling
65 John Keppel
66 John Upper
67 Philip Keppel
68 John Altmann

69 Anna Barbara Eisenmann
70 Maria Barbara Spingler
71 Barbara Dorn
72 Anna Margaretta Stahr
73 Margaretta Golt
74 Anna Maria Link
75 Catherina Link
76 Margaretta Dorn
77 Christina Margaretta Diemer
78 Magdalena Dorn
79 Christina Schneider
80 Sara Joehl
81 Catherina Mechling
82 Maria Jerian
83 Dorothea Henbach
84 Catherina Bernhart
85 Catherina Maria Miller
86 Margaretta Meyer
87 Hannah Gangwer
88 Susannah Altman
89 Maria Altman
90 Magdalena Kaszner
91 Thomas Leip and wife
92 Anna Maria
93 Anthony Ruff
94 Catherina Kesten
95 Barbara Brinken
96 Henry Kedin
97 Theobald Keppel
98 Frederich Reisz
99 Henry Heilmann
100 Barbara Scholl
101 Feronica Summisen
102 Catherina Tippis
103 Anna Maria Stupp
104 Christian Beisch
105 Christoph Amelang and wife
106 Catherina
107 Elizabeth Amelang
108 Barbara Hermann
109 Catherina Heinsen
110 Anna Maria Heinsen
111 John Mechling
112 Jacob Mechling
113 Jacob Fuchs and wife
114 Catherina
115 Jacob Steinmetz
116 Susannah Weber
117 Margaretta Bayer
118 Anna Maria Waken
119 Margaretta Kuehn
120 Peter Uber and wife
121 Maria
122 George J. Altmann and wife
123 Anna Catherina
124 Martin Lautenschlaeger
125 Rebecca Schoener

Communicants at the Herold's or Zion's Church in the year of our Lord, 1794, April 20.

1 John Bachman
2 Valentine Steiner
3 Michael Gangwer
4 Jacob Ruch
5 Dewalt Mechling
6 Conrad Hag and wife
7 Anna Elizabeth Hag
8 Anna Margaretta Hag
9 Ludwig Oddermann
10 Jacob Stroh and wife
11 Maria Catherina
12 Christian Ehret
13 Peter Miller and wife
14 Anna Catherina
15 John Ehret and wife
16 Anna Barbara
17 Nicholaus Miller and wife
18 Anna Catherina
19 Martin Froehlich and wife
20 Anna Margaretta
21 John Peter Miller and wife
22 Anna Margaretta

23 Adam Schneider
24 John Kunkel and wife
25 Anna Margaretta
26 John Peter Ruch and wife
27 Anna Margaretta
28 Christoph Uhrig and wife
29 Anna Catherina
30 John Peter Ruppert
31 Christian Eisenman and wife
32 Susannah
33 Bardel Kunsz and wife
34 Anna Christina
35 Jacob Baumgartner and wife
36 Anna Catherina
37 Christoph Fuchs and wife
38 Susannah
39 John Froehlich
40 John Peter Kunkel
41 Conrad Meyer
42 John Kunkel and wife
43 Anna Maria
44 George Zehner
45 John Mueckendoerfer
46 Frederich Maechling
47 Jacob Zehner
48 Bastian Kunkel
49 George Maechling
50 Frederich Keppel
51 Ludwig Keppel
52 Peter Keppel and wife
53 Anna Catherina
54 Henry Keppel
55 George Peter Altman
56 Anna Mag. Baumgaertner
57 Andrew Alms and wife
58 Anna .Catherina
59 Anna Maria Maechling
60 Anna Magdalena Bauman
61 Anna Catherina Waeldisen
62 Maria Barbara Altman
63 Anna Catherina 'Hinsel
64 Maria Magdalena Zehner
65 Anna Maria Schneider
66 Anna Margaretta Schmidt
67 Susannah Altman
68 Susannah Mueckendoerfer
69 Henry Schatz and wife
70 Eva
71 Ludwig Stautenhauer
72 Anna Maria Runscin
73 Anna Catherina Altman
74 Jacob Waelcker
75 Anna Margaretta Belinger
76 Henry Best and wife
77 Anna Margaretta
78 Anna Catherina Waelcker
79 Wilhelmina Haarbach
80 Christian Sacksman
81 Stephan Reinbold
82 Anna Catherina Best
83 Samuel Ritscher and wife
84 Juliana
85 Andrew Rosenstiehl
86 Nicholas Keppel
87 Michael Maechling and wife
88 Anna Maria
89 Daniel William and wife
90 Anna Christina
91 John Peter Eisenmann and
92 wife Anna Barbara
93 William Altman and wife
94 Anna Barbara
95 John Peter Uber and wife
96 Anna Maria
97 John Peter Altman
98 Christoph Beyer
99 Nicholas Scheurer and wife
100 Anna Maria
101 John Maechling
102 Philip Miller and wife
103 Anna Maria
104 Henry Eisenman and wife

105 Anna Christina
106 Jacob Friedle and wife
107 Anna Elizabeth
108 Martin Ritscher
109 John Altman and wife
110 Anna Elizabeth
111 George Kunsz
112 George Hag and wife
113 Anna Elizabeth
114 Conrad Link
115 Jacob Maechling and wife
116 Anna Maria
117 Jacob Hag and wife
118 Anna Catherina
119 John Maechling
120 Joseph Gangwer
121 John Schneider
122 John Ueber
123 John Miller
124 Philip Gangwer and wife
125 Anna Margaretta
126 John Gangwer
127 Maria Elizabeth
128 Nicholas Eisenmann and
129 wife Anna Catherina
130 Andrew Altman
131 Adam Steiner
132 Sibylla Trubes
133 Anna Margaretta Buerger
134 Anna Margaretta Scheurer
135 Anna Magdalena Dornis
136 Anna Catherina Bernhart
137 Elinor Keppel
138 Susannah Mahnsch
139 Susannah Fuchs
140 Anna Catherina Miller
141 Hannah Gangwer
142 Anna Maria Thiemer
143 Susannah Guebler
144 Anna Elizabeth Thiemer
145 Anna Catherina Mueller
146 Anna Catherina Kunsz
147 Anna Catherina Zehner
148 Anna Barbara Steiner
149 Anna Elizabeth Bricker
150 Anna Elizabeth Keppel
151 Susannah Schaerr
152 Anna Margaretta Dormit

Communicants in Zion Church
April 10, 1796

1 John Peter Miller and wife
2 Margaretta
3 William Altman and wife
4 Barbara
5 Sewalt Maechling
6 Jacob Miller and wife
7 Anna Maria
8 Jacob Seddhar
9 Martin Froelich and wife
10 Margaretta
11 Joseph Jaeger
12 Elizabeth Poersching
13 Susannah Margar. Altman
14 George Rosenstiehl
15 Jacob Rosenstiehl
16 Frederich Beyer and wife
17 Margaretta
18 Barbara Miehleisen
19 Susannah Mohneschmitt
20 Catherina Maria Miller
21 Elizabeth Miller
22 Michael Gangwer
23 Peter Stroh and wife
24 Margaretta
25 Ludwig Ottermann
26 Peter Fuchs
27 Nicholaus Miller and wife
28 Catherina
29 Peter Ruch and wife
30 Anna Margaretta
31 Conrad Hack
32 Adam Miller

33 Jacob Zehner and wife
34 Catherina
35 Samuel Wilnis and wife
36 Christina
37 William Best and wife
38 Catherina
39 John Andrew Holtz
40 George Zehner and wife
41 Anna Maria
42 Catherina Zehner
43 Elizabeth Zehner
44 Christian Eisenman and wife
45 Susannah
46 Jacob Zehner and wife
47 Susannah
48 George Zehner
49 John Miller
50 William Best
51 Jacob Kunsz
52 Christian Miller
53 Jacob Ruch
54 Henry Eisenmann and wife
55 Christina
56 Samuel Poersching
57 Lenora Keppel
5 Christina Marg. Thomas
59 Elizabeth Thiemer
60 Catherina Schmidt
61 Margaretta Sorny
62 Catherina Bastian
63 Maria Magdalena Zehner
64 Catherina Craepsz
65 Margaretta Schaeurer
66 Anna Maria Craepsz
67 Anna Maria Kunsz
68 Christina Kunsz
69 Magdalena Ruch
70 Sarah Schaerr
71 Hannah Gangwer
72 Valentine Steiner and wife
73 Catherina

74 Jacob Stroh and wife
75 Sarah
76 Henry Schatz and wife
77 Eva
78 John Bachman
79 Catherina Bachman
80 Philip Kunsz
81 Catherina Kunsz
82 John Kunsz
83 Henry Best and wife
84 Margaretta
85 Nicholaus Best and wife
86 Maria Catherina
87 Philip Oberny
88 Adam Steiner
89 Jacob Klingelschmidt and
90 wife Elizabeth
91 Michael Kreiger
92 William Altman and wife
93 Catherina
94 Christian Sachsman
95 Jacob Waelker
96 Jacob Friedle and wife
97 Elizabeth
98 Michael Zehner
99 Jacob Maechling
100 Philip Stoll and wife
101 Margaretta
102 Maria Magdalena Lutz
103 Frederich Maechling
104 Anthony Walter and wife
105 Sarah
106 George Hack and wife
107 Elizabeth
108 Jacob Mahneschmidt
109 Peter Ueber
110 Abraham Ueber
111 Jacob Schmidt
112 George Foszstell
113 John Maechling
114 Jacob Maechling

115 Anna Maria Bontz
116 Christina Kunsz
117 Margaretta Koehler
118 Catherina Bernhart
119 Anna Maria Acker
120 Margaretta Baerger
121 Margaretta Linenger
122 Margaretta Sornys
123 Ironica Sunner
124 Catherina Sunner
125 Catherina Mackendoerfer
126 Margaretta Bayer
127 Catherina Schauer
128 Catherina Klingelschmidt
129 Elizabeth Hack
130 Anna Maria Demon
131 Eva Kunsz
132 Catherina Fuchs
133 Susannah Steinmetz
134 Wilhelmina Haarbach
135 Susannah Holtz
136 Elizabeth Holtz
137 Christina Heyl
138 Maria Catherina Soergin
139 Peter Ueber and wife
140 Maria
141 Michael Maechling and wife
142 Anna Maria
143 Simon Ueber
144 Ludwig Keppel
145 Samuel Haak and wife
146 Maria
147 Catherina Hartman
148 Anna Margaretta Schaeubel
149 Anna Maria Keppel

Communion list, Zion Church
October 23, 1796

1 Valentine Steinêr
2 John Altman
3 Elizabeth, his wife
4 Margaretta Miller
5 William Altman
6 Maria Barbara, his wife
7 Frederick Steiner
8 Susannah, his wife
9 John Ehret
10 Barbara, his wife
11 David Altman
12 Susannah, his wife
13 Abraham Erdman
14 Sibilla, his wife
15 John Gongaware
16 Maria Elizabeth, his wife
17 Joseph Gongaware
18 Barbara, his wife
19 Conrad Poersching
20 Maria, his wife
21 Daniel Poersching
22 Christina, his wife
23 Ironica Summen
24 Elizabeth Poersching
25 Catherina Unsel
26 Anna Maria Miller
27 Salome Scheibel
28 Anna Maria Matheis
29 Susannah Maria Schmidt
30 Elizabeth Franz
31 Susannah Schaerris
32 Catherina Best
33 Margaretta Uhrig
34 Christina Uhrig
35 Magdalena Matheis
36 Anna Maria Ruch
37 Justina Stroh
38 John Peter Ruch
39 Jacob Baumgartner
40 Magdalena, his wife
41 John Andrew Holtz
42 Christian Ruch
43 Elizabeth, his wife
44 Michael Ruch
45 Lusia, his wife

46 Lenora Keppel
47 Hannah Gongaware
48 Magdalena Keppel
49 Susannah Weber
50 Adam Schmidt
51 John Jacob Steinmetz
52 Daniel Wilmer
53 Catherina Klingelschmidt
54 Catherina Baehr
55 Magdalena Gongaware

Communion List April 14, 1805

1 Henry Schatz
2 Elizabeth Schatz
3 John Gannewehr
4 Elizabeth, his wife
5 Peter Herold
6 Daniel Herold
7 Michael Gannewehr
8 John Bachman
9 Barbara Breinig
10 Michael Saddler
11 Elizabeth Saddler
12 John Peter Mueller
13 Margaretta Mueller
14 Christina Wengert
15 Adam Meyer
16 Catherina Meyer
17 Elizabeth Meyer
18 Jacob Mueller
19 Anna Maria Mueller
20 Christian Eisenmann
21 Susannah Eisenmann
22 Jacob Detthar
23 Peter Kaeppel
24 Catherina Kaeppel
25 Philip Fuchs
26 Christina Fuchs
27 Philip Mechling
28 Catherina Mechling
29 Peter Hansz
30 Anna Hansz
31 John Mueller
32 Nicholas Mueller
33 Peter Fuchs
34 Henry Kaeppel
35 Ludwig Kaeppel
36 Lenora Kaeppel
37 Margaretta Fuchs
38 Christina Loh
39 Magdalena Kaeppel
40 Catherina Schneider
41 Elizabeth Engen
42 Michael Eisenmann
43 Barbara Eisenmann
44 Michael Welker
45 Jacob Hausz
46 Anna Maria Hausz
47 Adam Bachman
48 Margaretta Bachmann
49 John Bachman
50 Barbara Bachman
51 Jacob Bachman
52 Catherina Bachman
53 Philip Steinmetz
54 Elizabeth Schmidt
55 Barbara Scholl
56 Catherina Miller

Communion List, May 10, 1812

1 Jacob Dethor
2 Peter Herold
3 John Mueller
4 Adam Wintling
5 Adam Bachman
6 Margaretta, his wife
7 Jacob Mueller
8 Anna Maria, his wife
9 John Stauch
10 Maria, his wife
11 John Bachman
12 Adam Meyer
13 Michael Gangwehr
14 Philip Fuchs

15 Christina, his wife
16 Anna Margaretta Fuchs
17 Andrew Eisenmann
18 Catherina, his wife
19 Elizabeth Eisenmann
20 David Dethor
21 Peter Fuchs
22 John Mueller
23 Susannah, his wife
24 Jacob Mueller
25 Adam Steiner
26 Daniel Herold
27 Samuel Ritscher
28 Christian Eisenmann
29 Susannah, his wife
30 Samuel Hummel
31 Jacob Bachman
32 Catherina, his wife
33 Catherina Herold
34 Elizabeth Herold
35 Susannah Herold
36 Barbara Mueller
37 Elizabeth Gangwehr
38 Anna Maria Altmann
39 Magdalena Steinmetz
40 Elenor Kaeppel
41 Salome Scheibel
42 Hanna Magdalena Brown
43 Barbara Altman
44 Rosina Bender
45 Michael Zundel
46 Jacob Hensz
47 Maria, his wife

Communion List April 15, 1821

1 John Stauch
2 Maria, his wife
3 John Adam Bachman
4 Margaretta, his wife
5 Christoph Krebs
6 Christian Eisenmann
7 Susannah, his wife
8 John Mueller
9 Adam Ehret
10 George Ehret
11 Christian Ehret
12 David Mueller
13 John Mueller
14 Michael Mueller
15 Catherina, his wife
16 George Eisenmann
17 Barbara, his wife
18 Elizabeth Ehret
19 Elizabeth Mueller
20 Maria Holzer
21 Daniel Stauch
22 Catherina Hochenhill
23 Elizabeth Zehner
24 Susannah Steiner
25 Peter Fuchs
26. Sarah, his wife
27 Margaretta Fuchs
28 Philip Fuchs
29 Christina, his wife
30 John Herold
31 Maria Klingelschmidt
32 Catherina Nelzin
33 Barbara Bachman
34 John Bachman
35 Jacob Bachman
36 Catherina, his wife
37 Michael Mueller
38 Susannah, his wife
39 John Stauch
40 Hannah, his wife
41 John Peter Mueller
42 Catherina, Heil
43 Henry Mueller
44 Catherina, his wife
45 John Schatz
46 Sarah, his wife
47 John Mueller
48 Sarah, his wife

49 Henry Kaeppel
50 Anna, his wife
51 John Mueller
52 Susannah, his wife
53 Susannah Eisenmann
54 Christina Schneider
55 Hannah Eisenmann
56 Elizabeth Rosenstiehl
57 Elizabeth Schumacher
58 Peter Eisenmann
59 Rosina Bender
60 Samuel Hommel
61 William Wintes
62 Catherina, his wife
63 Adam Wintes
64 Maria, his wife
65 Salome Scheibel
66 Andreas Rosenstiehl
67 Maria Aker
68 Catherina Krum
69 Susannah Aker
70 Catherina Aker
71 Catherina Musik
72 Peter Herold
73 Susannah Wenzel
74 Andrew Eisenmann
75 Catherina, his wife
76 Adam Steiner
77 Jacob Haensz
78 Israel Haensz
79 Lydia Haensz
80 Henry Steiner
81 Michael Haple

Communicants, May, 1831

1 Peter Fuchs
2 Sarah, his wife
3 Daniel Steiner
4 Maria, his wife
5 John Bachman
6 Susannah, his wife
7 Daniel Henrich
8 Elizabeth, his wife
9 John Miller
10 Elizabeth, his wife
11 Adam Bachman
12 Margaretta, his wife
13 Christian Altman
14 Barbara, his wife
15 Susannah Eisenmann
16 Catherina Eisenmann
17 Jacob Bachman
18 Catherina, his wife
19 Eva Schatz
20 Susannah Schatz
21 Catherina Stebson
22 Daniel Herold
23 Catherina, his wife
24 Peter Braecht
25 Hannah Ehret
26 Sarah Ros
27 John Bachman
28 Jacob Bachman
29 Jacob Bachman
30 Jacob Miller
31 Elizabeth Zuncel
32 Jacob Schatz
33 Esther, his wife
34 Barbara Miller
35 Catherina Heinrich
36 Jacob Haensz
37 Jacob Miller
38 Lydia Miller
39 William Wender
40 Catherina, his wife
41 John Herold
42 Catherina, his wife
43 Jacob Bachman
44 Jacob Haensz
45 Philip Fuchs
46 Christina, his wife
47 Peter Fuchs
48 Henry Miller

49 Catherina, his wife
50 George Eisenmann
51 Barbara, his wife
52 Henry Fuchs
53 Maria, his wife
54 John Fuch
55 Salome, his wife
56 Jacob Bender
57 Esther, his wife
58 Michael Miller
59 Susannah, his wife
60 Elizabeth Miller
61 John Stauch
62 Hannah, his wife
63 George Mayer
64 Peter Miller
65 Sarah, his wife
66 Rosina Bender
67 Christoph Krebs
68 John Schatz
69 Sarah, his wife
70 Ludwig Keppel
71 Catherina Schneider
72 Maria Keppel
73 Susannah Keppel
74 Catherina Keppel
75 Christian Eisenmann
76 Margaretta, his wife
77 Catherina Kner
78 Maria Miller
79 Adam Ehret
80 David Ehret
81 Lydia Baer
82 Barbara Bachman
83 Maria Baum
84 Maria Rorrer
85 Peter Miller
86 Frederich Haensz
87 Catherina, his wife
88 Susannah Baum
89 Susannah Wenzel
90 Philip Miller
91 Catherina, his wife
92 Daniel Runs

Communicants, May 17, 1840

1 Peter Bachman
2 Jacob Bachman
3 Susannah Kuns
4 Barbara Bachman
5 Susannah Krach
6 John P. Miller
7 Sarah Heisli
8 Margaretta Bachman
9 Margaretta Bachman
10 Henry Kunkel
11 Esther, his wife
12 George Eisenmann
13 Elizabeth Gangwer
14 Daniel Bachman
15 Susannah Lang
16 Hannah Eisenmann
17 David Kuns
18 Daniel Henrich
19 Elizabeth, his wife
20 Barbara Henrich
21 John L. Miller
22 Elizabeth, his wife
23 Henry Miller
24 Catherina, his wife
25 Jacob Haensz
26 Catherina, his wife
27 Peter Eisenmann
28 William Wendeck
29 Catherina, his wife
30 Jacob Wendeck
31 Catherina, Wendeck
32 Catherina Krach
33 John Eisenmann
34 Catherina Miller
35 Susannah Henrich
36 Benjamin Detar
37 Samuel Keppel

38 Catherina Keppel
39 Elizabeth Keppel
40 Elizabeth Detar
41 Susannah Detar
42 Lydia Detar
43 Pat. Tomas
44 Samuel Schmelser
45 Sarah, his wife
46 Margaret Schmidt
47 Daniel Altman
48 Maria, his wife
49 Joseph Eisenman
50 Philip Eisenman
51 Michael Miller
52 Susannah, his wife
53 Susannah Baum
54 John Miller
55 Susannah, his wife
56 Michael Eisenman
57 Elizabeth, his wife
58 Margaret Eisenmann
59 Jacob Miller
60 Daniel Miller
61 Jacob Schatz
62 Esther, his wife
63 Jacob Bachman
64 Sarah, his wife
65 George Miller
66 Esther, his wife
67 Jacob Miller
68 Maria, his wife
69 Andrew Eisenmann
70 Catherina, his wife
71 Susan Eisenman
72 Maria Eisenman
73 Henry Schmidt
74 Susan Mayer
75 Christina Weiman
76 Elizabeth Miller
77 George Krebs
78 Samuel Krebs
79 Sarah, his wife
80 Jacob Weiman
81 Christopher Krebbs
82 Levi Krebbs
83 Susannah Krebbs
84 Israel Haensz
85 Susannah, his wife
86 Joseph Miller
87 John Schatz
88 Sarah, his wife
89 Maria Bender
90 George Mayer
91 Catherina Schneider
92 Henry Steiner
93 Maria, his wife
94 Christian Mayer
95 Agnes Schneider
96 Fronica Scheily
97 Andrew Eisenman
98 Esther, his wife
99 Christian Altman
100 Barbara, his wife
101 Philip Fuchs
102 Christina, his wife
103 Maria Fuchs
104 John Knerr
105 Adam Steiner
106 Susan Wentzel
107 Leise Rosenstiehl
108 Susannah Menzch
109 John Herold
110 Catherina, his wife
111 Elizabeth Herold
112 Catherina Eisenman

Communicants, May 30, 1852

1 John Stauch
2 Elizabeth, his wife
3 John Miller
4 Maria Miller
5 Susannah Miller
6 Catherina Miller

7 John Bachman
8 Susannah Bachman
9 Margaretta Bachman
10 Peter Bachman
11 Susannah Wentzel
12 John Anderson
13 Maria, his wife
14 Daniel Bachman
15 Catherina, his wife
16 John Knerr
17 Elizabeth Bieker
18 George Eisenman
19 Sarah, his wife
20 Henry Miller
21 Catherina, his wife
22 Maria Mayer
23 Samuel Krebbs
24 Sarah, his wife
25 Levi Stauch
26 Esther Stauch
27 Joseph Steiner
28 Susannah Steiner
29 Jacob Steiner
30 Jun, his wife
31 Elizabeth Steiner
32 Elizabeth Nybbel
33 John Steiner
34 Sophia, his wife
35 Emanuel Kuns
36 Jacob Fuchs
37 Elizabeth, his wife
38 Tobias Henrich
39 George Becker
40 John Miller
41 John Krebbs
42 Susannah Baum
43 Catherina Wentzel
44 William Heinrich
45 Henry Bachman
46 Leah, his wife
47 Maria Wentzel
48 David Steiner
49 Sarah, his wife
50 George Miller
51 David Mileisa
52 Lewit Bachman
53 Lydia Henrich
54 Jacob Herold
55 Ruben Kuns
56 Jonas Eisenmann
57 Andrew Eisenmann
58 Esther, his wife
59 Michael Steiner
60 Lawina Henrich
61 Joseph Schmidt
62 Lydia, his wife
63 Margaret Wentzel
64 Emmanuel Schmelcer
65 David Miller
66 John Herold
67 Elizabeth, his wife
68 Catherina Herold
68 Elizabeth Lang
70 Isaac Keppel
71 Henry Gudlin
72 Hannah, his wife
73 John Miller
74 Jacob Steiner
75 Maria, his wife
76 Jacob Altman
77 Leah, his wife
78 Samuel Schmeltzer
79 Sarah, his wife
80 Joseph Detar
81 Joseph Miller
82 Abraham Altman
83 Susannah Wentzel
84 Maria Bender
85 Samuel Herold
86 Michael Miller
87 Susannah, his wife
88 George Mayer

89 Cyrus Eisenman
90 Catherina Schneider
91 Maria Steiner
92 Ferniz Nole
93 Debora Jung
94 Daniel Henrich
95 Elizabeth, his wife
96 Sarah Henrich
97 John Herold
98 Leah Bear
99 Daniel Schneider
100 Catherina, his wife
101 Michael Miller
102 Leah, his wife
103 Leonard Miller
104 Lucinda, his wife
105 David Kuns
106 Georgia Wendek
107 Lydia Weis
108 Maria Mileisa
109 Susannah Mileisa
110 John Eisenmann
111 Susannah Eisenmann
112 Joseph Gangwer
113 Lydia, his wife
114 Elizabeth
115 Jacob Becker
116 Elizabeth, his wife
117 Henry Fuchs
118 Maria, his wife
119 Lydia Fuchs
120 Jacob Bayer
121 Benjamin Detar
122 Daniel Williams
123 Nicholas Miller
124 Elizabeth, his wife
125 Reuben Herold
126 Henry Blank
127 Louisa, his wife
128 Christian Altman
129 Barbara, his wife
130 Henry Steiner
131 Lovina Steiner
132 Magdalena Steiner
133 Maria Steiner
134 Maria Steiner
135 Lydia Bear
136 Michael Eisenman
137 Elizabeth, his wife
138 George Eisenman
139 Catherina Eisenman
140 Joseph Eisenman
141 Elizabeth, his wife
142 Catherina Eisenman
143 Susannah Eisenman
144 Lydia Altman
145 Hannah Altman
146 Sarah Eisenman
147 Maria Detar
148 Lovina Detar
150 Margaretta Rifer
151 Susannah Detar
152 Elizabeth Kuns
153 Maria Bear
154 Esther Eisenman
155 Leah Altman
156 Susannah Kuns
157 Susannah Kuns
158 Betty Masenstein
159 Adlina Madier
160 Benjamin Eisenman
161 Catherina, his wife
162 Maria Tomas
163 Anna Bratrich
164 John Seatz
165 Anna, his wife
166 Michael Haehns
167 Susannah, his wife
168 Catherina Haehns
169 Leah Haehns
170 Jacob Altman
171 John Schatz

172 Sarah, his wife
173 Maria Miller
174 Mrs. Welsh
175 Anna Miller
176 Maria Muehleisen
177 Mrs. Steiner
178 Margaret Sadler
179 Sarah Bambach
180 Lovina Heasly
181 Elizabeth Aeret

May 11, 1862

1 John J. Weinman
2 Catherina, his wife
3 John Weinman
4 George Weinman
5 Regina Weinman
6 Catherina Strobel
7 John Loughner
8 Harriet Loughner
9 Susannah Steiner
10 Mary Steiner
11 Andrew Wineman
12 Carolina, his wife
13 Lucy Ehret
14 Lydia Bear
15 Eli McCartney
16 Elizabeth McCartney
17 Jacob Altman
18 Leah Altman
19 Jacob Eisaman
20 John Stough
21 Elizabeth Stough
22 David Smith
23 Elizabeth Smith
24 Mary Wentzle
25 Mary Low
26 Susannah Baum
27 Ester Shotts
28 Lovina Haines
29 Elizabeth Bricker
30 Elizabeth Nipple
31 Anna Fox
32 Susanna Long
33 Elizabeth Eisaman
34 Julian Farver
35 Elizabeth Kuhnz
36 Lyda Wise
37 Mary McIntire
38 Hannah Goodlin
39 Sarah Long
40 Andrew Eisaman
41 Lewis Eisaman
42 Esther Eisaman
43 Catherina Eisaman
44 Susannah Eisaman
45 Samuel Smeltzer
46 Sarah Smeltzer
47 Sarah Smeltzer
48 Susannah Smeltzer
49 Joseph Miller
50 Daniel Henry
51 Elizabeth Henry
52 Margaret Wentzel
53 Susannah Wentzel
54 Amos Bierer
55 Maria Bierer
56 Henry Miller
57 John H. Miller
58 John Henry
59 Henry Miller
60 John Miller
61 Daniel Miller
62 Christian Altman
63 Barbara Altman
64 Oliver Miller
65 John Miller
66 Mary Altman
67 Catherina, Miller
68 Peter Altman
69 Leah Altman
70 Michael Eisaman
71 Elizabeth Eisaman

72 Joseph Gongawere
73 Lydia Gongawere
74 Elizabeth Gongawere
75 Mary Painter
76 Jacob Errett
77 Susana Errett
78 Solomon Fry
79 Susan Fry
80 William Altman
81 Catherina Altman
82 Joseph Smith
83 Lucinda Smith
84 David Kuhns
85 John Fox
86 Mary Fox
87 Daniel Steiner
88 Adam Miller
89 John Fox
90 Hannah Allshouse
91 Susanna Wentzle
92 Lyda Anna Hoops
93 Maria Eisaman
94 Reuben Kuhns
95 Sarah Kuhns
96 Mary Anna Long
97 Simon Eisaman
98 Franklin J. Baker
99 Maria Baker
100 Lucinda Miller
101 Adam Shotz
102 Catherina Walthour
103 Sarah Errett
104 Jacob Harrold
105 Harriet Eisaman
106 Leah Henry
107 Benjamin Eisaman
108 Catherina Eisaman
109 Albert Allshous
110 Luceta Allshous
111 Adam Baughman
112 John Myers
113 Mary Thomas
114 Harriet Rohrer
115 John Shotz
116 Anne Shotz
117 Sarah Shotz
118 Elizabeth Harrold
119 Joseph Eisaman
120 Catherina Eisaman
121 Lewis Gangaware
122 Simon Miller
123 Sophia Miller
124 Nicholas Miller
125 George Myers
126 Catherina Keener
127 Conrad Miller
128 Sarah E. Harrold
129 Hannah Harrold
130 Israel Haines
131 Sarah Haines
132 Ellen Kuhns
133 Hester A. M. Shotts
134 John Harrold
135 Sarah Jane Harrold
136 Margaretta Baughman
137 Simon Detar
138 Albert M. Zundel
139 Susanna Zundel
140 Daniel Altman
141 Caroline Zundel
142 Michael J. Miller
143 Leah Miller
144 Joseph Smith
145 Jacob Altman
146 Elizabeth Harrold
147 Lydia Henry
148 Susannah Miller
149 Jacob Miller
150 Mary Miller
151 George Stall
152 Christina Stall
153 George Eisenmann

154 Catherine Eisenmann
155 Peter Brought
156 George A. Eisaman
157 Sarah Eisaman
158 Kate Keener
159 Barbara Staul
160 Lovina Henry
161 Michael Fox
162 Joseph Fox

APPENDIX C.

Confirmants

(Full Lists of all Confirmants, 1792-1862)

Record of the Confirmants who, in May 26, 1792, in Hempfield Township, Westmoreland County, in the Herold's or Zion's Church, by Pastor Steck, Evangelical Lutheran preacher, were confirmed and blessed, and on the following day, the 27 of May, for the first time, partook of the Lord's Supper.

No.	Name	Age
1	Andrew Dormeyer	18
2	John George Stemmetz	16
3	John George Ottermann	16
4	Christoph Amelang	17
5	John Muecknendoerfer	18
6	John Peter Kunkel	19
7	John Fridchmann	17
8	John George Zehner	17
9	John Jacob Zehner	17
10	John Jacob Dormyer	15
11	John Miller	17
12	Sebastian Kunkel	18
13	Martin Ritcher	16
14	John Wolff	18
15	Abraham Uber	14
16	Anna Maria Diemer	16
17	Anna Maria Adolph	18
18	Anna Margaretta Ruch	16
19	Anna Elizabeth Best	17
20	Anna Elizabeth Diemer	15
21	Anna Catherina Hartmann	18
22	Anna Margaretta Eisenmann	13
23	Anna Catherina Eisenmann	18
24	Anna Margaretta Hagen	15
25	Anna Barbara Steiner	18
26	Anna Catherina Miller	16
27	Anna Catherina Ritshert	15
28	Susannah Kueblern	14
29	Anna Elizabeth Ruch	15
30	Anna Catherina Bachman	16
31	Anna Magdalena Bissen	16
32	Anna Maria Keppel	14
33	Anna Maria Kunsz	15
34	Maria Catherina Zehner	16
35	Maria Magdalena Zehner	15
36	Anna Margaretta Williamsen	15
37	Susannah Scherrer	16
38	Susannah Mueckendoerfer	17
39	Susannah Urich	17
40	Anna Maria Amelang	18
41	Susannah Beyer	17
42	Maria Barbara Altman	16
43	Rosina Hartman	16

Confirmed April 20, 1794

No.	Name	Age
1	Christophel Schaeurer	19
2	John Jacob Laester	18
3	John Jacob Mahnaschmidt	17
4	—— —— Mahnaschmidt	16
5	John William Best	15
6	John Philip Klingenschmidt	17
7	John Philip Beyer	16
8	John Daniel Saeuberling	17
9	John Jacob Kunsz	15
10	Henry Kunsz	17
11	John Ehret	16
12	John George Rosenstiehl	18
13	John —— Rosenstiehl	15
14	Christian Mueller	16
15	John Jacob Baeumgartner	20
16	Franz Baeuerly	36
17	Anna Catherina Schaeurer	15
18	Anna Catherina Ruppert	17
19	Anna Catherina Uhrig	14
20	Sarah Schaerris	15
21	Anna Elizabeth Linten	14
22	Anna Catherina Klingenschmidt	15
23	Anna Magdalena Ruch	15
24	Anna Maria Wolff	17
25	Anna Elizabeth Beyer	14
26	Susannah Margaretta Sauberling	15
27	Eva Catherina Kunsz	15
28	Anna Catherina Huber	15
29	Anna Barbara Kunkel	14
30	Anna Maria Bachmann	14
31	Maria Elizabeth Zehner	15
32	Anna Catherina Mattheis	17
33	Anna Magdalena Mattheis	16
34	Anna Catherina Juck	17
35	Anna Elizabeth Juck	15
36	Anna Elizabeth Spengler	14
37	Rosina Baumgaertner	22
38	Anna Maria Brinis	16

Confirmants of the Herold's or Zion's Church, in the year of our Lord 1796, April 9, and on the 10th of April, they took communion.

No.	Name	Age
1	Sowald Maechling	17
2	Peter Ruch	17
3	John Steiner	16
4	Samuel Williams	17
5	Thomas Altmann	25
6	Conrad Frischmann	18
7	Michael Zehner	16
8	Peter Schmidt	20
9	Christian Zehner	15
10	John Geiger	18
11	Philip Mechling	16
12	Philip Stemmetz	19
13	Peter Fuchs	16
14	William Hack	14
15	Samuel Miller	17
16	Christian Sacksmann	17
17	Christian Herold	18
18	Matthew Sacksmann	21
19	Peter Sacksmann	23
20	Michael Wallintin	29
21	Justin Margaretta Stoh	15
22	Anna Maria Ruch	15
23	Christina Jaeger	16
24	Elizabeth Guldisen	19
25	Magdalena Laeppel	17
26	Elizabeth Geiger	13
27	Franzina Mermann	16
28	Catherina Best	15
29	Magdalena Ganewehr	15
30	Susannah Dhaemer	16
31	Amelia Hacking	16
32	Catherina Mechling	14
33	Magdalena Hartmann	15
34	Anna Maria Gutakunst	18
35	Elizabeth Rohrer	17
36	Anna Margaretta Uhrig	19
37	Christina Wilhelm	16

No.	Name	Age
38	Christina Uhrig	13
39	Catherina Naeuberling	15
40	Nahemy Williams	14
41	Barbara Sacksmann	19
42	Anna Maria Sacksmann	15
43	Catherina Mayer	17
44	Margaretta Staebel	16
45	Christina Boersching	19
46	Elizabeth Hatg	19
47	Elizabeth Bermes	19

Confirmants, April 8, 1798

No.	Name	Age
1	Christian Mahnenschmidt	15
2	Philip Fuchs	16
3	Michael Ruch	17
4	Henry Mitbor	18
5	Henry Zaehner	16
6	Ludwig Keppel	18
7	Bernhart Miller	17
8	Michael Aper	17
9	Michael Hock	14
10	Jacob Meckendoerfer	18
11	Michael Matheus	18
12	Frederich Walter	22
13	Susannah Ruch	13
14	Elizabeth Loeppel	16
15	Anna Maria Aber	15
16	Anna Maria Altmann	17
17	Christina Stroh	16
18	Elizabeth Struthan	18
19	Anna Maria Meckendoerfer	15
20	Eva Bachmann	16
21	Margaretta Bossert	14
22	Margaretta Miller	15
23	Julianna Stoll	18

Confirmants on April 19, 1801

No.	Name	Age
1	Jacob Erdmann	17
2	Michael Wolker	17
3	Andrew Wahener	21
4	Jacob Roder	19
5	John Bachmann	22
6	Jacob Bachmann	25
7	Martin Koter	16
8	John Wagner	17
1	Elizabeth Erdmann	15
2	Christina Mueller	15
3	Elizabeth Klingenschmidt	16
4	Elizabeth Schatz	15
5	Catherina Errit	18
6	Elizabeth Kraebs	14
7	Anna Hartmann	16
8	Susannah Wagner	15
9	Magdalena Koter	17
10	Christina Wagner	15
11	Anna Maria Fuchs	16
12	Maria Hartmann	15
13	Elizabeth Hartmann	13
14	Elizabeth Imber	20

Confirmants, April 13, 1805

No.	Name	Age
1	Henry Mueller	16
2	Theobald Brauthoefer	20
3	John Mueller	17
4	David Sadtler	16
5	Jacob Mueller	15
6	Abraham Meyer	22
7	Daniel Schmidt	19
8	Samuel Loh	23
9	Hannah Schatz	14
10	Magdalena Steinmetz	15
11	Anna Steinmetz	17
12	Susan Eisenmann	19
13	Catherina Fuchs	16
14	Susannah Indher	19
15	Susannah Meyer	19
16	Susannah Schmidt	17
17	Maria Salome Breyen	19
18	Maria Widdern	21

Confirmants, April 20, 1817

No.	Name	Age
1	John George Herold	20
2	Peter Eisenmann	17
3	Henry Steiner	20

No.	Name	Age
4	Michael Mueller	17
5	John Herold	18
6	George Eisenmann	17
7	David Mueller	17
8	William Altman	17
9	Philip Dethar	18
10	Martin Branthoefer	24
11	William Wintel	28
12	Jacob Baer	28
13	Catherina Eisenmann	16
14	Catherina Steiner	18
15	Catherina Bachman	17
16	Elizabeth Herold	17
17	Hannah Mueller	15
18	Susannah Wintel	18
19	Eva Bachman	17
20	Elizabeth Schneider	19
21	Susannah Mueller	17
22	Anna Maria Schneider	17
23	Elizabeth Rosenstiehl	15
24	Elizabeth Dethar	16
25	Anna Maria Haensz	18
26	Anna Maria Welschen	31
27	Magdalena Dethar	24
28	Eva Koenig	21

Confirmants, May 16, 1819

No.	Name	Age
1	Adam Wendel	18
2	Daniel Stauch	18
3	Israel Haensz	19
4	John Mueller	18
5	Michael Lagly	19
6	John Bachman	17
7	Peter Schmidt	20
8	Daniel Hesz	26
9	Lydia Haensz	17
10	Maria Steiner	18
11	Hannah Eisenmann	16
12	Barbara Laegly	18
13	Maria Gangaware	16
14	Catherina Hockenhill	18
15	Barbara Bachmann	16
16	Susannah Schatz	15
17	Elizabeth Mueller	17
18	Elizabeth Branthoefer	16
19	Elizabeth Schmidt	19

Confirmants, April 15, 1821

No.	Name	Age
1	George Acker	20
2	Samuel Stauch	19
3	Michael Eisenmann	18
4	George Walter	18
5	Conrad Hockenhill	17
6	Henry Bachman	17
7	John Peter Mueller	16
8	David Schmidt	20
9	Peter Pracht	26
10	David Ehret	22
11	Hannah Haensz	17
12	Elizabeth Steiner	18
13	Anna Maria Haerner	17
14	Sarah Steiner	16
15	Anna Maria Pahr	16
16	Anna Nelzin	17

Confirmants, May 11, 1823

No.	Name	Age
1	Jacob Steiner	22
2	George Stauch	18
3	Daniel Steiner	20
4	Henry Fuchs	19
5	Christian Altmann	22
6	Peter Krebs	20
7	Philip Mueller	19
8	Jacob Mueller	21
9	Sarah Haensz	17
10	Hannah Steiner	19
11	Esther Bachman	18
12	Anna Bachman	15
13	Esther Schaz	16
14	Catherina Krebs	18

Confirmants, May 8, 1825

No.	Name	Age
1	Joseph Stauch	18
2	Jacob Altman	20

No.	Name	Age
3	John Fuchs	18
4	Joseph Gangware	19
5	Philip Mueller	18
6	John Mueller	19
7	George Mayer	21
8	Frederick Haensz	18
9	Jacob Schaz	28
10	David Kistler	27
11	John Mayer	26
12	Maria Magdalena Hohenhill	17
13	Catherina Mayer	18
14	Maria Eisenmann	16
15	Maria Mueller	17
16	Catherina Eisenmann	18
17	Salome Kreps	17
18	Anna Catherina Zündel	16
19	Maria Steiner	17
20	Maria Keppel	19
21	Anna Kreps	17
22	Catherina Keppel	20
23	Leah Steiner	17
24	Maria Rosenstiehl	18
25	Elizabeth Steiner	19
26	Lydia Mueller	17
27	Lydia Musik	18
28	Anna Listler	19
29	Barbara Altmann	19
30	Elizabeth Schmidt	18

Confirmants, May 14, 1827

No.	Name	Age
1	Peter Miller	19
2	Adam Bachman	18
3	John Bachman	18
4	Simon Miller	17
5	Henry Schmidt	19
6	Daniel Henry	26
7	John Werner	28
8	Jacob Ferwer	41
9	Sarah Fuchs	17
10	Salmi Miller	17
11	Elizabeth Miller	16
12	Maria Margaretta Fuchs	19

Confirmants, March 3, 1829

No.	Name	Age
1	Joseph Steiner	20
2	Joseph Kreps	19
3	Peter Fuchs	16
4	John Eisenmann	18
5	Jacob Miller	17
6	Jacob Bachman	17
7	Jacob Haensz	17
8	George Haensz	20
9	Jacob Bachmann	17
10	Jacob Bachmann	18
11	Joseph Miller	18
12	Levi Kreps	18
13	Daniel Altmann	17
14	Abraham Hoster	22
15	George Kolp	31
16	Jacob Bendner	25
17	Maria Steiner	18
18	Elizabeth Zingel	15
19	Anna Maria Miller	16
20	Elizabeth Miller	—
21	Anna Barbara Hans	16
22	Elizabeth Kuns	18
23	Susannah Bachman	19
24	Susannah Eisenmann	17
25	Margaretta Kaufmann	23

Confirmants, Oct. 23, 1831

No.	Name	Age
1	Benjamin Eisenmann	17
2	George Miller	18
3	Michael Bachmann	17
4	Daniel Bachmann	28
5	Peter Bachmann	16
6	Samuel Keppel	20
7	Philip Keppel	22
8	David Landes	26
9	Bernhard Kraus	30
10	Michael Schultz	27
11	William Rihm	25

No.	Name	Age
12	Alexander Nelson, with baptism	36
13	Robert Myers	17
14	Susannah Eisenmann	16
15	Sarah Miller	18
16	Lydia Detar	16
17	Maria Hanselman	36
18	Susannah Miller	16
19	Esther Kuhns	19
20	Sarah Schmelzer	21
21	Sarah Bachmann	17
22	Maria Krebs	16
23	Elizabeth Wendick	16
24	Susannah Bachman	20
25	Elizabeth Krack, with baptism	18
26	Susannah Eisenman	19
27	Catherina 'Hansz	17
28	Hannah Miller	17
29	Esther Bernhart	16
30	Maria Bachman	15
31	Catherina Herman	22
32	Priscilla Mayer	22

Confirmants, May 26, 1833

No.	Name	Age
1	Jacob Zunzel	21
2	Samuel Eisaman	20
3	Andrew Eisaman	18
4	Michael Miller	17
5	Esther Haensz	17
6	Susannah Bachman	15
7	Lucinda Bachman	15
8	Margaret Fuchs	18
9	Anna Maria Miller	17
10	Magdalena Kreps	16
11	Esther Miller	15
12	Anna Maria Eisaman	15
13	Susannah Miller	16
14	Henrietta Bohver	16
15	Lucinda Mayer	20

Confirmants, May 21, 1836

No.	Name	Age
1	Joseph Eisaman	20
2	Leonard Miller	16
3	John Miller	18
4	Jacob von Dyk	20
5	David Keppel	20
6	Benjamin Detter	19
7	Samuel Krebs	18
8	Jacob Waiman	17
9	John Heil	25
10	Catherina Von Dyk	17
11	Elizabeth Fuchs	18
12	Anna Schmidt	19
13	Elizabeth Keppel	19
14	Margaretta Schmidt	16
15	Juliana Schmidt	17
16	Veronica Keppel	19
17	Elizabeth Schaester	19
18	Nora Kuhns	19
19	Hannah Eisaman	16
20	Margaret Miller	16
21	Maria Dettor	18
22	Rebecca Keppel	28

Confirmants, May, 1839

No.	Name	Age
1	John Anderson	18
2	George Ehret	19
3	Philip Eisaman	21
4	George Kreps	19
5	Benjamin Miller	20
6	Daniel Bachman	19
7	Philip Steiner	25
8	Daniel Schneider	36
9	Michael Keener	24
10	Frederick Shoff	29
11	Henry Schatz	21
12	Elias Schmelzer	18
13	David Kuhns	19
14	George Mayer	20
15	Leah Kreps	17
16	Susannah Kreps	16

No.	Name	Age
17	Catherina Miller	16
18	Lucinda Schmidt	19
19	Caroline Eisaman	16
20	Elizabeth Miller	17
21	Elizabeth Long	17
22	Maria Fuchs	18
23	Elizabeth Herold	19
24	Maria Ellis	20
25	Susannah Detar	17
26	Margaretta Bachman	16
27	Rebecca Heinrich	16
28	Esther Eisaman	19
29	Christina Regina Weiman	16
30	Maria Eisaman	19
31	Agnes Schneider	16
32	Elizabeth Detar	18
33	Susannah Mayer	16
34	Jeremiah Lantzenheiser	18
35	Elizabeth Rosenstiehl	21
36	Elizabeth Schmeltzer	21

Confirmants, May 14, 1842

No.	Name	Age
1	Conrad Miller	—
2	John Wendel	—
3	Michael Miller	—
4	Jacob Herold	—
5	John Nicholas Miller	—
6	Levi Eisenman	—
7	Joseph Stough	—
8	John Steiner	—
9	Daniel Eisenman	—
10	Henry Miller	—
11	Catherina Schneider	—
12	Catherina Eisaman	—
13	Sarah Wendel	—
14	Susannah Fuchs	—
15	Leah Herold	—
16	Nora Anna Schatz	—
17	Nora Hehns	—
18	Esther Eisaman	—
19	Maria Miller	—
20	Lovina Fuchs	—
21	Susannah Baughman	—
22	Susannah Fuchs	—
23	Catherina Miller	—
24	Rebecca Kepple	—
25	Margaretta Heisle	—

Confirmants, May 10, 1845

No.	Name	Age
1	Jacob Steiner	—
2	Henry Hehnes	—
3	Jacob Eisaman	—
4	Jacob Steiner	—
5	Jacob Stauch	—
6	Abraham Miller	—
7	Solomon Eisaman	—
8	Abraham Eisaman	—
9	John Fuchs	—
10	Jacob Baer	—
11	John Heinrich	—
12	George Ehret	—
13	Henry Schneider	—
14	Henry Baughman	—
15	Elias Moyer	—
16	John Lang	—
17	Thomas Herold	—
18	Jacob Walter	—
19	Joseph Farington (baptized)	—
20	Samuel Low	—
21	Abraham Munsch	—
22	Anna Eisaman	—
23	Leah Herold	—
24	Catherina Hehns	—
25	Lovina Steiner	—
26	Susannah Fuchs	—
27	Magdalena Hehns	—
28	Lucia Fuchs	—
29	Lydia Fuchs	—
30	Elizabeth Schmidt	—
31	Maria Altman	—
32	Anna Maria Anderson	—
33	Maria Stauch	—

No.	Name	Age
34	Susannah Baughman	—
35	Catherina Black	—
36	Elizabeth Steiner	—
37	Sophia Steiner	—
38	Sarah Farington (baptized)	—
39	Elizabeth Heinrich	—
40	Elizabeth Schatz	—
41	Jean Merchant	—
42	Margaret Antre	—
43	Mary Steiner	—

Confirmants, May 5, 1848

No.	Name	Age
1	John Herold	—
2	David Steiner	—
3	Michael Steiner	—
4	John Miller	—
5	Peter Miehleisen	—
6	Levi Stauch	—
7	Isaac Baer	—
8	Emanuel Detar	—
9	Tobias Heinrich	—
10	Levi Baughman	—
11	James McEnter (baptized)	—
12	Daniel Kuhns	—
13	Josiah Wendel	—
14	Isaac Altshaus (baptized)	—
15	Reuben Herold	—
16	John Schatz	—
17	Lovina Hehns	—
18	Magdalena Steiner	—
19	Leah Steiner	—
20	Elizabeth Rosenstiehl	—
21	Leah Altman	—
22	Ellanor Altman	—
23	Anna Stauch	—
24	Nora Heinrich	—
25	Maria Erret	—
26	Susannah Miller	—
27	Louisa Kreps	—
28	Lovina Detar	—
29	Lovina Hielsle (baptized)	—
30	Jean Kreps	—
31	Catherina Detar	—
32	Francisca Noel	—

Confirmants, May 4, 1850
By J. Mechling.

No.	Name	Age
1	Simon Herold	—
2	Cyrus Eisenman	—
3	George Miller	—
4	David Miehleisen	—
5	John Stauch	—
6	Joseph Miller	—
7	Jonas Eisaman	—
8	Peter Miller	—
9	Michael Rosenstiehl	—
10	Jacob Mayer	—
11	William Heinrich	—
12	Reuben Kuhns	—
13	Jacob Fux	—
14	Joshua Datauer	—
15	Peter Fux	—
16	Reuben Altman	—
17	Emanuel Schmeltzer	—
18	Louis Rathebach	—
19	Daniel Schmeltzer	—
20	John Kreps	—
21	Catherina Herrold	—
22	Maria Ann. Steiner	—
23	Lucy Hehns	—
24	Elizabeth Steiner	—
25	Catherina Miller	—
26	Susannah Altman	—
27	Sarah Maria Eisaman	—
28	Hannah Catherina Altman	—
29	Susannah Catherina Steiner	—
30	Maria Catherina Mensch	—
31	Maria Christina Steiner	—
32	Susannah Miehleisen	—
33	Sarah Maertin	—
34	Maria Catherina Keppel	—
35	Sarah Jean Alshaus	—

Confirmants, May 29, 1852

No.	Name	Age
1	Obadiah Eisaman	21
2	Henry Edwin Jung	19
3	Elias Schatz	20
4	Abraham M. Altman	17
5	John Altman	18
6	John Peter Fuchs	19
7	Simon Miehleisen	18
8	Joseph Altman	19
9	Joseph Heinrich	18
10	Jacob Erit	20
11	Lebens Alshaus	21
12	John Steiner	17
13	David Altman	27
14	Hettie Eisaman	16
15	Solomon Altman	16
16	Sarah Catherina Fuchs	20
17	Leah Eisaman	18
18	Lucinda Altman	16
19	Elizabeth Bigelo	17
20	Sarah Baughman	16
21	Florinda Miehleisen	19
22	Lovina Kuhns	21
23	Henrietta Evans	17
24	Fronic S. Schmidt	30
25	Margaretta Keppel	27

Confirmants May 24, 1856

By J. Mechling.

No.	Name	Age
1	Joseph Eisaman	18
2	Ludwig Herold	20
3	Michael Schneider	19
4	John Boch	18
5	David Boch	21
6	John Jacob Strobel	15
7	John Jacob Haehns	20
8	Joseph Schmidt	20
9	Jacobus Jung	22
10	George W. Jung	18
11	Robert Mayer	20
12	Reuben Haehns	19
13	Jacob Altman	17
14	Peter Baughman	18
15	Joseph Fuchs	19
16	John Miller	19
17	David Schmidt	19
18	Ludwig Eret	26
19	Peter Schmeltzer	20
20	Gebhart Mechling	22
21	Maria Ann Fuchs	17
22	Maria Eisaman	17
23	Sarah Kreps	17
24	Maria Schmidt	17
25	Elizabeth Miehleisen	18
26	Susannah Stauch	16
27	Susannah Baughman	17
28	Sarah Schmidt	16
29	Susannah Schmeltzer	19
30	Carolina Elter	23

Confirmants, May 22, 1858

By J. Mechling

No.	Name	Age
1	Louis Gangwer	18
2	Joseph Herold	18
3	Jacob Harrer	18
4	Carl Rohrbach	18
5	Andrew Bosh	18
6	Simon Peter Steiner	20
7	Zacharias Buhl	20
8	Michael Fuchs	20
9	Henry Fuchs	25
10	Daniel Altman	17
11	Albert Zundel	19
12	George Krimer	18
13	Henry Schneider	19
14	John Schmeltzer	19
15	Benjamin Altman	20
16	Cyrus Altman	20
17	Lewis Schmidt	19
18	Catherina Eisaman	18
19	Catherina Bosh	16
20	Elizabeth Sarah Fuchs	18

No.	Name	Age
21	Caroline Zundel	14
22	Harriet Turner	18
23	Catherina Heil	22
24	Susannah Mayer	16
25	Susannah Baughman	18
26	Elizabeth Charlotte Kinner	18
27	Catherina Schmeltzer	18
28	Ellen Weis	16

Confirmants, May 12, 1860

No.	Name	Age
1	Adam Miller	19
2	Oliver Miller	18
3	Simon Eisaman	19
4	Henry Strowel	17
5	Henry Kiener	18
6	Adam Baughman	18
7	Daniel Steiner	17
8	Henry Eret	20
9	William Walthauer	17
10	John Fuchs	19
11	Lucetta Eisaman	18
12	Henrietta Eisaman	18
13	Elizabeth Herold	18
14	Caroline Barbara Schmidt	16
15	Sarah Eret	18
16	Sarah Jean Kieuer	16
17	Catherina M. Walthauer	16
18	Ellanor Schmidt	17
19	Margaretta Baughman	16
20	Sarah Elizabeth Herrold	16
21	Anna Catherina Strowel	16
22	Sarah Schmeltzer	17

Confirmants, May 10, 1862

No.	Name	Age
1	Samuel Miller	18
2	Albert Eisaman	19
3	Nathanael Miller	16
4	Frederick Heinrich	17
5	Alphaeus Altman	18
6	John Altman	23
7	Henry Mayer	20
8	John Buhrer	17
9	Ludwig Frey	20
10	Harrison Miller	18
11	Susannah Miller	18
12	Susannah Eisaman	17
13	Lucinda Zundel	16
14	Maria Altman	19
15	Caroline Eisenmann	18
16	Maria Strobel	15
17	Eleanor Altman	18
18	Elizabeth Hiesle	16
19	Margaretta Baughman	18
20	Maria N. Schatz	15
21	Margaretta N. Buehrer	19
22	Elizabeth Eisaman	19

APPENDIX D

Taufschein

Immanuel—(Taufschein translated). See Cut, page 31.
(Written in rhyme)

What I, your beloved Uncle, from a true heart, now (repent?) That is only a small gift. Take care of your soul, and think that you through the Sacrament of Baptism by Jesus are received. It is only water which is externally used, but the blood of Jesus Christ internally, so that your soul, virtuous and clean, may enter the Kingdom of heaven. Through grace you are born anew. You are chosen to be an heir of heaven through Jesus Christ the Son of God, who from the throne of high heaven, came down and humbled Himself that we might with Him enter the Kingdom and live in happiness with Him forever. Through Baptism we may taste of blessedness in time through faith, that when He sits on His throne; that we may be rulers forever; to eternity proclaim Him as the true Son of God, thrice holy. Jesus "Make us ready," to your rejoicing and blessedness. So speak we in thy name one happiness full of faith. Amen. Amen.

Parents were the honorable Peter Eisenmann and Justina his beloved wife, nee Altman.

John George Eisenmann, born 28th of May in the year of our Lord 1788 and on the 13th of July was through the washing of Holy Baptism, baptized into the congregation of Christ as a living member, and as a young branch received.

Baptism Witnesses were, in this sacred ordinance, the honorable John Peter Eisenmann and Anna Barbara, his wife.

My child since you are born in this world
God has proclaimed you to His pleasure tent
Therefore thank Him with heart and soul
And praise God and His love
Then as thy ....possession
Only His favor and gift.
The Baptism gives you new life
To live in that new life forever.
Here in time and there in eternity
Remain true to your covenant
Then you will enter heaven
By Jesus Christ, the Son of God
Fall heir to the happy throne. Amen.

Made by Karl Sheibeler, Schoolmaster, Hempfield, Township, Westmoreland County, 1788.

MOTTOES:

on border of Taufschein.

1 "Do not fall into sin."
2 Love humility, seek peace.
3 Never seek to be great.
4 Speak little but hear much.
5 Don't pry into secrets.
6 Let the little ones be without sorrow.
7 Keep out of the way of grown-up folks.
8 Weep with those that weep.
9 Be satisfied with your own.

10 Don't be too slow to go to work,
11 If you owe work to anyone.
12 With all your power be mild to the poor.
13 Learn to save and keep it.
14 Prepare thyself to do for all good things.
15 Think earnestly of your death.
16 Then you will be heir of heaven.
17 Trust in God and continue in prayer.

APPENDIX E.

Annual Settlements

Today, the 15th of February, 1793 we have, the undersigned Church Council, met in peace and agreeableness in Zions Church, Hempfield Township, State of Pennsylvania.

Today the fifteenth day of February, 1793, I hereby acknowledge that I, from the congregation of Zions Church and with thanks received, 6 lb. 6 s. 6 p. which I spent for the following things.

He paid to Samuel Mau for Greement and Banden to write		9 s.	
He paid to Jacob Bender for deed of church	4 lbs.	10 s.	9 p.
He paid to Jacob Bender for the same		7 s.	6 p.
He paid for nails for church yard		11 s.	3 p.
He paid for glass in schoolhouse		8 s.	
Total	6 lbs.	6 s.	6 d.

Which I hereby sign with my own hand, I witness and undersign by the above date by witnesses.

Michael Gangwer
Karl Scheibeler } witnesses.

Anthony Altman.

So done in peace and harmony.

Anthony Altman holds in treasury balance of 53 lbs. 12 s. 6 d.

Anthony Altman.

John Michael Steck, President
Jacob Zehner
John Bachmann
J. Meyer
Karl Scheibeler, Schoolmaster
Valentine Steiner
John Jacob Altman
William Altman

Jacob Stroh
Michael Gangwer
Peter Eisenmann
John Gundel
Martin Fraelig
Michael Ruch

Today, the sixth of December, 1793 we, the undersigned, the Elders and Deacons, assembled made report and we delivered 4 lbs. 5 s. ½ d. to William Altman after all costs and expenses were paid. The above date these things were done before witnesses.

John Michael Steck, Preacher
Michael Gangwer
John Bachman
Nicholas Altmann
John Weyandt
Nicholaus Lang
Jacob Barnes
Christopher Schneider

Today, January 2, 1795, we, the undersigned, have settled the accounts of the church and also the land which the Pastor Luetge bought for the sum of 60 lbs. which money Andrew A. Amans held as trustee, but at the present in the hands of the elected trustees, but that money is not yet used for building purposes.

Nicholaus Allerman	33 lbs.	16 s.	2 d.
John Nicholaus Miller			
Anthony Altman	6 lbs.		10 d.
John Peter Altman	4 lbs.	2 s.	6 d.
John Michael Ruch	4 lbs.		

These men owed the Zion's Church.

Anton Uhlrich Luetge
Philip Knauss
Jacob Stroh
Jacob Hehner   I of Adam Moyer of
Michael Ruch   5 lbs. 2 s. 6 d.

All undersigned in the presence of witnesses of the above date.

John Michael Steck, Preacher
Valentine Steiner
Henry Schatz
Michael Gangwer
John Bachman
Christoph Schneider

Today, January 2, 1794, have we, the undersigned, Deacons and Elders held a settlement of church accounts, and there was 3 lbs. 1 s. handed in by Nicholaus Miller for alms, after all bills were paid.

John Michael Steck, Pastor
Valentine Steiner
Henry Schatz
Anthony Allemann
Michael Gangwer
John Bachman
Christoph Schneider
Nicholaus Alleman

Today, January 2, 1796, was held the Church and Alms settlement at the schoolhouse by the Zion's Church by the Elders and deacons of both congregations. Nicholas Molle had in hand Alms to the amount of 4 lbs. 13 s. 9 d.

Witness:

John William Weber
John Michael Steck, Preacher
Valentine Steiner
Michael Gangwer
Frederick Heinrich
Frederich Mahmenschmidt
Peter Miller

Today, January 2, 1796, the Deacons, Elders and Manager held a meeting concerning the church funds.

Philip Wentzel was elected manager and received 6 lbs. 11 s. 45½ d. in the presence of John William Weber.

John Michael Steck
Valentine Steiner
Michael Gangwer
Frederick Henrich
Christian Michael Schmidt
Peter Miller

On the 22nd of January, 1796, Nicholaus Alleman paid the sum of 33 lbs. 16 s. ½ d. in presence of witnesses:

Christian Malynan Schmidt
John Thomas
Peter Miller
John Altman

On the 22nd of January, 1796, Philip Wentzel as manager received on church money in gold 27 lbs. 1 s. ½ d. Witnesses:

Christian Mahnenschmidt
John Thomas
Peter Miller
John Altman

The 30th of December, in the year of our Lord 1796, was held the Church and Alms settlement, at the schoolhouse near Zion's Church, in Hempfield Township, Westmoreland County, by Elders and Deacons of both congregations. Alms money was 1 lb. 11 s. 11 d. This was done in peace and unity at above date which we sign with our own hands.

John Michael Steck, Preacher
Peter Miller
John Thomas
Michael Gangwer
Frederick Henrich

February 18, 1797, Nicholaus Miller as manager received Alms money, 3 lbs. 10 s. 4½ d. Witnesses:

Christian Mahnenschmidt
John Thomas
Frederick Henrich
William Altman

Nicholaus Miller was elected Alms-trustee of both congregations.
The Alms in 1800 amounted to 20 lbs. 4 s. 5 d.
The Alms in 1802, 5 lbs. 4 s. 9 d.

(The joint meetings ended)

Date August 2, 1805, the elders and deacons had a meeting in Zion's Church in the presence of the Pastor Michael Steck. An account was given of the Alms money and after all was settled they found in notes and cash in hand 30 lbs. 12 s. 8 d., and gave John Baughman, manager, the money. (Signed by officers).

INDEX

A — Page

Academies ....179 ff.
Allen, Fort 87, 165
Augsburg Confession.115, 132, 133

B

Bank of North America 9
Baptisms List 33
Appendix A
Beayen, Capt. 18
Bissel, Israel 6
Blane, Lieut. 23
Bounty 60
Bouquet ....17, 23 ff.
Brady, Capt. 65
Braddock's Defeat 18
Brown, Enoch ....169 ff.
Bruegel, G. A. 125
Brush Creek 177
Bushyager, George 42, 177
Byerly, Andrew ....20, 24 ff.
Byerly, Flight of Family ....22 ff.

C

Cannon, Lieut. John 17
Carlisle 23
Catechetical System ......112 ff.
Cemeteries 159
Census, Early 2
Census, German 3
Church, Log 41
Church, Stone ....99 ff.
Clapham Massacre 21
Clark Expedition 74

Page

Colleges ....179 ff.
Colonists, German .... 1 ff.
Communion List 35
Appendix B
Confirmation List 35
Appendix C
Connolly .... 46 ff.
Crawford Expedition 74

D

Definite Platform 115
Detars 20
DeVitri 18
Domestic and Foreign Mission Society 106
Dow, Lieut. 24
Dunmore's War 46, 48
Duquesne, Fort, Capture of.. 15

E

Ecuyer, Capt. 21
Education 164
Ehrenfeldt, A. C. ....128 ff.
Eisenmann, John George 31
Appendix D........... 103
English District of the Joint Synod of Ohio 123
Ev. Lutheran District Synod of Ohio 130

F

Fabian, Peter 2
Forbes, Gen. ....15, 18 ff.
Forbes Road ....

Page

Fort Allen 47
Fort Pitt 20
Fort Stanwix, Council of ... 28
Fort Wayne 118
Frankean Synod 118
French and Indian War 13
Frontier, Germans on 7

G

Gage, Gen. 27
General Council ....119 ff.
General Synod 114, 131
Germania, Rush's .... 9 ff.
Germans, Characteristics of .9 ff.
Germans, Early Prosperity of 18
Germans and Pennsylvania Independence ....75 ff.
Germantown 44
Girty, Simon 16
Glenn, J. O. 141
Gnadenhuetten 16
Good Purpose 30, 110
Goshocking 16
Grant, Major 18
Greensburg ....178 ff.
Greensburg Seminary 180

H

Hamilton, Gov. 58
Hanna, Robert 45
Hanna's Town Burned 74
Hanna's Town Resolutions.49 ff.
Hanover Resolutions 51
Harmon, Andrew 20
Hartman, Regina ....66 ff.
Heckewelder 16
Henry Massacre ....63 ff.
Herkimer, Gen. 25
Herold, Christopher 20
Herold, Daniel 20
Herold, John 20
Heins 2

Page

Highlanders ....23 ff.
Huffnagle, Michael 74

I

Indian Captives ....65, 66 ff.
Indian Ravages 48, 61, 62

J

Johnson, Col. John ....55 ff.
Johnson, Sir William 28
Joint Synod of Ohio ......122 ff.

K

Kepple's Blockhouse 88
Kimmel 18, 20
Klingensmith's House 89
Kohn, E. H. 141
Krauth, Charles Porterfield . 116
Kunzmann, J. C. 137

L

Lame Indian, Story of .....81 ff.
Language, Pennsylvania German ....181 ff.
Lederer, John 2
Lochry, Archibald 61, 74
Ludwig, Christoph 9
Ludwig, Maria 69
Luetge, Anton Ulrich 32, 35, 37 ff.
Luther, Heinrich 2

M

MacDonald, Donald 70
Marchand's Blockhouse 88
Massacre of Christian Indians ....16 ff.
McDowell's Blockhouse 88
Mechling, Jonas ....108 ff.
Mecklenburg resolutions 53
Melanchthon Synod 118
Membership, Old Zion .....143 ff.
Meyer, Balthasar ....
............30 ff., 36, 37, 164 ff.
Military Permit 19
Miller, Mrs. Salome 36

Page
Miller, Peter 20
Minuit, Peter 1
Music 60

N

Nagel's Berks County "Dutchmen," 25
National Lutheran Council.. 134
New Purchase 28

O

Ohio Company 17
Ourry Wendel 23

P

Palatinates 25
Patriotism 162
Passavant 108
Pastorius 44
Pittsburg, Early Inhabitants. 21
Pittsburg Synod ......106, 114 ff.
Pittsburg Synod, General Synod 120
Plan of Union 114
Pontiac's Conspiracy 20
Population, 1776 2
Population, German, 1775 2
Post, Frederick 15, 18
Printz, John 1
Property Affairs 110
Pulpit, Old 42

R

Rangers ....24 ff.
Redemptioners 46, 167
Reformed Pastors 161
Regiments in Revolution 54
Relations with Reformed 110
Renegades 77
Revers 39
Rifle 25
Rodenbaugh, Michael 20
Royal American Regiment... ....23, 25 ff.

Page
Rudebaugh, Christopher 20
Rugh's Blockhouse 87
Rush, Dr. Benjamin ....9 ff.

S

Sarver, Jonathan 139
Scalps 58, 59, 60
Schell, Johann Christian ....70 ff.
Schlatter, Michael 27
Schmucker, Dr. .... 115 ff.
Schoolhouse ....35 ff., 40
Senecas 60
Settlers, Early 19
Sharswood, Justice 130
Scheibeler, Karl ..33 ff., 42, 168 ff.
Slavery 178
Smith, Enoch 127
Social life ....90 ff.
Sprecher, Dr. 118
Stauch, Johannes 178
St. Clair, Arthur 19
Steck, Johann Michael ......95 ff.
Steck, Michael Johann ....104 ff.
Steuben, Baron ....56 ff.
Stokeley's Blockhouse 88
Sunday School ....155 ff.
Superstition 12
Swiss 25
Synod 105

T

Taufschein 31, 168
Appendix D
Teachers at Herold's School. 174
Testimony of the Pittsburg Synod 116
Tories 76
Trunkey, Judge 120

U

Ulery, William F. 128
United Lutheran Church ..134 ff.

Page

W

Wagle, John 20
Waldseemueller 1
Walther, Dr. 119
Walthour, Christopher 20
Walthour, Fort 80
Walthour, Fort, Petition 78
Washington, George 167
Washington's Body guard... 55
Weber, Rev. John William .. 30
Weiser, Conrad ....13 ff.
Wheeling Convention 122
Williamson, Col. David .....16 ff.
Wilson, Woodrow 163
Wismer, Isaack 142
Woodstock Resolutions 52
Wyandots 16

Y

Yorktown 56
Yount, J. A. 141

Z

Zane, Elizabeth ....69 ff.
Zeisberger, David 16
Zuber, William H. 139
Zundel, H. M. 157
Zundel, John A. 151
Zundel, Johann Michael ....
............36 ff., 42, 171 ff., 177
Zundel, W. A. 153